JULIE WALTERS
SERIOUSLY FUNNY

THE UNAUTHORISED BIOGRAPHY

Lucy Ellis and Bryony Sutherland

For Clare and Ted Ellis

First published in Great Britain in 2003 by
Virgin Books Ltd
Thames Wharf Studios
Rainville Road
London W6 9HA

A catalogue record for this book is available from the British Library.

ISBN 1 85227 068 3

Typeset by Phoenix Photosetting, Chatham, Kent
Printed and bound in Great Britain by Mackays of Chatham, Chatham, Kent

CONTENTS

ACKNOWLEDGEMENTS

Julie Walters's unbreakable spirit has been an inspiration. When work commenced on this book, the project was daunting to say the least: Julie's career is as diverse as it is long, but, worse still, my partner-in-crime, Bryony, went on maternity leave. However, the research was a pleasure, as the films were as different as the many characters I interviewed, and the story fell into place.

Of course, it was not all plain sailing and I would particularly like to thank my husband, Elton Thrussell, whose faith, encouragement and understanding have been immeasurable. Congratulations to Bryony and Frankie on the birth of their beautiful son, Finlay Peter Sutherland, and thank you, Bryony, for coming back to work!

Sadly, we were unable to interview Julie Walters herself, but, in piecing together her staggering achievements, Atomic were delighted to speak to the following people: Michael Abbensetts, Michael Angelis, Ellie Beavan, Mary Bodfish, Mike Bradwell, Gary Cady, Alexander Clements, Wendy Craig, Giles Foster, John Goldschmidt, Glenys Hopkins, Dusty Hughes, Alan Igbon, Marigold and Mark Kingston, Pat King, Andrew Lancel, Robert Lang, Mike Leigh, Derek Lister, Hugh Lloyd, Richard Loncraine, Stephen Moore, Penelope Nice, Nathaniel Parker, Jane Parnum, Chris Rankin, Crissy Rock, David Ross, Peter Sasdy, Alyson Spiro, Ewan Stewart, Simon Stokes, Baz Taylor, Sophie Thursfield, Marc Warren, Erika Welsh, Peter Whitfield, Dorothy Williams, Snoo Wilson and Jacky Wollaston. Some interviewees have requested anonymity and we have respected their wishes.

Special thanks must go to Clare Ellis for her tireless genealogy, but we have also received fabulous support from the rest of our research team: Angela Blundell, Mike Brady, Hilary and Steven Field, Sue Gibbons, Ann Maguire, Ros Merkin, Trisha O'Neill and Barbara Thrussell, and the staff at Equity, Holly Lodge Grammar School, Queen Elizabeth Hospital, Manchester Polytechnic, Everyman Theatre, Colindale Newspaper Library and the British Library, St Pancras.

Thank you to everyone at Virgin Books who made this book possible, particularly Kirstie Addis and Stuart Slater.

Miscellaneous mentions go to Pretty Nic, Melissa Whitelaw, Steven Gordon, John Prater, the Fountain Café, David Lamb to the Slaughter and Titty Spick 'n' Span. We mourn the loss of troubadour Tim, batty Freda, Ivy and Drew.

If last year was incredible – this one has been something else!

Lucy Ellis, April 2003

LIST OF ILLUSTRATIONS

Holly Lodge Grammar School school photo (courtesy of Sue Gibbens)
A Midsummer Night's Dream (courtesy of Mary Bodfish)
The Pig and the Junkle (Liverpool Everyman Theatre)
Alan Bennett (Rex Features)
Alan Bleasdale (Rex Features)
With Michael Caine in *Educating Rita* (Acorn Pictures Ltd/The Kobal Collection)
The premiere of *Educating Rita* (Rex Features)
As Christine Painter in *Personal Services* (Zenith/UIP/Vestron/The Kobal Collection)
With Phil Collins in *Buster* (Hemdale-Movie Group-NFH/Tri Start/The Kobal Collection)
On stage in *The Rose Tattoo* (© Robbie Jack/Corbis)
Wide-Eyed and Legless/The Wedding Gift (© Howard Jacqueline/Corbis Sygma)
With Matthew Walker and Laura Sadler in *Intimate Relations* (Handmade/Boxer/The Kobal Collection)
With Brenda Blethyn in *Girl's Night* (Granada/Showtime Networks/The Kobal Collection/Tepper, Randy)
With Joanne Whalley and Victoria Hamilton in *Before You Go* (Capitol/Isle of Man Film/The Kobal Collection)
With Jamie Bell in *Billy Elliot* (Tiger Aspect/Working Title)
Calendar Girls on the beach (Rex Features)
With husband Grant (Rex Features)
With her family at the second *Harry Potter* premiere (Rex Features)

PROLOGUE: A NATIONAL TREASURE

*'I remember someone saying that acting was about being dishonest and
that prickled me. It's the opposite: it's a way of trying to find the real
truth and the reality of the person you're playing.'* – Julie Walters

Julie Walters employs this straight-talking interpretation in life, tackling
her changing issues with assured candour. Fate has thrown her many
curve balls, but she has taken them all in her stride.

Born into poverty in Birmingham in 1950, Julie had a tough
upbringing. Her strict, emotionally undemonstrative mother, Mary, had
high ambitions for her three children and consequently pushed them
from an early age. Julie was the only girl and was intended to become a
well-behaved, 'proper' lady. The mischievous youngster, however, had
other ideas and loved being the centre of attention.

Julie caused havoc throughout her education and brief spell at
nursing college: she played truant, initiated pranks and took every
opportunity to make light of a situation. It turned out that she was
simply bored and her latent desire to entertain turned into an overwhelming passion for acting.

To that end, she joined the drama course at Manchester Polytechnic,
followed by a couple of years at Liverpool's Everyman Theatre. There she
formed many strong friendships, including one with the playwright Alan
Bleasdale, with whom she has worked countless times. Once she found
her vocation, the actress never shied away from work, turning her hand
to numerous genres and undertaking a strenuous schedule.

Julie's forte is her talent for mixing drama with comedy. She can be
agonisingly emotive and side-splittingly funny at the drop of a hat. That
is not to say she doesn't work hard, but that she has an innate ability to
touch the genuine emotion of a character, and portray that feeling with a
sincere realism. Actresses with loftier aspirations might view playing
'ordinary women' as a lack of ambition, but Julie pours her heart and soul
into every part.

On top of her being a true pro, the overwhelming – if repetitive –
observation from all her colleagues is that she is 'great fun'. And there is
no clearer way to put it: she retains a refreshingly rosy outlook on life and

makes work, on and off set, a barrel of laughs. She can ease the toughest and most tense scene, ad lib with the best stand-up comics and wring the hilarity dry from a comedic moment. Her skill as a raconteur, combined with her uncontainable *joie de vivre*, makes her irresistible.

As she worked hard, so she played hard. Julie was always up for a good night out: she drank, she smoked, she ate takeaways and slept on other people's floors. Commitment, to anyone or anything, did not appeal. Then she found fame with the smash-hit film *Educating Rita* and the parties became fancier and wilder.

Although courted by Hollywood, Julie remains true to the roots of her profession and chooses roles on merit, not money. While this is very noble, it means that, unfortunately, she doesn't necessarily receive the international recognition she deserves. Thankfully, the recent globally award-winning film *Billy Elliot* helped to correct the public's under-estimation of this fine actress.

Perhaps the saddest thing is that Julie Walters was typecast at a young age as an old biddy, a worrying mother and a frumpy housewife. Her modesty means that she isn't scared to appear as a hag, but make-up, padding and wigs often hide her beauty. She is petite, standing at just five foot three and a half, and boasts a slender figure, wonderful cheekbones and captivating smile.

Julie has certainly never been short of male admirers and had two five-year relationships in her teens and twenties. However, raised an independent woman, she heeded her mother's mantra: never rely on a man for anything. It was not until her late thirties that, without looking, she met Grant, a man with whom she felt she could spend the rest of her life. In her typically blunt fashion, rather than race him up the aisle, she asked if he would father her children. Their daughter, Maisie, was born two years shy of Julie's fortieth birthday.

For someone who lived a carefree life, had never settled down and was wholly unmaternal, motherhood hit Julie like a ton of bricks. She was engulfed by her new compassion and suddenly became committed to helping various children's charities. The couple's world was turned upside down when Maisie was diagnosed with leukaemia at two years of age.

Understandably, Julie wanted to work less and look after her daughter, but, as Grant was a student and she was the main breadwinner, she was forced to continue working.

It was possibly the hardest thing she had ever done. But, as with everything in her life, when interviewed about this decision she was honest and open, freely admitting that at times she was jealous of Grant's relationship with their daughter.

Suddenly, the actress's outlook changed. She undertook only work that she felt was really worthy, and preferably filmed nearby. Nevertheless, she will always jump at the chance to work with Alan Bleasdale or Victoria Wood, considers both big and small screen equally and, although nervous of stage work, continually returns to the boards.

Despite her OBE, four BAFTA awards and two Oscar nominations, what Julie fails to come to terms with is her celebrity. 'When I think of the future I think of doing my washing, so I've something to wear tomorrow,' she says.

She is, and always has been, utterly grounded. At the beginning of her fame, Julie attended a theatre award ceremony where she was honoured for her role in the stage version of *Educating Rita*. On the journey home, Julie and her colleagues noticed an old woman slip and fall into the gutter. Still in her finery and clutching her award, Julie leaped from the car and took charge of the situation. Drawing on her nursing skills, she checked the woman's vital signs and insisted on taking her to hospital herself.

Such a selfless action is typical of Julie.

This is the story of a fun-loving Brummie girl who has achieved immeasurable success in her profession, while remaining remarkably down-to-earth.

1. UKULELES, MANGLES AND BLOOMERS

At 6 a.m. on Wednesday, 22 February 1950, Mary Walters went into labour. None of her previous deliveries had been easy. This was her fourth time and she had a high temperature and flu symptoms. Accompanied by her husband, Thomas, on an uncomfortable bus ride, when Mary finally reached St Chad's Hospital in Birmingham, it was established that the baby was in distress – the umbilical cord had become wrapped around its neck. As both mother and baby's conditions deteriorated, the hospital priest was summoned. Thomas was presented with an impossible predicament: should he save his wife or his unborn child?

Thankfully, he was spared the agonising decision as Mary finally gave birth to their second daughter. The girl's name was registered as Julia Mary Walters on 8 March in Edgbaston. The complicated and traumatic birth was the first of many hurdles for Julie, as she soon became known.

Her mother, Mary Bridget O'Brien, was born in 1915 and had a strict Catholic upbringing on a farm in County Mayo, Republic of Ireland. In her girlhood, she initially inherited her father's low opinion of women, including of her own mother, whom she deemed foolish. Frustrated by her parents' rural lifestyle, Mary ran away to England, where she struggled to prove her father's antiquated, sexist attitude wrong.

Despite her ambitions, she settled in Birmingham, gaining menial employment as a barmaid. Soon Mary was courted by Thomas Walters, a humble builder and decorator, five years her senior and hailing from a large family. When Thomas proposed, Mary accepted and, although she had broken familial ties, wrote to her parents with the joyous news.

'Come home at once,' came the scathing reply from her pious mother. 'A daughter of mine marrying a man in overalls!'

Mary would have none of it, and promptly married Thomas on 12 February 1941. She had retained her Catholicism and, although her groom was not especially religious, the wedding took place at her local church, St Patrick's on Dudley Road, next to the canal. The newlyweds moved into 69 Bishopton Road in Smethwick, a town a few miles west of the city, and all communication with Mary's parents was severed.

Birmingham was one of Britain's most important industrial sites during the twentieth century and, at the outbreak of World War Two, its manufacturing might was called upon to produce planes, vehicles, engines and ammunition. Consequently, the city became one of the

Luftwaffe's primary targets and suffered not only Britain's first air raid, but also regular attacks throughout 1941 and 1942. Much of the city centre was flattened, more than six thousand homes were lost and some five thousand civilians were killed or injured. Patriotic Thomas laid down his paintbrush and rallied to help his country, taking on work as a machine-tool setter for army tank parts.

A year after their marriage, Mary discovered she was pregnant, and their first child, Thomas Patrick, was born on 30 October 1942. Sadly, this coincided with the death of Mary's father, Thomas O'Brien; her mother sold the farm in Ireland and arrived on Mary's doorstep, expecting to be cared for in her retirement.

Problems arose immediately as the two headstrong women clashed. Furthermore, Mary's mother wouldn't speak to Thomas Sr, whom she considered beneath her, and resented Thomas Jr, simply because he had arrived first.

Two years later, the family expanded further with another boy, Kevan John (known as Kevin), born on 28 December 1944. After the war ended, life resumed some normality as Thomas returned to his decorating business and Mary took on work as a post office clerk. Their third child, a girl, was born on 7 November 1947. She was named Mary, but tragically died just minutes later, leaving a family in mourning. It was to this troubled background that Julie entered the Walters clan a few years later.

After Julie's birth, family life continued in the end-of-terrace property in Bishopton Road. The attractive street led directly down to Warley Woods and Lightwoods Park, a large open area with playing fields. 'Smethwick was, and still is, a place of contrasts,' explains Julie's childhood friend, Mary Bodfish. 'In the northern end it resembles its Black Country neighbours, which at the time were severely affected by the closure of several big engineering works, putting thousands of people out of work.

'At the southern end in Bearwood, where Julie grew up, many people commuted into Birmingham and it remained relatively prosperous. It is a bustling, densely packed residential district, only three miles from the city centre, with long streets of well-maintained terraced houses, built in the late nineteenth and early twentieth centuries to provide housing for the upper working class. It has retained its character remarkably well.'

Despite outward appearances, the Walterses were far from wealthy. With an ageing mother-in-law to support on top of his own family, Thomas worked long hours, while Mary juggled her work with running the household. This was not the flourishing lifestyle she had dreamed of back in Ireland. 'My mother had three children, no washing machine and a mangle in the garden', says Julie. 'For somebody with plenty of ambition, it must have been awful.' Not only was Mary intelligent, but she had always wanted to see the world.

Mary's thwarted aspiration manifested itself in striving for her offspring's success. Unfortunately for the children, this meant a firm upbringing without any display of affection. 'I was loved all right, but she didn't show it,' Julie continues. 'I think she was judgemental in a genetic way. Because she felt frustrated, none of us could ever be good enough, either.'

By contrast, Julie's father was creative, funny and endlessly supportive of the children's fantasies. 'I was emotionally much closer to him,' she says. 'He was very gentle, whereas she was full of unspent passion. So she passed her drive on to me.'

While Mary provided Julie's momentum, Thomas encouraged her first flirtation with entertaining. The curtains cutting across the bay window at the front of the house created a miniature stage for the vivacious toddler. 'I was given a ukulele, when I was three: terrible!' she laughs. 'Coming out from behind the curtains at home, throwing them back and doing the show. It was just my desire to show off.'

Julie began with some simplistic impressions of her relatives and moved on to the stars she saw on television. Despite her age, the child could act, make people laugh and belt out gutsy numbers in the guise of the sensual Eartha Kitt and the flamboyant Shirley Bassey. Few could resist Julie's big brown eyes gazing up through her auburn fringe. Thomas, a pianist himself, applauded wholeheartedly, along with the rest of the audience, including her paternal aunts and uncles, and next-door neighbour, Mrs Price.

Mary's response, however, was dismissive: 'Acting? No good will come of it.'

Aged four, Julie was enrolled in the local Catholic primary school in Smethwick. There she made friends easily, amusing them with her routines, but it was her home life that demanded the most attention. Her grandmother became increasingly senile and Thomas and Mary struggled to look after her.

Julie describes the septuagenarian as 'a tall, rather stately woman, with iron-grey plaited headphones and one yellow tooth in the middle of an otherwise vacant upper set'. As she had suffered two strokes since her arrival, Thomas and Kevin regularly joked, 'At the third stroke she will be seventy-something.'

Grandma was in a fairly permanent state of mental confusion, and her sporadic moments of clarity were even more upsetting, as she gazed at her surroundings in bewilderment and cried at her confusion.

Julie and her brothers thought their grandmother's erratic behaviour (which included frequently turning up at the local post office in the middle of the night, wearing nothing but pink, urine-soaked bloomers) was hysterical. However, the reality of living with such constant worry was extremely distressing for Mary and only served to make her more distant.

Not one for mother–daughter heart-to-hearts at the best of times, Mary certainly did not discuss the delicate subject of the birds and the bees. Julie remembers her confusion as a youngster when she caught her father wearing only his pyjama top.

'I knew I'd seen a lot of dark hair where his jacket ended and his pyjama bottoms should have begun,' she says, 'but I could have sworn there was something else. Extra. *Dangling*.' Unsure whether she had just imagined the extra appendage, Julie broached the subject with her mother. The inquisitive little girl asked point-blank if her father was the same as she was 'down there'. While pushing her tangled sheets through the mangle, Mary curtly responded in her thick Irish accent, 'Yeees!'

Julie was positively relieved by the news, since she had not cared for what she saw. Furthermore, she says, 'It also meant that what I'd *definitely* seen when my brother was in the bath would drop off in time and he'd get better.'

And so she was left with a perverse understanding of male and female sexual characteristics. Undeterred by her mother's brusque manner on the topic, Julie was as curious as ever and found one of her father's condoms under her parents' bed. She and a friend spent a hilarious afternoon taking turns to blow up this 'special balloon', much to her mother's dismay.

Mary felt strongly that her mischievous daughter needed firmer guidance than that offered by the local primary school. Although the family had no spare cash, she was determined to send Julie to St Paul's private Roman Catholic school, so they scrimped and saved to afford what she perceived as the best all-round education.

St Paul's was tucked away in an affluent residential area on Vernon Road, Smethwick, and backed on to the picturesque Edgbaston Reservoir. Run by foreboding nuns, the new school came as quite a shock to the six-year-old. The yellow-trimmed blue and white uniform had to be worn exactly according to the rules. There was to be no childish behaviour and the faith was revered.

Julie was still intrigued by sex, not least due to her mother's reluctance on the subject, but found that her new tutors only confused matters further. 'During my early schooldays, the bundle of misunderstandings was compounded by the nuns,' she says. She was bewildered with the dos and don'ts: chocolate should be avoided because it was a stimulant; patent-leather shoes might reflect up her skirt; and girls shouldn't cross their legs 'because you never saw the Virgin Mary cross hers'. Julie says, 'I personally have never seen the Virgin Mary cross anything.'

On arrival at St Paul's, Julie realised that all the other pupils were quite posh and, with her heavy Black Country accent, she stood out like a sore thumb. The naturally affable girl was uncharacteristically shunned. 'I had a dreadful time,' she says. 'I've never been so unhappy in my life.'

Socialising aside, her real problems arose in elocution classes. 'I refused to pronounce bath "barth", instead of the hard, flat "a" sound I used. My dad said "bath" the way I did, and it was as if I was betraying him and all he stood for, saying it wasn't good enough. And I deeply resented that. I couldn't bring myself to say "barth".'

Her tutors believed they had a valuable job to do and were determined to succeed, at all costs. 'The nuns, through fair means or foul, wanted only the best for the girls – but it didn't always work out that way,' recalls a former pupil, Margaret Sheils.

'I was hit and hit in elocution lessons by these nuns,' winces Julie. 'One in particular I'd kill if I met her now. So I wrote "electric chair, electric chair, electric chair" right across my elocution book.' The experience gave her nightmares; she was particularly unhappy given that she'd liked her previous school – an ordinary school where her speech was the same as the other children's.

Like the misguided nuns, Mary sought only what was best for her children: she wanted the boys to be academic and Julie to be a lady, and was unaware that her daughter was so unhappy. 'She had three of us to look after and our grandmother, plus a full-time job – she did what she thought was best. She must have been deeply disappointed,' acknowledges Julie.

Forced to endure St Paul's for a further five years, the normally happy-go-lucky girl became insecure and was left with a residual hatred towards her persecutors, and a suspicion of organised religion. 'Those nuns were obviously deeply unhappy people, but they had no right to take it out on the children,' according to Julie. 'I'll never forget them.'

While Julie was growing up, so too was the country. The 1950s had been an era of considerable change for Britain, combining postwar rebuilding with expansion for the future. An important link between the north and south was made when the M1 motorway, joining Birmingham to London, opened in 1959. Hailed by the minister for transport as 'a magnificent motorway opening up a new era in road travel, in keeping with the new, exciting, scientific age in which we live', the road was actually quite treacherous: there was no speed limit, central reservation, crash barriers or lighting. Nonetheless, the Walterses used it to maintain contact with Thomas's family in the capital.

'One day we were all piled into my father's little grey Ford Esquire Estate with instructions to sit on Grandma should she take a peculiar turn,' recounts Julie. The children were relieved to find their eccentric relative remained serene throughout the journey. 'The only hitch was when she disappeared at one of our frequent toilet stops – essential, as Grandma was incontinent – and turned up crying twenty minutes later, a pair of soggy bloomers around her ankles.'

Evidently the excursion itself passed without any further hiccups until the return trip. Julie's aunt had provided various magazines for the long drive, but Grandma painstakingly ripped each one to shreds so that the back of the car soon resembled a hamster's nest. Oblivious of her surroundings, she then wanted to get up and make a cup of tea.

'For God's sake, sit on her!' shouted Thomas.

'A scuffle ensued, which lasted the remainder of the journey,' Julie continues. 'Tiny scraps of paper flying everywhere. We must have looked from the outside like one of those snowstorm paperweights that had been shaken violently.'

The family were exhausted by the time they finally reached Smethwick, at which point Grandma instantly calmed down and said, 'We've landed – *now* are you happy?'

Today Julie executes the anecdote with keen comic detail, but the fact remained that Grandma was proving hard work. After a full day at the post office, Mary didn't know what to expect when she returned to the house – on more than one occasion she found her mother sitting in the middle of the living room, head to toe in black dust, amid the entire contents of the coalhouse. Julie remembers, 'Even more strongly etched in my memory is my poor mother's weary face as she uttered the words, "May the great God look to me."'

While her parents were struggling with their draining duties, Julie continued to find humour and entertainment in all situations. As she got older, her amateur shows developed into grander affairs and she transferred her performances to the garage with help from her brothers. Though the only theatre she had been to were productions at her mother's office, television also had an effect on a young Julie: 'I used to think arrogantly, I can do those parts, all of them – and better! It wasn't a desire to be famous or a film star: I just wanted to be on the stage.'

2. THE SUBVERSIVE MOTH

In 1961 Mary Walters finally saw how withdrawn and unhappy her daughter was at St Paul's and agreed to send her to a different senior school. The relief felt by Julie was matched by the financial easing on the family, and life looked up.

Julie joined Holly Lodge Grammar School for Girls that autumn. 'You were considered to be quite bright to pass the eleven-plus and go to the grammar school,' recalls former student Jacky Wollaston, née Barron. 'It invoked much jealousy and rivalry from the pupils at the local comprehensive school, Smethwick Hall.'

Holly Lodge was founded in 1922 and moved to new premises on its present-day site five years later. Set at the end of an extended driveway, there are two schools within the same grounds: the boys' grammar and the girls' grammar, tantalisingly facing each other. In Julie's day, the pupils were expressly forbidden from mixing, particularly while traversing the lengthy path to and from the Holly Lane entrance.

The main girls' school buildings formed a long rectangle, in the centre of which was a sacrosanct plot of grass. The structure was very traditional and the decoration old-fashioned, with lots of oak panelling. The most impressive part of the school was the large assembly hall: it boasted a generous stage edged by rich velvet curtains, extensive panels of school honours and an imposing balcony bearing the Smethwick coat of arms in its centre. On the floor above was the school library, which had a series of half-railed French windows opening out into the hall.

Although the school was predominantly Church of England, Julie was obliged by Mary to maintain her faith, despite her recent trauma with the nuns at St Paul's. 'Catholic girls attended a service in the library while one for the rest of the school took place in the hall,' explains Julie's school friend Mary Bodfish. 'For the secular part of each morning's proceedings the French windows were opened and the Catholic girls crowded over the railings to listen.'

Holly Lodge was run by the headmistress, Miss Mary Fisher. She was only the second female head teacher and was considered to be very much 'old school', still wearing a mortar board and gown. The girls were divided into three houses, Da Vinci, Copernicus and Erasmus, and pupils were separated into an antiquated system of an academic group (bound for the civil service) and a commercial group (secretarial/clerical). 'I believe Julie Walters was in the commercial group,' recalls a fellow student, Dorothy Williams. 'Very few pupils went on to university simply because we were not encouraged to do so in those days.'

The dress code was as strict and exacting as the education. The school's colours were navy-blue and gold, and the winter uniform comprised a navy-blue gymslip or tunic (later replaced by a pleated skirt), a white shirt, a navy and gold tie and a slung purse. The summer uniform was a pale-blue and white dress, which was universally detested. Outside, pupils had to wear a blazer and beret displaying the town's coat of arms. 'Berets were hated by each and every one of us and were taken off as soon as we reached the school gates,' says Jacky Wollaston, 'but woe betide you if a teacher spotted you – it was one hundred lines or detention.'

However rigid Holly Lodge seemed, it was a dream come true in comparison with St Paul's, and Julie was eternally grateful. 'I might have been very different had I remained at the Catholic school,' she says. 'Fortunately, I was eventually switched to a girls' grammar school and never looked back.' Indeed, Julie quickly returned to her former cheerful self and soon became known in her new surroundings as an exuberant character.

Pupils from the Bearwood area of Smethwick travelled together on the X27 Midland Red bus. 'This bus was an institution,' remembers another former student, Elizabeth Skros. 'I caught it in Wigorn Road along with Julie. So many friends were won and lost during the course of the journey to Forster Street.'

The X27 picked up pupils of both sexes for Holly Lodge's two schools, but again they were segregated: boys upstairs, girls downstairs. While most students conformed to this rule, a few girls forming the 'in-crowd' used to sneak upstairs. Naturally, Julie was one of them.

Having stowed away on the upper deck, rather than keep quiet, the rebellious prepubescent held court. Christine Lewis-Smith, an older pupil, says, 'Julie was always the comedienne on the school bus – upstairs with the boys where the girls weren't really allowed to go!'

While Julie flaunted her impish nature, she also developed her passion for showing off in a constructive way: during acting classes. Her drama teacher, Miss Claudia Williams, channelled the young girl's focus and encouraged her flair. 'Acting was very important to me at school,' remembers Julie. 'I preferred it to lessons.'

In the summer of 1962, the joint school play was *A Midsummer Night's Dream*. The annual event always caused much excitement, because it was the one legitimate opportunity to mix with the boys, and for this play the invitation was uniquely extended to first-year girls. The giggling gaggle featured as the fairies, but Julie's reputation preceded her.

'You're playing Moth because you're a nuisance,' said the producer, Mr Hodgetts. The boys' school tutor often honed excellent performances out of some promising young performers and was determined to preserve some control over his rebellious charge.

Rather than cause trouble, Julie was content to behave, as she was finally in the limelight. 'I loved being the centre of attention and I wanted to act, but I had no idea how to achieve my ambition,' she says.

This was her real test after hours of practice on her makeshift stage in the garage and she thoroughly enjoyed herself, as did her audience. 'I witnessed Julie's stage debut, as my elder brother was in the cast,' recalls Mary Bodfish. 'It was an excellent production, at which I was utterly entranced.'

Acting aside, Julie wasn't particularly interested in school. In fact, she became more concerned with the opposite sex. She was a slight, pretty girl with an unruly mass of chestnut curls. As she grew older, like most girls of her age, Julie adhered to the latest trends. Holly Lodge pupils were allowed to swap their tunics for a pleated skirt in the second year and many, including Julie, folded their skirts several times at the waistband to create indecently mini versions. She also carried the unwieldy wicker baskets that were all the rage, even though they snagged her tights as she walked. She was even known to experiment with the latest extravagant hairdos. 'Most of the girls folded their beret in half and pinned it to the back of their heads with hair grips so as not to mess their beehive hairstyles,' remembers Erika Welsh.

Most of the classrooms overlooked the playing fields and tennis courts and during the summer the girls would sit and gawp at the sixth-form boys. Aside from the annual play, there was to be no contact between the two schools and the prefects waged a daily war to force the girls to walk on one side of the drive and the boys on the other. To the hormonal teenagers, this rule was like a red rag to a bull, and Julie was no exception.

'I went to Holly Lodge Boys' School and was in the same year as Julie,' recalls David Llewellyn. 'When I walked up the drive to school, one of the girls used to hide behind the trees and jump out at me! She would pull funny faces and do silly characters. I think she had a crush on me, as this was a regular occurrence, but I was a tall and gawky lad and, at that age, didn't want to be seen to be interested in girls. We never spoke, but I'm sure that it was Julie.'

David could be right because, under the influence of her mother, Julie seemed not to know how to display affection and almost certainly opted for uncontrollable vivacity. Other sources confirm that Julie wasn't backward in coming forward as an adolescent. Craig Barney was also in the same year and Julie attended many of his birthday parties. His sister, Zita, remembers, 'him hiding under the table whilst she tried to kiss him!'

Considering Julie's assertion that it 'was with great ignorance that I entered puberty', she made up for her lack of knowledge with bravado, drawn from her outgoing nature and the company she kept. Her best friend was Mary Marshall and the pair hung around in a small clique, notorious for their high jinks.

'Although Holly Lodge was a grammar school, it failed to bring out the best in its pupils academically, leading to quite a few of them expressing their intelligence in less than conventional ways!' explains Dorothy Williams. 'There were about seven hundred girls there, and you were very much a small fish in a big pond. Showing off was one way of getting attention. Julie was probably bored and underachieving, as was I and just about everyone else I knew who went there.'

'It was simple high spirits,' Mary Bodfish elaborates. 'I recall her as a girl full of vitality, with a lively mind. She was always at the centre of a group of friends, extracting as much fun as possible out of any situation. She loved to laugh.'

Holly Lodge saw a period of upheaval in the early 1960s, which unfortunately served to make disciplinary matters worse. Miss Fisher retired as headmistress, but her successor, Miss O'Neill, suffered a nervous breakdown not long after taking up the post. The institution was in its last phase as a grammar school and the staff were concerned about their future. Consequently, the standard of teaching varied from poor to excellent, and the girls received a somewhat uneven education.

A high proportion of the teachers were female, but the geography teacher, a token male called Mr Taylor, was one of Julie's favourites. He was a fairly young and talented teacher who was well liked by all the girls. In her bid for attention, Julie pushed him to the limit, just as she did with all the staff. 'I have a vivid memory of him insisting on her piping down and behaving herself in the school dining room, when her comments and jokes had created too much of an uproar at her dinner table!' laughs Mary Bodfish.

Although not an academic, Julie was good at English, taught by Mr Whitby-James, and French, instructed by Madame Sviedre, but it was the physical subjects in which she excelled. Along with a new science and arts block, a modern gymnasium was opened at Holly Lodge during this period. Julie enjoyed sport because she was able to expel some of her pent-up energy and fool around simultaneously.

'The cloakrooms were at basement level and were a mix of cagelike fixtures, for storing PE equipment, and central-heating pipes,' says Jacky Wollaston. 'It was very dark and dismal there, but, almost without exception, girls used to swing on the steel bars which ran across the room at a height of around seven feet. If you were caught, you were given a hundred lines: "I must not swing on the bars", or maybe detention for a second offence.' No prizes for guessing one teenager who often flouted this rule!

To be fair, Julie was a dedicated sportswoman and took part in several disciplines. The school houses took part in annual sporting contests, but then the three-house system was reorganised, disrupting formed friendships and alliances. The pupils were divided into four groups, named after local ranges of hills (and given appropriate nicknames by the girls): Clent ('clotty Clent'), Lickey ('lousy Lickey'), Malvern ('mouldy Malvern') and Wenlock ('weedy Wenlock').

'Julie was captain of the Wenlock sports team at one stage,' recalls Erika Welsh. 'At the end of the summer term we had the school sports day, which was held at Hagley playing fields, when all four houses competed against each other. One year Julie made me enter the hurdles race, as we were so short of runners. I was quite small and, when I checked these hurdles out, I couldn't even high-jump them, never mind race and hurdle them, so I hid in the toilets. I was mortified to hear my name being called out several times over the Tannoy system to line up for the race.

'She gave me a real telling-off for that. "It's competing that counts, not winning," she said, but I wasn't about to make a complete prat of myself for Julie Walters, or anybody for that matter.'

Decked out in the standard gym uniform of a white polo shirt and 'big blue knickers', Julie took part in field events, such as the high jump. She excelled at track events, even representing her county, Worcestershire, in running. 'She was very sporty,' recalls another ex-pupil, Judith Ganecki. 'We always seemed to compete in the same athletic events, but she was always that centimetre ahead of me. We also played in the same basketball team.' Julie tried her hand at all games and joined the First XI hockey team for a while. 'I believe Julie was quite good at hockey,' says her teammate Dorothy Williams, 'but she got hit in the face once, as did we all!'

Like all teenagers, Julie was often embarrassed by the behaviour of her parents. This was exacerbated by the fact that, while she was going through puberty, her mother hit the menopause and the two hormonal women frequently went head to head.

Although Mary refused to discuss matters of a sexual nature, she revelled in humiliating her daughter with fairly graphic details of her birth. When Julie was laid up in bed with flu on her fifteenth birthday, Mary seized her opportunity. 'Fifteen years ago today, I woke at six a.m. and knew I was in trouble,' she hollered up the stairs in her thick Irish brogue.

'Why?' Julie asked wearily.

Lowering her voice, Mary placed special emphasis on her vocabulary. 'Because I was Passing Your Motions. I had Asian flu.'

Mary described how she had eaten a 'fish dinner' and promptly brought it back up. Before returning to the kitchen, she concluded her tale by casually mentioning that baby Julie had been in distress and Thomas was asked to choose whom he should save. Julie had never heard the last part of the saga before and it wasn't until a couple of years later that she found the courage to enquire what her father's response was.

'Well, I had to choose your mother,' he said, matter-of-factly. 'Imagine how she'd have felt if I'd chosen you.' Julie wasn't surprised by the twist because she was used to a lack of affection.

Family conversations more often revolved around practical subjects. 'I'm interested in politics,' Julie says. 'I'm interested in what's going on in the world, how people behave and how your life is often in the hands of other people.'

Mary was keen that Julie should not forget her Irish heritage and made her aware of the country's problems, long before 1969. 'My mother was always going on about absentee landlords and the English. It was fascinating,' she says. Within a few years, the Unionist–Republican issue erupted in rioting on the streets of Northern Ireland and continued until the early 1970s, when the IRA turned their attentions to England's capital and major cities.

There were changes closer to home as Asian families began to move into Birmingham during the 1960s, settling in west Smethwick near Holly Lodge. 'The number of houses being bought by Asians in nearby Marshall Street became a focus of local concern, nominally over property values,' recalls Mary Bodfish. 'Smethwick hit the headlines when some homeowners in this street requested the local council to buy any properties that came on to the market, presumably so control could then be exercised over who occupied them. There was political uproar, and Smethwick was in the national spotlight at the 1964 general election, when a racist slogan was used to highlight the Labour Party's immigration policy and a local Conservative councillor overturned a large Labour majority.'

Living in Bearwood, the Walterses were largely untouched by the developments, but Holly Lodge school witnessed an influx of Asian girls in the 1967 academic intake. Open-minded Julie did not view these pupils any differently from her other friends and amiably continued with her assortment of teenage activities.

It was Julie's grandmother who was problematic, discouraging many of her peers from visiting her home. Her erratic ways unnerved Julie's friends, but even worse was her unmistakable odour. 'I was so used to it I didn't really notice it, but any unsuspecting visitor sitting in Grandma's chair was in for a shock,' laughs Julie. 'It was like sitting on a sponge and squelched with wee-wee at the slightest pressure.'

Despite the racial upheaval, Smethwick in the 1960s was quite a close-knit community. Gangs of teenagers would hang out in the parks, the bandstand in Warley Woods at the end of Julie's road being a favourite venue.

'We were invited through the school to join a youth club to boost numbers there,' says Jacky Wollaston. 'As it was King Arthur's *Boys'* Club, quite a few of the girls went, but not many of us remained members, as the novelty soon wore off.

'Thimblemill Baths was the "in" place to be seen. In winter they closed the swimming baths and boarded the floor. On Tuesday and Wednesday evenings there were discos. Tuesdays were usually fairly quiet and cost two shillings [10 pence], but Wednesdays were far better and cost two shillings and sixpence [12½ pence]. On Saturday evenings, live groups performed for an entrance fee between five and ten shillings [25–50 pence], according to who they were. The Who played there one time, that cost ten shillings.

'Fairly near to Smethwick is West Bromwich and the home of another frequently visited club – the Adelphi – but this burned down in the 1970s and never reopened. Birmingham was a bus ride away, which added unnecessary expense. Besides, parents generally weren't too keen on allowing their teenage girls to venture that far – the city was too dangerous for young girls in the opinion of most.' The area had been rebuilt after World War Two and became a modern municipality, boasting a fine shopping centre, plenty of dining venues and ample pubs for entertainment. 'As we grew up,' continues Jacky, 'the lure of the bright lights saw most of us visiting the clubs – the Rum Runner, Sloopy's, the Opposite Lock and Barbarella's, to name but a few.'

All these activities cost money and the Walterses were far from wealthy. Requiring some form of paid employment, fifteen-year-old Julie managed to land herself a dream job: helping her friend, Christine Saranczuk, in a local confectionery outlet every Sunday. 'The shop was called the Bon Bon, Smethwick always having been very Continental in its outlook,' laughs Julie.

Predictably for two teenagers, they consumed as much as they sold, although the owner never complained. 'In between sampling the stock we used to spend hours using the phone in the shop to call every single person we knew,' she continues, proving she was always up to mischief. 'Once we had exhausted our list of friends, we used to resort to random numbers and play tricks on them.'

She recalls that one of the girls would say into the phone, 'Hello, I'm from the GPO and we need to test your line. Would you mind whistling into your phone?'

The greatest problem for the pair was the difficulty of simultaneously laughing and eating. 'Work in the Bon Bon wasn't as much a first job for me as a passport to heaven,' Julie concludes.

Back at school, Julie's free spirit sometimes affected other students, as well as the teachers. During the Easter break in 1965, Julie and a friend, Jennifer Moss, were allowed on a trip to Paris with some of the sixth-formers. Their escapades proved a great annoyance to the rest of the party.

'They were always the last to meet the coach on the day trips,' recalls Dorothy Rogers, 'and one day in Versailles we'd been round the palace and there was no sign of them. We waited for hours until they came tearing round the corner, eating lollies which they'd been buying while we were all sitting on the bus.'

Prefects were almost as officious as teachers and Julie did not discriminate as to the target of her pranks. One prefect's chair was unceremoniously sabotaged. Two former prefects, Anne Baker and Glenys Hopkins (née Peters), remember her high jinks well. 'Julie was two years below me at school and I was her form prefect at one point,' says Anne. 'This involved "minding" the class while the staff were in a meeting. I remember Julie because she was high-spirited and lively.'

'I recall her as a very lovable rogue,' adds Glenys. 'Julie was a cheeky rebel who flouted those silly school rules.'

Fun though Julie's antics seemed to her peers, Mary Bodfish points out, 'She was well known throughout the school. This was a characteristic that not all of the teaching staff considered appropriate in a grammar-school girl, who should have been working seriously for her O levels.'

Julie scraped through her exams, passing just four O levels. Over the summer of 1966, she took on part-time work at the C&A retailers in Birmingham. Oddly, the branch already had an employee called Julie Walters, so the sixteen-year-old had to assume a pseudonym and was given the surname Bishop for administrative purposes.

The work was so mind-numbing, she found herself playing up once more. 'For some inexplicable reason my job title was "packer", but in fact all I ever seemed to do was *unpack* clothes,' she says. They spent their eight-hour days in what Julie described as a 'windowless caged compound, well away from the customers, concentrating on the main task in hand.' As her daily mission seemed to be messing around, unsurprisingly, however, Julie's service was short-lived.

Beginning to despair of her uneducated, unemployable daughter, Mary Walters forced Julie to give her future some serious thought. When she failed to come up with anything other than her enjoyment of entertaining, her mother guided her with a heavy hand towards nursing: a worthwhile, 'proper' profession with secure prospects.

'Because I was at the teenage stage of only caring about the day ahead rather than my long-term future, I didn't bother to disagree with her choice,' says Julie. With overwhelming indifference, she simultaneously applied for the SRN course at the Queen Elizabeth School of Nursing in Birmingham, and dutifully entered the sixth form at Holly Lodge.

In September 1966, Julie's drama teacher, Miss Claudia Williams, had been appointed headmistress of Holly Lodge. Her first main task was to oversee the transformation from single-sex grammar school to co-education comprehensive the following year.

This period also spelled the end of an era for Julie. Rather than struggle through the sixth form, the errant pupil more often than not bunked off classes. The few times she showed up for lessons, the teachers invariably wished she hadn't, as she turned the classroom upside down. Over the summer of 1967 Julie undertook another selection of part-time jobs, including work in a shoe shop and a cigarette factory, before returning to Holly Lodge for the final charade.

Eventually Miss Williams felt that the level of disruption Julie caused was no longer tolerable, particularly considering she was clearly not making satisfactory progress towards her A levels.

'Mr Taylor, the deputy head, approached me on one of my rare appearances in school and told me that I wasn't required back the following term,' recalls Julie.

She was expelled aged seventeen.

'Not for anything appalling,' she justifies, 'I just wasn't there very much, and they said I was subversive – I had to go and look that up in the dictionary!'

Jacky remembers, 'We knew she was "asked to leave", but the reasons were kept very quiet – it was almost unheard of for anyone to be in that position. It was quite a scandal and rumours were spread, but that is all they were.'

Fortuitously, Julie had already received her acceptance on to the nursing course at the Queen Elizabeth Hospital, so she moulded the truth to fit.

'I explained very convincingly to Mum that there was no need for me to stay on at school because I wanted to start nursing right away,' she elucidates.

The nursing course wasn't due to start for a while, so, to try to make amends, she quietly took on work as a clerk in the Midland Assurance office in Birmingham. However, she found office work extremely arduous. 'The dullness and sterility of the job almost drove me crazy,' she recalled in the *Observer*. 'I really felt as if I was doing time in prison rather than working for a living.' She was one of two juniors: the other, Lynn, was two years younger.

In order to get through their days, Lynn and Julie mucked around. One of their favourite activities was searching through the many thousands of files in the office for funny names. 'Discovering fantastic names like Agnes Bottoms and my personal favourite, Cornelius Crack, in a mound of manila files could reduce us both to tear-stained and shoulder-heaving hysterics,' continued Julie.

Julie also admitted that, when she couldn't find anything to laugh about and the job became depressing, she developed a unique way of lightening her workload: she rather unconventionally 'filed' bundles of correspondence pertaining to old records down the toilet! The whole experience was an eye-opener for Julie: not only did she discover that she was not cut out for office work, but also that she had inherited Mary Walters's independence.

Julie's partner in crime, Lynn,* had a very different outlook on life. 'She was a big girl full of good fun, with a voice like a foghorn,' says Julie,

---

* When Julie first recounted this story in *Baby Talk*, the friend's name was Lynn, but in a more recent elaboration of the events in *Julie Walters Is an Alien*, the same friend was called Sue – during interviews for this biography, the name Carol was alternatively suggested.

'and her one and only ambition was to be married. She was simply passing time until that wonderful day arrived.'

To Julie, this was impossible to imagine. Mary had been so determined that her daughter should lead the full life she, Mary, had missed out on, that she had also put her off marriage completely. Her mother had drummed into her that a woman should never rely on a man for anything.

Julie concluded that, when she had seen Lynn three years later up Smethwick High Street, Lynn had been pushing a pram with a baby and a toddler in it. 'Lynn had a huge black eye, her face had hardened and she looked utterly run down . . . The fun, the dreams, the hope and the youth had gone.'

3. MY MASTURBATOR HAS BROKEN

In May 1968 Julie joined the nursing course at the Queen Elizabeth Hospital in Edgbaston, Birmingham. The entry requirements were five O levels, including English, but, failing that, an applicant was allowed to take the GNC (General Nursing Council) test, which was a glorified IQ test. Julie scraped in.

'At the time there were three entry groups a year,' recalls her fellow trainee Pat King (née Peters), 'and we were set number two hundred and forty. We were considered a small set as there were only about sixty of us. The QE was on a par with the big teaching hospitals in London, so it was quite a feather in our caps to be accepted for training.

'Our course consisted of eight weeks of PTS (Preliminary Training School), where we had one day on the wards and the rest of the week in school. Then we had eight weeks of one day at school and the rest of the week on the wards – we all used to pray the coach taking us for our one day would break down.'

It was compulsory for nurses to 'live in' until their third year, which was actually quite an exciting prospect. 'That was the big lure – being away from home and the freedom that offered in those days,' says another student, Jane Parnum (née Tydeman).

'The QE site was on Cadbury family land and for the initial sixteen weeks we lived in two old houses donated by the Cadbury family,' continues Pat. 'There was a surgical side (Cadbury's Chocolate, the west wing) and a medical side (Vincents Toffees, the east wing). [Evidently Julie's sweet tooth had followed her from her days at the Bon Bon!] It was built in the 1930s and dedicated to the Queen Mother – a bronze statue stands in the entrance hall.'

According to Pat, 'The two houses were beautiful places, in wonderful grounds, and there were about four or five of us in a room. We formed firm friendships with our roommates. Julie was one of the girls who shared a house with us. She looked like a little girl, with her short curly hair and deep-set brown eyes.' Julie, much to her mother's chagrin, hunched her shoulders and had trimmed her long locks, but inwardly she was still the same.

'She was very friendly. She was very funny and could always be relied upon to do lots of crazy things. I remember one day we found an old piano in an outbuilding and she gave us an impression of Shirley Bassey.' Clearly, Julie had maintained her musical ability alongside her comedy streak.

When the trainees moved to the hospital on a permanent basis, they lived in the nurses' accommodation, a building directly opposite the QE hospital called Nuffield House. But the freedom they thought they had attained was suddenly far from their reach. 'The nursing homes were often guarded by officious matrons and porters,' says Jane Parnum, 'so a lot of nocturnal entrances were done in a variety of ways!'

As the rules became stricter, so Julie tried harder to break them.

'We were only allowed one late pass a week,' says Pat. 'We had to sign in at the night porter's office and woe betide you if you didn't have a late pass. The rest of the time we had to be in by nine forty-five p.m., and the doors were shut and bolted by ten p.m. The only way into the nurses' home after that was through a subterranean tunnel from the hospital.

'I believe Julie got very adept at climbing through the dining room window, which a friend would leave open. Then all she had to do was dodge the night warden, who patrolled the corridors of the nurses' home. My friend Liz Oliver [née Etheridge] went out with her a couple of times. One time, they spent the whole night convincing two fellers that they were Russian, and could only understand a "leetle ingleesh"!'

The nurses didn't always leave the campus to let their hair down. 'At the QE there was a fantastic social life and many dances were held in the social club,' says Jane. 'On top of this, there was a police section house and many invites were given for the students to turn up at their parties!'

Back on the wards, Julie's tomfoolery continued to land her in trouble as the teachers failed to find her so amusing. 'The uniform code was very strict,' explains Pat. 'We wore yellow, double-breasted dresses in our first year – designed by Norman Hartnell, the Queen's designer, as our tutors took great delight in telling us. The day Julie turned up for class with her hair in bunches and no stockings on will always be remembered for the expression on the tutor's face! Miss Cooper sent Julie away to put her hair right and change.'

Outfit aside, Julie approached the nursing course in a similar manner to her previous education and employment. 'I quite enjoyed it in a showing-off sort of a way,' she admits, 'doing a soft-shoe shuffle up the ward, eating the patients' grapes, and waiting for the senior staff to go off so I could do a bit of a show.'

She was up to her usual tricks as soon as the coast was clear.

'Washing bed pans was often a time for great hilarity, out of earshot and eyesight of those in charge,' recalls Jane. 'Night duty was also a time for many practical jokes: dressing up in a sheet and hanging out of the window, or going down fire escapes and frightening friends in other wards.

Jane especially recalls one elaborate prank that she believes involved Julie Walters among others. 'There was a junior doctor who had bought a car, a brand-new Mini. As part of the Rag Week events, a number of medical students and student nurses carried the car to the lift and took it to the top floor. Then they carried it up the stairs to the roof.

'They decorated it and took a Polaroid photo, which they left in the doctor's pigeonhole with a suggestion that money donated to Rag Week would ensure its safe return, or at least more information of its whereabouts. The whole escapade caused a lot of hilarity, as this doctor was not well liked and the powers-that-be felt that they could, or would, not do any more than reprimand those caught.'

Through Julie's relentless pursuit of the limelight, she began to realise where her future lay. 'I finally admitted to myself something I think I had known for a long time,' she said. 'I didn't want to be a nurse for the rest of my life, or do any other conventional job for that matter. What I really wanted to be was an actress.'

This revelation seems rather unprecedented as there is no family history of acting, but somehow, Julie instinctively knew that she would be happy only on stage.

She still remembers her epiphany: locked in her bathroom, mouthing the words, 'I want to be an actress.' She says she felt both fulfilled and sad, 'because I doubted I could ever say them to my parents in a million years.' Worse than not being able to tell Thomas and Mary about her career choice, Julie had no idea how to get started.

Her first foray was as fruitless as it was inventive. 'I looked under "D" for "Drama" in the telephone directory,' she continued. 'There was just one listing, for the British Drama League, and they were very snooty and unhelpful when I gave them a call.'

All was not lost, though, as she was afforded a couple of theatrical opportunities while still a nurse that didn't involve illicit shenanigans.

'Twice a year the hospital held a small revue,' recalls Jane, 'where budding actors and impressionists performed humorous sketches about the people in the hospital, mainly doctors and nurses, and were largely to do with rumoured or embellished events.

'I remember one about the bedpan washer, a comparatively new device called the macerator. A staff nurse phoned a porter for some jobs to be done in the ward, but he was rather unenthusiastic and gave her a long estimation time for completion. She phoned a little later and said, "My masturbator has broken" – a mispronunciation of "macerator" – and the porter said, "I'll be up in a few minutes."

'Other skits usually involved making fun of medical and nursing personnel who really have to be known to be thoroughly understood. For instance, there was a certain orthopaedic sister who used to lecture students on the way she wanted the beds made and which way the wheels should point – when you were handing over to the next shift you would point the wheels a certain way, to help you remember which side the patient had his operation or problem. So the sketches were about changing the direction of the wheels.

'The revues proved great fun and were very well attended, although the seniors would often censor them.' Needless to say, Julie was always the star in such shows and held her peers in hysterics with her observant impressions and innate comic timing.

The frustrated actress was not content to restrict the hilarity to these biannual performances and often found ways to make simple daily chores amusing. Julie often recounts one mirthful miscommunication, in which an elderly deaf man admitted to her ward drank some disinfectant, mistakenly thinking it was his medicine.

But it wasn't all fun and games. 'I did save someone who had a heart attack,' says Julie sombrely. Equally, not every case was a success story and Julie had to cope with the unwavering certainty of mortality

She was shocked when she witnessed one man being given a death sentence with the diagnosis of leukaemia. 'The man was big,' she told *Woman's Own*. 'I can still picture him now. He just broke down when they told him he had leukaemia. I've never forgotten it.'

Julie was not a natural nurse and admits she was terrified of most procedures because of her lack of medical confidence. Technical ability aside, she undoubtedly enjoyed the care aspect and developed an overactive bedside manner.

'I did get a real pleasure from looking after the patients and I found myself getting so close to many of them that I'd often go round and kiss them all goodnight after late shift,' she recalled.

While her behaviour was endearing, it was rather unethical and Julie would have been reprimanded had she been caught. Ingratiating herself so firmly with her patients was important to the young nurse, but the inevitable experiences with death were consequently more per-sonal. 'It was devastating to come back from my days off to find an empty bed where forty-eight hours ago there had been someone I had washed, fed, laughed and joked with for days, sometimes weeks, on end,' she says.

The physical work, such as lifting and turning patients, added a bit of muscle to Julie's slender frame, and she blossomed into a very attractive young woman. An emancipated woman of the 1960s, Julie started taking the contraceptive pill, on the off chance that she would find herself a boyfriend.

Of course, this predated concerns about the safety of the pill, let alone sexually transmitted diseases. Julie was on a dangerous prescription with too much oestrogen. 'At the beginning of each month I would wake every morning mildly irritated, and by the end of each month I wanted to smash every breakable object in the house,' she admits.

Despite her mood swings, Julie seduced a young lad named David Thompson, and the pair embarked on a long-term relationship. 'I didn't even realise that I had a vagina,' Julie joked of her naïveté. She then found that losing her virginity was so drawn-out and painful that 'I thought, Oh, I see: the man actually has to make the hole by pounding away with his penis!'

The couple enjoyed a blissful summer together but, in September 1968, David went to Manchester Polytechnic to read sociology. Suddenly he became a little highbrow for Julie.

'He'd say things to me like, "Do you condone apartheid, then?" I'd mumble "No", but then I'd have to go and look up "condone", and look up "apartheid",' she says. However, Julie could see – past the conceit – that David was clearly relishing his studies.

That Christmas, Julie, a struggling student, had to take on part-time work. She became a waitress at the unusually named United Cattle Products Restaurant in Birmingham. 'It wasn't really a great deal of fun because the head waitress thought all students were layabouts and scroungers, and she tried to make our lives a misery,' she recalled in *Julie Walters Is an Alien*.

'There were a few bright moments about my time there – one special day when the Welsh Lothario himself, Tom Jones, strode into the place in a tight-trousered way and asked to sample our fine cuisine.' The singer, at the height of his first dalliance with fame, having just signed a deal for his hit TV show, *This Is Tom Jones*, was pleased with his fare and left a whole pound as a tip.

The visit from The Voice aside, Julie was thoroughly depressed by the way her life was panning out. By now, she categorically knew that she wanted to be an actress, yet there she was, taking on menial holiday work to supplement her uninspiring career as a nurse.

In May 1969, Julie had made it to the second year of her course, and her uniform was decorated with blue epaulettes. Nursing still wasn't her choice, but she just didn't know how to make the move. When David returned to college, he stumbled across the answer: Manchester offered a drama course.

'I knew immediately that this was exactly the right thing for me to be doing, so I wrote to them,' says Julie. She kept the information from her family, fearing her mother's response, and nervously waited for the results of her application. Finally she was summoned to her first audition.

'I didn't know anything about actors or the theatre. I'd never even been to the theatre at home,' she admits. 'I hardly knew anything about plays. I thought Clemence Dane* was a man. For my audition I rewrote some of *Juno and the Paycock*, putting some of my own jokes in without really thinking. How naïve can you get!'

Julie instinctively turned to Sean O'Casey's play about an Irish family's struggles and, despite her attempts to bastardise the work, she was granted a further meeting with the professors.

In her interview she was asked why she wanted to be an actress but was quick to correct the error. '"I *am* an actress," I told the interviewing board. "If you don't choose to take me on, that is another matter, but I'm still an actress. That is what I am."'

Her arrogance belied her anxiety and again she was forced to play the waiting game. Eventually, news from Manchester Poly arrived: she had been accepted on the course, due to start the following September.

Julie wasted no time and immediately handed in her notice at the Queen Elizabeth Hospital. 'I was overjoyed,' she continues, 'but the hospital was utterly outraged that I should even consider giving up nursing for the theatre and phoned my mother to convince her to stop me.'

The hospital's clerk received the full co-operation of Mary Walters, who was furious to find that her daughter was deserting a secure career for seemingly impossible dreams. Julie remained steadfast in her decision, but tackling her intimidating mother on the issue was another matter. She enlisted the help of her father and two brothers before facing the music.

---

* Clemence Dane was the pseudonym for the actress, novelist and screenwriter, Winifred Ashton.

'What have we reared?' raged Mary. 'You're giving up a respectable job to go up there! You'll be in the gutter before you're twenty. Great God, will you look at her!'

The three men literally had to hold the two women apart.

'Oh, that did cause trouble,' Julie told the *TV Times*. 'She went potty! Nothing I ever did was good enough for her and I resented it.' Julie felt she and her brothers continually tried to please their mother, but she didn't see it.

Julie recalled that she would say, ' "If I said something was good enough, you'd have stopped trying. So I never said it." She did it with the best of intentions. But all it made us feel was that we weren't good enough.'

Mary's logic had worked, however: Julie was resolute.

4. IN THE RIGHT GEAR

Julie moved to Manchester and lived with David Thompson. Her mother had predicted she would be 'in the gutter' before she was twenty. 'She was right,' admits Julie, 'but I rather liked it!'

Less than one hundred miles north of Birmingham, Manchester is a lively cosmopolitan city renowned as one of the major commercial, educational and cultural centres of northwest England. In the early 1970s, it also boasted a thriving pub and club scene, and much of the social life revolved around the student campus – by all accounts Julie and David enjoyed themselves to the full.

Moreover, Julie was thrilled to be finally following her dream, as opposed to her mother's. It wasn't great literature or having seen Shakespeare that motivated her, as she explained to the *Observer*, 'It was more just wanting to understand what the people around me were really like, what went on inside their heads, why they said all the strange things they did.'

In September 1970, the budding actress enrolled at Manchester Polytechnic. 'Previously, it wasn't specifically a drama school,' explains a fellow student, David Ross. 'It was a drama school which had a teaching qualification at the end of it. It was easier to get a grant for Manchester Poly because of the teaching qualification, as some authorities looked upon that as more acceptable than just a drama college where you went solely to be an actor.'

Alexander Clements has tutored the course ever since Julie's arrival. 'Very soon after that, the National Council for Drama Training was founded,' he elaborates. 'It was set up between [the actors' union] Equity and the drama schools to validate professional courses, so the teaching element was dropped. We started to change it quickly and Julie Walters was one of the first people who auditioned for that new course. We were subsequently validated and very gradually got to be known and respected in the profession.

'It has always been a fairly traditional course. It was mainly practical and very focused; there was a lot of discussion about texts and obviously some theatre history. Instead of spreading wide and doing a lot of disciplines, our course tended to concentrate very hard on acting.

'It was quite a long day: students would carry on until at least six p.m., sometimes much later. In the morning, they would have had voice and specialised classes, like phonetics. The afternoon would have been occupied by acting classes, which were always centred on a workshop of some sort, such as a character exercise looking at Chekhov or Ibsen.

'The texts given to the students, even in the early stages, were quite heavy projects. In the second year they moved on to Brecht and aspects of English theatre, such as Restoration. Then in the third year they would perform endless plays for the public.'

Despite the regimented hard work, Julie was in her element. 'It felt fabulous,' she says. 'Suddenly I was in the right gear, instead of just grinding along in second.'

Having found her calling, Julie was ready to commit herself fully. All those years spent larking about because she wasn't interested in her studies fell away and suddenly she was 100 per cent engaged.

'Julie was a full, rich, human being,' says Alexander Clements. 'She was always fun but always ready to work. She just felt that it was a really good thing to be doing what she was doing – although she did find some of the voice work rather amusing because the deep-breathing exercises involved quite a lot of lying down and being quiet in the dark! But she was diligent and got on with it – her voice developed and she obviously hasn't lost it.'

Clements discovered that, as well as applying herself to the craft, Julie had a natural talent for acting. 'She was intelligent and understood things readily,' he continues. 'She was not somebody who required a lot of explanation, though she would ask questions. You knew where you were with Julie. She wouldn't just say, "Yes, I understand," when plainly she didn't: she would always ask questions, and that was very reassuring. She was very practical and a good influence on people.'

Not only did Julie have a good grasp of the work, but this wasn't her first time away from home and she wasn't struggling to find accommodation. Many first-year pupils miss classes as they come to terms with their new lifestyle, but Julie was already two steps ahead.

'Sometimes with drama students you get an awful lot of fuss,' says Clements, 'but you never got that with Julie. I think her contact with nursing gave her grounding, and she was fairly humble in many ways.'

For all her sensibility in class, Julie still revelled in the same carefree, fun-loving social life. As always, she made friends easily and was often found out drinking and partying with a crowd. Moreover, she had turned into a good-looking woman and attracted her fair share of male attention. 'I was a third-year by the time Julie joined college as a first year,' says David Ross, 'so we didn't particularly interact at that time. But I remember seeing her on campus, well, because she was a very attractive girl! She had quite a good shape to her and, although she was a diminutive girl, she had a big bust. She was very popular and easy to get on with, so she was usually with a group of friends.'

Julie quickly surrounded herself with new friends, mostly actors, and was often seen hanging around with a fellow actor, Matthew Kelly. She also made a good impression on her tutors – so good that, when they were looking for someone to chaperone prospective students around campus on open day, they thought of her. It was in this official capacity that Julie Walters first met Victoria Wood.

Although shy as a teenager, Victoria Wood was determined to break into show business. To this end she had attended numerous auditions for drama schools, but had failed every time. After her performance of the death scene from *Romeo and Juliet* at Manchester Poly, she joined the tour of the Capitol Building, where she would hopefully be studying.

Julie certainly looked the part of an ambitious thespian, dressed in a leotard, and simply thrived in the role of guide, entertaining her young charges with a torrent of amusing anecdotes.

When someone asked Julie what she did before arriving at the Poly, Victoria recalls, 'She just launched into this huge impression of being a nurse and how she used to wheel commodes down the ward, with lots of acting out and showing off. I was quite mesmerised by her. She had these teeny weeny eyes, tons of eye shadow and tons of hair.'

In complete contrast, Julie remembers Victoria as a 'little girl with glasses who was being quietly sick in the corner'. Unfortunately, Manchester Poly turned out to be yet another rejection for Victoria.

Conversely, Julie went from strength to strength and completed her first year with flying colours, trying her hand at all media. 'One thing that was unusual about our course,' says Alexander Clements, 'was that we managed to fit in some television work. This was so that the actors could understand some of the basic differences between stage acting and television acting, and so much of that has to do with dynamics and understanding the different energies.

'Julie was in a production of *Summer Folk* by Maxim Gorky, and they took a chunk of that and televised it on black-and-white television. She played a doctor, and the language she was using was RP [received pronunciation], so this was a well-spoken middle-class character. And she was good in it, very convincing. People often see Julie as an actress with an accent, but she can play other characters as well – in fact she's got a wide capability.'

'We would teach voice work and tackle all sorts of accents for plays. We were one of the few drama schools who taught phonetics, and we've always stuck to it. We feel it sets actors up to cope with accents and pronunciations of difficult names, particularly if they have to work in a Russian play or something like that – if you put it down phonetically, people pick it up very quickly. Indeed, Julie worked hard at it and had a good repertoire.'

Julie would later boast of her vocal range: 'I can do Irish, Welsh, Mancunian, Scouse, Brummie, Cockney, and New York Jewish lesbian.'

After a flourishing first year, Julie's world was rocked when her father died of heart failure on 24 July 1971. He was only 61 and had been in good health, other than having high blood pressure, until the incident. At 21, Julie was not long an adult herself and felt that she had never really got to know him.

Shaken by the loss, she stayed with her family in Smethwick for a while during the summer, but life had to continue and she returned to Manchester Poly. There, her second year followed the same positive bent as the first. She performed well in class and sustained her concentration, as well as her active social life.

'At the end of the summer term 1972, we did a public production to get the students used to doing performances for their third year,' explains Clements. 'I'd recently worked in Ireland at the Abbey Theatre and got a great enthusiasm for Irish theatre, so we presented *Playboy of the Western World* by John Millington Synge in the Library Theatre.'

The comedy in three acts, first produced in 1907, is one of Synge's most famous works, and a masterpiece of the Irish literary renaissance. It sent shock waves through the dramatic world of the time, pushing the limits of decency and stoking an already red-hot nationalistic fire. It was certainly controversial and almost caused riots in some areas.

However, the combination of Synge's sophisticated rhetoric, which playfully satirises the Irish braggart, and authentic brogue, makes *Playboy* a complex work. 'I was anxiously looking around for someone to cast as Pegeen Mike, the leading lady, thinking, This is daft; this play is so difficult,' says Clements. 'But when I chose Julie, I couldn't have chosen anyone better.

'When I think about it now, she had an Irish look about her – she had long dark hair and she wasn't waiflike – but, because she came from Birmingham, I had no idea she had any Irish connections. She turned out to be the obvious casting for Pegeen Mike.' Clements could not believe his good fortune, but the coincidences continued.

'Then we went into it, and the play is set in County Mayo,' he continues. 'Lo and behold – that's where Julie's mother came from. It was uncanny! So the accent was greatly helped because Julie could use her mother as a good example.

'Of course, she knew all about how people would have behaved in western Ireland. Religion was incredibly strong at that time, so there was holy water inside each door and people would dip their fingers in the holy water and cross themselves on entering and leaving the house. I had read up on all that information, but Julie was there saying, "Oh yes, my mother said when they went back to Ireland this is what they did." She knew all about this world.'

Julie was excited about the part, feeling that she was really able to draw on a primary source. This was the first but by no means the last time she tapped into her mother for inspiration. Julie's performance was magnificent, particularly in such a demanding role, and Clements was clearly moved.

'She was very sensitive,' he says. 'She understood the humility and passion of the character. Often, as an actor, you use what's closest to you without even knowing it, and I think you could see in her work that someone had been strict with her. Some of the tough characters that she takes on – you can see that she's somebody who knows about these women.'

Four years into their relationship, David Thompson felt he was ready to make more of a commitment and proposed to his girlfriend. Caught up in the romance of the moment, Julie went against her ingrained attitude, decided it would be a wonderful idea and graciously accepted.

Plans were already in full swing when reality set in. Julie realised about a fortnight before the wedding that she couldn't go through with it. 'I sat up in bed and said: "I can't do this. I know it will break up". I can remember thinking at the time that I still had too much to do in my life to get married,' she told the *Star*. Her upbringing had included the belief that 'you never know what's around the corner.' Julie had also succumbed to her mother's attitude: 'Her views were soundly etched into my thinking: "Never rely on any man".

'I was too interested in acting and showing off to settle down. David and I were together nearly five years . . . it was heartbreaking.'

Alexander Clements, for one, could see that she was too focused on her career to settle down. 'I think she was very happy to be doing artistic work,' he says. 'That's what she wanted to do and she wasn't going to let anything stop her.'

Heartbroken as she was, Julie did not have time to mourn the split as she entered her third year and the pace rapidly increased. She no longer took classes: instead the students produced countless plays for the public, preparing for their future.

'Rehearsals would go on until late, to eight or nine p.m., and so any socialising was pretty impossible,' concedes Clements. 'It was crazy, but she always had tremendous energy. She didn't tire easily and was able to keep delivering.'

Clements also directed Julie in *Love on the Dole*, adapted from Walter Greenwood's first novel, published in 1933. 'She didn't have such a big and important part in that play – she was just one of the gossips who reads tea leaves – but she was great and brought a lot to it,' he says. 'The reading of the tea leaves is a scene I can still remember, while other bits of it are not so clear. But that's the sign of somebody who's a good actor, when their work stays with you for years and years, even if it's only a small role.'

Julie also proved her worth among her fellow actors in the crucial last year. 'She was very good with people,' he continues. 'That really seemed to help with the group, having somebody who had good communication skills. It released people who might have a few kinks of inhibition and the whole thing went much more smoothly.'

After an exhausting year of hard work, Julie graduated from Manchester Polytechnic. Yet her thirst for experience was far from quenched and the actress returned for a year's postgraduate course in 1973.

'The one-year diploma was run in conjunction with Manchester University Drama Department and the Stables Theatre Club,' explains Clements. 'There was a mix of people from different backgrounds and other drama courses, and they worked together as a professional company for a year.'

Julie continued appearing in roles, both large and small, in endless plays on campus and at the theatre, during the ten-month period. Finally, in the summer of 1974, she left the safety of Manchester Polytechnic to brave the world as a working actress.

5. RISE AND FALL

During her postgraduate year, Julie had branched out and worked with actors from the surrounding areas. Having spoken to many people in her field, she was particularly keen to be involved in Liverpool's Everyman Theatre.

Founded in 1961, the Everyman was opened to rival the well-established Playhouse Theatre in the city. Seeking individuality, the new company produced plays written by Liverpudlian authors, focusing on the lives of local people. To this end one of the house playwrights was Willy Russell.

Russell was born in Shiston in 1947, and was from a 'thinking' working-class background. He persevered in his dream to become a writer. He finally broke through in 1972 with *Keep Your Eyes Down* and the following year joined the Everyman, where he achieved critical acclaim with *John, Paul, George, Ringo . . . and Bert*.

The play, based on the Beatles' rise and fall, was so successful that it transferred to London, taking with it the majority of the company Consequently, the Everyman was desperately seeking a new ensemble and held auditions in London in July 1974. Fresh out of Manchester Polytechnic and the Stables Theatre, Julie and her fellow student Matthew Kelly eagerly attended the trials.

They both passed with flying colours and were excited to be joining the thirteen-strong company which comprised returning actors Nick Stringer and Katherine Fahy, and newcomers Kevin Lloyd, Del Henney, Nicholas Woodeson, David Peart, Nicholas Le Prevost, Michael Radcliffe, Bill Rigby, Roger Philips and Stephanie Fayerman.

The troupe arrived in Liverpool on 18 September and were immediately called upon for a photo shoot and press conference to drum up local interest. Then they were rushed straight to rehearsals at Hope Hall, as they were due to open the 1974–5 season on 9 October, just three weeks later. This was the Everyman's tenth-anniversary season, undertaken by a new artistic director, Jonathan Pryce. The first production was Shakespeare's comedy, *The Taming of the Shrew*.

'We were in for surprises from the very start of Jonathan Pryce's production . . . it was one of the funniest and most inventive box of tricks I've seen yet from that talented company,' raved Colin Voakes from Radio Merseyside. The brightly lit set included blow-ups of comic strips and send-ups of adverts. In keeping with the contemporary theme, the cast were all dressed provocatively (Petruchio was a Hell's Angel, for example, and the servant was a sexy French maid) and Shakespeare's masterpiece was crammed with horseplay and fiendishly funny asides. 'For bubbling fun, I heartily recommend this vital production,' Voakes concluded.

Julie Walters made her debut for the Everyman as a modern-day Bianca, Kate's pretty sister, who's not allowed to wed until her bitchy sibling is taken off the family's hands. She minced on stage in a floral pink dress and knee-length white socks, with her long hair tied in bunches by big, floppy bows.

This was Julie's first real test outside college. She was understandably nervous about joining the ranks of the Everyman and sought solace in her past. 'On my first nights, which are the worst experiences you ever go through, I always think, I wish I was still a nurse washing people's bums!'

Not only was she stunning to look at in every sense of the word, but she also wowed her audience. 'Julie Walters gives us a sweet Bianca with just a hint of wickedness,' reported Ed Townsend in the *Birkenhead News*.

The Taming of the Shrew ran until 2 November, but the schedule was relentless. When not performing on stage at the Everyman, actors were encouraged to join Vanload, the theatre's touring company.

Set up the previous year, Vanload was a new concept allowing actors to work outside the parameters of the theatre, thus gaining first-hand experience of their audience. Furthermore, it meant that plays were taken to people where, and when, they wanted them. The shows were all designed to be put on out of the theatre and each production adapted to the venue, be it a school, political club, community centre, youth club or public house. 'We were doing this pub theatre project, where we performed in the roughest pubs in Liverpool,' elaborates Julie. 'We had a deal with the pub landlords: no one had to pay to come in and we just did the show.'

One BBC producer praised the work in the *Liverpool Daily Post*, saying, 'Actors have to be very competent and very tough to succeed in this field. And Vanload do succeed ... In this kind of environment they are close to the audience and must contend with people coming and going and ordering pints.'

This expansion venture was feasible only after a substantially increased grant from the Merseyside Arts Association. Directed by Geoffrey Durham, a.k.a. the Great Soprendo, Vanload proved very successful and reached an audience of two thousand within its first six weeks.

Julie rented a room in Liverpool above Geoffrey and, as she often popped in for a chat, it was no surprise that she accepted the challenge to join Vanload. Her first taste of this hands-on acting was in a blue version of *Dick Whittington*. With Matthew Kelly in the lead role, Julie saucily stole the show as his feline sidekick.

'A more bawdy, boisterous, bumptious, belly-based pantomime it is difficult to imagine!' exclaimed Bill Bowder in the *Liverpool Echo*, of the good clean, dirty fun. He described the plot: Dick '(no prizes for guessing how that name could be misconstrued)', a thick Wigan schoolboy of 35 years old who leaves his parents to go to Liverpool but finds it difficult to recognise his pussycat '(again, no prizes)'.

The second act seemed to lose the plot a little, but bounced along regardless with some corrupted music hall standards. The show was a smash, with Matthew and Julie excelling themselves, and toured the full round of Merseyside clubs and pubs.

No sooner had she finished *Dick Whittington* than Julie started her next project. She was back at the theatre for Everyman's Christmas production: an all-singing, all-dancing revue entitled *Cantril Tales*. Boasting an impressive line-up of writers, including Willy Russell, Chris Bond, Adrian Henri, Adrian Mitchell and George Costigan, the director Jonathan Pryce created an updated *Canterbury Tales*, set in and around Liverpool.

'Geoffrey Chaucer arrives by time machine at the worst pub on the Cantril Farm overspill estate, Liverpool, where he is as welcome as a soggy crisp,' summarised Gillian Linscott of the *Guardian*.

> *The show that the Everyman builds round the idea is, on the other hand, as welcome as a hangover cure. How often do you find seasonal entertainment that is shoutingly funny, sometimes touching, contains at least one nearly new Irish joke and is just rude enough to justify leaving the kids at home? The Everyman's high reputation for Christmas shows should be pushed even higher by this one.*

Not only did the Everyman end the year on a high, but Julie triumphed in Adrian Mitchell's sophisticated tale of Southport Sally: 'She puts over a torch song like a one-woman attack on the power crisis.'

Julie had clearly not lost her vocal ability. The *Stage* concurred that her voice was good and that she 'made a plaintive groupie, disguising herself as a man to be near her idol only to find that he would have preferred her as a boy. This tale had form, shape and flow, highlighting the evening.'

In January 1975 Alan Dossor returned as artistic director of the Everyman Theatre after a three-month break. He opened the second half of the season with the British premiere of Mike Stott's *Funny Peculiar*. The comedy had been performed in Hamburg the previous year where it caused a furore, owing to its explicit content, and Dossor was delighted with the script: 'I read it first on the train and found it impossible not to laugh out loud.'

Marketed by the Everyman as 'clean, hilariously funny and about fellatio', *Funny Peculiar* is a complicated tale of sexual frustration in a small village in the Pennines, where gossip is rife. Nicholas Le Prevost stole the show as the lead, Trevor Tinsley, with a magnificent straight-faced comic performance. Julie was his all-knowing wife Irene, and Katherine Fahy his lover. Other parts were portrayed by Nick Stringer, Eileen O'Brien and David Peart.

Again, the company could do no wrong and received rave reviews. 'Here is two-and-a-half hours of gutsy, funny sex, open-hearted and unrestrained,' appraised the *Stage*. 'A new, original play destined for popularity.' The original run from 30 January to 15 February was extended a further week owing to popular demand, and there were even rumours about a London transfer. Of course, Julie was far too busy to fantasise about any such event because she was straight back in rehearsals, frantically preparing for the March production.

Her next appearance was in *The Pig and the Junkle*, a play by Brian Patten aimed at seven- to nine-year-olds. It is a magical tale of a boy living in Liverpool's derelict city centre, who conjures up a fantastic dream jungle from the nearby junk yards: 'junkle'. In this imaginative world he meets a pompous flower, a polite elephant, a pig who wants to be de-pigged, an erratic robot, evil bamboons and a wise jesting doll. Although this was Julie's first production aimed at children, she seized the chance to become the polite elephant who always forgets and is fond of a song and dance, despite the cumbersome outfit of a round wire-framed pink body and a trailing trunk.

'What I want is for this play to help kids use their imagination,' said Brian Patten. 'I know that by using my imagination I have got further than I might have done.'

While Alan Dossor was praised for his careful direction, Ralph Steadman and Graham Barkworth's dramatic design, using colour, music, lighting, costume and character provided an afternoon of enchantment. However, *The Pig and the Junkle* cost twice as much as the regular adult productions in the theatre.

Though sporting her elephant attire in matinées from 27 February to 15 March, Julie somehow had also to squeeze in rehearsals for her next outing with Vanload, which commenced on Friday, 21 March, at the Masonic on Berry Street.

Scully is the saga of a Liverpool youth, whose anarchic adventures challenge the authority of those responsible for the impoverished society in which he lives. The author, Alan Bleasdale, was a drama teacher at a comprehensive school in Liverpool when he achieved something of a coup: his first two plays debuted at both of Liverpool's repertory theatres at the same time. While Vanload toured with *Scully* for two weeks, the Playhouse Theatre presented *Fat Harold and the Lady 26* from 1 April 1975.

'We all wanted to do *Scully*,' says Julie. 'I think Alan was very shy of us all, but I have a memory of him being around in the background.' As a playwright, Bleasdale was very keen to be involved in the production and took it upon himself to attend rehearsals, giving advice and help to the actors where necessary.

He warmed to Julie instantly. 'She was the first person I'd ever seen laugh out loud at my work,' he told the *Observer*. 'Even when [Julie's] playing the wildest comedy . . . people know that at the end of the day . . . it's always somehow real, and that's a very rare quality.'

As Martyn Lumley reviewed her in the Liverpool *Daily Post* – 'A lovely performance from Julie Walters as Scully's heavy drinking Irish gran' – she was already comfortable playing crazy little old ladies. Julie's ability to act three times her age, no doubt drawn from years of watching and mimicking her senile grandmother, was exaggerated by her natural stoop, old clothes, a wig and make-up. She was a hit.

But it was Pete Postlethwaite, five years her senior yet playing her grandson Scully, who really captured her attention with his dark hair and strong features. The pair connected and sparked a romance, which soon became quite involved.

As their relationship blossomed, it is not surprising that the couple were cast as husband and wife in Bertolt Brecht's version of the Shakespeare tragedy, *Coriolanus*. The production was exceptional and even merited a review in the *Times Educational Supplement*. Although Julie was not singled out, the review was complimentary: 'As Coriolanus, Peter Postlethwaite is tough, unglamorous but commanding, while Keith Washington as the Volsci general is exotic and earringed, stalking the stage like a cunning vulture. Both performances are excellent.'

The play was presented at the Everyman Theatre throughout April and Julie continued to work at breakneck pace as she moved on to the May production. It is amazing that she coped, but her passion clearly saw her through.

The Everyman Theatre was proud to support up-and-coming writers, as much as, if not more than, actors. On the back of the success of *John,*

Paul, George, Ringo . . . and Bert, which had gone into film production after its run in London, they were keen to commission Willy Russell to write another play.

The result, Russell's second full-length stage play, was *Breezeblock Park*, described by its author as 'a comedy of bad manners'. Set at Christmas, it shows the forced festivities of three families – the spouses and offspring of two sisters and a brother – living on a council housing estate in Liverpool. The friendships are superficial and the goodwill spiked, each family aiming for materialistic one-upmanship. The clan rally together only when one of the children upsets proceedings by announcing she wants to leave her job, become a student and live with her boyfriend. Oh, and she's pregnant.

Again directed by Alan Dossor, *Breezeblock Park* was another fashionable favourite, extending the run to the end of May 1975, effectively closing the season. Everyone was eager to see Russell's second offering, but at the end of the day it received mixed reviews. The cast and direction were praised to the hilt, but Russell was occasionally attacked. Although he had again humorously and fairly accurately depicted Liverpool family life, critics claimed the characters were not fully formed and the play lacked the spark of the Beatles piece.

'The comic spirit of *Breezeblock Park* is exceptionally well caught under Alan Dossor's lively direction by a splendid cast . . . Willy Russell's characters, however stereotyped, are always entertaining and authentic in expression and attitudes,' wrote Philip Radcliffe in the *Sunday Times*.

Michael Coveney also felt that the play was flawed, but, 'indulgently directed by Alan Dossor, who has secured some excellently observed performances from Julie Walters as Tommy's appalling wife, Kevin Lloyd as Tommy himself and Nick Stringer as the loathsomely humourless Ted. Graham Barkworth's [set] design is suitably and unremittingly atrocious.'

Andrew Veitch of the *Guardian* concluded that the audience 'only came for Willy Russell's next play, not the play itself', but agreed that 'in spite of all this there are some fine touches by Julie Walters as Vera, a particularly dense lady, Kevin Lloyd as her brash flash husband Tommy, Jane Wood as Reeny and Eileen O'Brien as Betty'.

Julie certainly seemed to shine. 'Walters, a gum chewing daft and innocently happy young married, produces the best observed study of the evening,' claimed Philip Key of the *Daily Post*.

Sadly, Alan Dossor's reign as artistic director of the Everyman ended on this awkward note. 'I've been here five years now and really I have done all I wanted to do,' he said. 'This is like an ending to all that – a natural act.'

With the hectic season over, Julie was free to do whatever she liked. Certainly not one to rest on her laurels, the actress was keen to improve her skills and, on the basis that practice makes perfect, spent the summer at the Aberystwyth University Theatre. Before returning to the Everyman, she also found time to try something different and accepted work on a couple of radio plays.

'In 1975 I was the director of the Cambridge Theatre Company, which was a touring theatre company,' explains Robert Lang. 'If I was doing a radio play I would be looking at the others in the cast, thinking I might want him or her to come and work for us. Julie recorded one of these pieces, Edward Bond's *Bingo*, and on the front page of the script there is the cast list. I scribbled little things on it. Against Julie I wrote, "V.G." and "rather pretty", so she obviously stood out, even on just two or three days working together.'

A half-hour play would probably be completed in a day, and heavy, hour-long titles such as Bond's would probably take two or three days, all of which was paid for by the BBC. Despite his high opinion of Julie, Lang never did ask her to join him at Cambridge. However, she was so successful on radio that she undertook more work, including another Edward Bond piece, *Week Ending*.

Julie's second season with the Everyman Theatre saw John Roche succeeding as artistic director. Julie, George Costigan and Bill Nighy were the only three returning actors and they were joined by Carolyn Pickles, Mary McCusker, David Fielder, Robert Benfield, David Maybury, Philip Wilde, Les Miller, Ian Redford, Hugh Armstrong, Rory Maclaine and James Masters.

John Roche also chose an Edward Bond play, and opened with the mammoth work, *Edward Lear*, on 7 October 1975. It was a brave choice, since *Lear* had received a poor reception at the Royal Court in 1971. Nevertheless, Roche was confident that his version, only its second telling, would succeed, because he considered it to be 'one of the most amazing plays to have appeared in the last twenty years'.

Roche was hideously mistaken and the reviews were unanimously scathing. 'The Everyman has bitten off more than it can chew,' claimed Stephen Dixon of the *Guardian*. 'If you're looking for enjoyment then be warned, Edward Bond's play *Lear* is like having every tooth slowly ripped out,' slated Martyn Lumley of the *Liverpool Daily Post*, although he spotted the hidden talent, Julie Walters and Carolyn Pickles: 'Dressed like two nightmarish ugly sisters from *Cinderella*, [they] give spine chilling studies in evil as the daughters.'

Joe Riley from the *Liverpool Echo* agreed on both points: 'I'm not surprised that people walked out of the Everyman Theatre's production of *Lear* last night ... [although] Carolyn Pickles and Julie Walters ... achieve considerable impact.'

A strong return for Walters, but a disastrous start for Roche.

His next production was an adaptation of Ken Kesey's *One Flew Over the Cuckoo's Nest*, with Julie Walters playing Nurse Flynn Bandy in November of 1975. It fared little better and the critics waited with teeth bared for the Christmas offering.

Straight afterwards, the Everyman presented a month of matinées of Bernard Shaw's *Androcles and the Lion* from 18 November. The series was aimed at junior- and middle-school children, but evening performances for adults were included in the last week.

The company hoped that for this production a change of director to Roland Jaquarello of the Abbey Theatre, Dublin, and specially commissioned music by Stanley Reynolds and Rick Juckes might break the bad run. There was no such luck.

'We had conversations conducted on swinging trapezes, songs, strange sound effects, a couple chatting on a see-saw, gladiators in black plastic and even a chase through the auditorium,' described Philip Key of the *Post*. 'Alas it was to no avail – rigor mortis seems to have set into the play with its moralistic tone and stilted dialogue.'

Joe Riley of the *Liverpool Echo* was no less cutting. 'In a season that's not exactly proved memorable, things seem to have hit a new all time low ... who knows, perhaps most of the Everyman company actually find their version really funny.'

Not even Julie's appearance as a tennis player in long white socks, short white skirt, white vest top, boater and two braids could save the day. That hard-working, successful Christmas of the previous year seemed a million miles away from the succession of bad plays. But things were about to change.

6. DUSTY, SNOO AND VICTORIA TOO

Hope Hall closed in 1976 for refurbishment and the Everyman Theatre temporarily moved to Fleet Street in Liverpool's city centre. Julie relocated, too: her site was the bright lights of London as her career suddenly sky-rocketed.

The rumours about a London transfer of Mike Stott's hilarious play, *Funny Peculiar*, proved correct. Although it took some while in planning, Alan Dossor and his crew finally arrived at the Mermaid Theatre just under a year after their first performance in Liverpool. Nestling on the north bank of the Thames, among the city's warehouses, the Mermaid opened in 1959 and combined modern features such as a revolving stage, cinema projectors and stereophonic sound equipment with a Victorian setting. (Unfortunately, the theatre is now struggling for survival.)

A few of the cast travelled to the capital, including Julie, her boyfriend Pete Postlethwaite, Eileen O'Brien and Matthew Kelly, but they needed a 'big name' to attract the fickle London audiences. Richard Beckinsale, a well-known TV personality from *The Lovers*, *Rising Damp* and *Porridge*, was brought in to fill the lead.

Tapping into the liberated and carefree attitude of London's new generation of theatregoers, the play was a hit when it opened on 22 January 1976. Liz Brown from the Mermaid's press department wrote to Pam Flynn, the publicity officer for the Everyman, in February, saying, 'You'll be glad to hear the production is doing great business after those smashing reviews.'

Indeed, *Funny Peculiar* proved so popular that it transferred to the famous Garrick Theatre in London's West End on 28 April, where it ran for a further fifteen months. There, the theatre programme was illustrated with cartoons drawn by Susan P Place depicting witty innuendos, based on an idea by McGill. With a year and a half in London, it was an unmitigated success. (Sadly, Richard Beckinsale died shortly afterwards of a heart attack, aged just 31.)

While the British struggled through the terrible drought of 1976, Julie lapped up the praise and watched her career soar. While in London, she and Pete rented a flat together in Soho and, making the most of the exciting nightlife, the pair had a great time living and working in the City.

In 1977, when Julie began to look for her next project after *Funny Peculiar*, she ran into an old friend. Alan Bleasdale had co-written a six-part television series called *Watchwords*. Julie briefly joined the cast, which included Tony Haygarth, Adrian Henri, Roger McGough, Andy Roberts and Andrew Schofield for this BBC production.

'When it comes to her talent as an actress, at first you think it's pure instinct,' Bleasdale told *Reader's Digest*. 'But the more you get to know her, the more you realise that there's a considerable amount of intellect working away underneath the surface, as well as a huge amount of courage.'

The Everyman Theatre reopened in Liverpool on 21 September 1977, but Julie hardly looked back as her life was now firmly rooted in London.

Based on the achievements of *Funny Peculiar*, the Mermaid Theatre looked to transfer another of the Everyman Theatre's home-grown productions to London. The resident playwright Willy Russell had made a name for himself with the runaway *John, Paul, George, Ringo . . . and Bert*, and so they chose his second work, the previously poorly received *Breezeblock Park*, as their next showcase.

It had been two years since the Liverpool premiere and some of the cast were otherwise engaged, but many of the Everyman Company travelled to the city to participate, albeit in different roles. Julie retained her role of Vera, but this time her husband, Tommy, was played by Pete Postlethwaite.

The other major change in the cast was the female lead, Betty, and again the Mermaid felt they needed to enlist the services of an established actress. Wendy Craig, the star of countless stage shows and films, was perhaps best known for her television work in *Not in Front of the Children* and *And Mother Makes Three*, which became *And Mother Makes Five*. She was invited to play the central character.

'I was brought in as a "name" to bring the play to the West End,' recalls Wendy, 'and that's never a very good circumstance to be asked to do anything. I just felt that it was unfair on the person who was playing the part in Liverpool that they weren't asked to do it in the West End. It made one feel a little awkward and a little self-conscious, but at the same time it was such a lovely part that I couldn't find it in my heart to turn it down.

'I knew Willy Russell's reputation was very good and that he was an up-and-coming and exciting writer. That very much influenced my decision to take the role – I wanted to be working in that milieu.

'Before I did the show I went to see Willy and he showed me around Liverpool. He was really lovely and couldn't have been nicer – that helped enormously.' Having seen the location that inspired the play, Wendy still had several major obstacles to overcome.

'I had to adopt a Liverpudlian accent. Fortunately Carla Lane [with whom Wendy had worked on *And Mother Makes Five*] helped me with that. But I just kept thinking, Am I going to be able to do this? Can I really fit into this already run-in play?

'And I think they were a little wary of me. They were perfectly polite and nice, but I never felt as though I belonged – I am not from Liverpool and they all were, or had at least worked there together.'

Alan Dossor directed the mix-and-match cast and rehearsals started in August. As most of the cast knew the play, if not their individual parts, fairly well, their schedule was reasonably relaxed for three weeks. 'Alan was very nice,' enthuses Wendy, 'and a brilliant director. I think he was just trying to revive the production and keep it strong.'

Breezeblock Park opened on 12 September 1977 and, once again, the reviews were lacklustre. 'Willy Russell's newish play aspires, I think, to be a tragicomedy,' wrote Stephen Gilbert. 'But the terms of the comedy prevent the achievement of tragedy, leaving the comedy looking distinctly tawdry and churlish.'

On the whole it was deemed to be Russell's fault as the script was flawed, but Gilbert also took a swipe at the actors. Still, he was impressed with one member of the cast: 'Julie Walters, the empty-headed sister-in-law, is amusing as she runs amok with the awful knowledge of Sandra's pregnancy.'

'I think it *was* a flawed play,' admits Wendy today, 'but nevertheless a good play. It was a very funny, very sad, wry look at Liverpudlian suburban life. I seem to remember that some of the criticism was that it was patronising towards the lower-middle classes, and I think Willy was hurt by that – he meant it to be sincere.'

Despite the disparagement, the cast from the Everyman managed to enjoy themselves. 'They were very funny and there were plenty of laughs and jokes,' recalls Wendy. 'There was a certain sense of humour flying around.' The gang continued with their usual partying in town, but, unfortunately for Wendy, she felt somewhat shunned by the clique and consequently remembers it as an unhappy time. 'I tried to be sociable but I never really felt I fitted in. It was an established group and I was an outsider. Not belonging to the area from which they came and their whole manner and way of speech, it was hard to break in.'

Still, Wendy recalls that it was Julie who was particularly warm and welcoming, trying to involve her as much as she could. Regardless, the more experienced actress was bowled over by Julie's ability on stage. 'I was just amazed at her talent – she was quite brilliant in the play. I used to gasp every night as I watched her, because she was so good in the role.

She played an awkward, shy, plain person and she made her so funny. She had this radiance.'

Without rave reviews, the play lasted its limited run and closed. Wendy says, 'I remember it being over and breathing a sigh of relief!'

Always one to keep her options open, Julie returned to the small screen, appearing in several programmes throughout 1978.

On the back of the success of *Funny Peculiar*, Mike Stott was invited to contribute to the BBC's *Play For Today* series. His piece, *Soldiers Talking Cleanly*, was a military comedy featuring Bob Mason, Stephen Moore and Ewan Stewart. 'It was my first telly and I had a tiny little scene right at the beginning of it,' says Ewan. 'It was literally as the title said – soldiers talking about their job – only it had to be clean because they couldn't eff and blind on telly.' Julie landed one of the two female roles, not least because her friend Alan Dossor was the director.

'I remember her from that time anyway,' continues Ewan, 'because *Soldiers Talking Cleanly* followed on from a play I was doing, *Flying Blind*, at the Royal Court. They were both directed by Alan, which is how I got the part. Julie was going out with Pete Postlethwaite at the time, and he was in the play too. We used to socialise at their flat in Soho.'

Julie was next seen in the second series of *Empire Road*, British television's first black soap opera. Written by Michael Abbensetts (considered by many to be the best black playwright to emerge from his generation), the landmark series focused on the daily lives of a couple in Handsworth, Birmingham. Julie appeared as Miss Watson in Episode 6, 'Blues in the Night'. The following year, Abbensetts received an award for Outstanding Contribution to Literature.

Moving into sitcom, Julie made a fleeting appearance on the long-running *The Liver Birds*. Created by Carla Lane and Myra Taylor, the series became a recognised part of Liverpool history, charting the trials, tribulations and love lives of two women sharing a flat on Huskisson Street.

Through a couple of changes of cast, Julie was reunited with a former Everyman performer, Elizabeth Estensen, who played Carol. Michael Angelis was cast as her brother, Lucien Boswell. 'The first thing I did with Julie was *The Liver Birds*,' he recalls. 'It was my first comedy series, a weekly sitcom with Nerys Hughes and Elizabeth Estensen.'

Over time, Julie also had small roles in *Getaway*, *Green Card* and *Club Havana*, the last being, a *Second City Firsts* play for the BBC. Still reasonably new to television, Julie was preoccupied with her performance. 'I know it sounds terrible but I can't watch anything else but myself,' she says. 'I think, What a terrible piece of acting, or, Oh my God, I look too gross!'

In May 1978, Julie returned to the theatre and was soon making waves once again. This time the playwright was the brilliant Snoo Wilson. 'I wrote *Glad Hand* long before word processors,' laughs Snoo of the tale. 'It's about a South African who tries to recreate the appearance of the Antichrist by hiring a defunct oil tanker and engaging people to re-enact the cowboy strike of 1888. I was desperate for the Royal Shakespeare Company to do it and when I told a taxi to take me to Soho where the typist was waiting to transcribe the latest lot of foul papers, I must have bewitched him with my psychic beams, because he drove me straight to the Aldwych, which was the London home of the RSC at the time.'

Fate worked in Snoo's favour and Stuart Burge of the RSC did indeed commission *Glad Hand*. Max Stafford-Clark edited Snoo's messy drafts, then directed it at the Royal Court.

'Julie was both our first choices for the lead,' continues the playwright. 'I can't remember first hearing of Julie Walters, but my gratitude and admiration were more or less instantaneous when she started doing parts in my plays.

'Julie's ornery character as brothel madam and shipwrecked survivor was based on the gloriously intransigent *Time Out* journalist and personal friend, Mandy Merck – now it can be told! Also in the cast were the amazingly talented Nick Le Prevost [from the Everyman Theatre] and Julian Hough who played the ship's faith healer.' (As a footnote, Snoo says of Hough, 'Julian became schizophrenic and ended his life trying to cross the Guildford bypass on foot.')

'There are two strong memories I have. One of when Julie arrived, shipwrecked after a collision with the aforementioned oil tanker, with her hapless protégé in tow. Then her later induction scene with the brilliant Di Patrick as Sylvia Hooley, as she tries to educate her into the ways of "getting on" in the Wild West, via whoring.'

The play was described by the *Sunday Telegraph* as, 'a full-blooded theatrical experience which is also – praise be – good fun to watch. Its energetic, imaginative nonsense spills out ideas, situations, crises, comedy and political harangue in a firework display of non sequitur, whiz-bang high spirits.'

Opening on 11 May, *Glad Hand* was a success and enjoyed an extended run of six weeks and a mini-tour.

After the humiliating flop of *Breezeblock Park*, a second time around, Julie was pleased to be back in a positive position. Her appearance in

Glad Hand earned her a job at the Bush Theatre, which changed her life.

Established in April 1972 in the upstairs dining room of the Bush Hotel, Shepherd's Bush Green, the theatre had come into its own since Dusty Hughes was appointed artistic director in 1976. 'I transformed it into a fully professional theatre,' he says, 'paying Equity wages with a properly defined policy of being a producing house for the best new playwrights and actors.'

The theatre quickly built a reputation for being 'one of the liveliest centres of new writing' and became internationally renowned for discovering new talent, leading the *Sunday Times* to proclaim rightly, 'What happens at The Bush today is at the very heart of tomorrow's theatre.'

During the summer of 1978, Dusty conceived the idea of producing a show based on the news stories from one particular week. 'We decided that most of the interesting stories had death in them,' he elaborates, 'so that became the theme. A snapshot of that week in Britain. It was an evening of short plays, some of which had music, and sharp satirical songs.

'The budgets were tiny because, in order to attract good people, we had to pay wages, which ate up most of our cash. So the set was very simple – with most of the money spent on props.'

He gathered a core of writers: Snoo Wilson, Ken Campbell, Nigel Baldwin and Ron Hutchinson, and a cast ensemble comprising Alison Fiske, John Fiske, Godfrey Jackman, Philip Jackson, Clive Merrison and one Julie Walters. 'I knew Julie because of her work at the Royal Court with Snoo, and she had always said she was keen to work at the Bush Theatre,' he recalls.

'I liked her enormously because she's very down-to-earth, hates bullshit, and is always good-natured. I think at the time she didn't trust her immense talent, but she has that knack of always being sympathetic without being sentimental. She approached every challenge as if it was a live hand grenade, but always made you laugh. "Oh, God, I don't know about that, Dusty, I can't do that," she'd say, then of course she'd give it a go and be great.'

Dusty had spotted another rising new talent performing at the Institute of Contemporary Arts: Victoria Wood. 'I reviewed one of her first ever gigs for *Time Out* and thought she was a star, so I knew her work well,' he adds. To her own accompaniment on the piano, Victoria's jaunty tunes, which often belied her prickly and poignant lyrics, were extremely popular. Her regular themes were of unrequited love and tedious and mismatched relationships, and she often found humour in the minutiae of humdrum suburban life.

Impressed, Dusty invited her to join his group as both a writer and performer. Although relatively unknown at the time, Victoria was proud of her individuality on stage, and worried that a company-based run of three weeks would stifle rather than stimulate her fledgling career. Yet she was intrigued and reluctantly agreed to attend an initial meeting.

The troupe gathered, rather unconventionally, at Snoo's house. 'I was trying to put the roof of a guard's van on in my garden – I inveigled Dusty into having a cast meeting at my house so the cast could all push the roof on!' Julie typically mucked in and thought it was a riot, but, to Snoo, Victoria came across as snobbish and refused to help on the grounds that manual labour was beneath her.

When they eventually got down to theatre business, Victoria was still not keen on the project, but unexpectedly changed her mind. The reason? She recognised the person with the 'teeny weeny eyes' sitting next to her.

'Suddenly the face from the past, and the face in front of me, blended into one,' recalls Victoria. That Julie had left such an impression from almost a decade earlier told the comedienne that she was something special.

'It was obvious that Julie and Victoria would become friends,' recalls Dusty. The two northern lasses forged an instant and enduring friendship and were often to be found gassing over lunch at a café in Shepherd's Bush. They discovered that they shared not only a sense of humour, but also a similar background: they were both the youngest of four and had suffered unhappy educations, and their mothers were equally difficult women of Irish descent.

In at the Death was the name of the show and, as per Dusty's original concept, the writers were asked to provide compositions on mortality as represented in the newspapers during the first week of June. While Ken Campbell leafed through the *Malaysian New Straits Times* and Nigel Baldwin turned to the *Holyhead and Anglesey Chronicle*, Victoria preferred more pertinent pieces and focused her attention on the national stories as told by the tabloids.

The show ran at the Bush Theatre from 13 July to 6 August 1978 and for the most part was well received. Some critics found the fascination of the macabre, grisly and gory too bitter to digest. Others welcomed the opportunity to see something fresh and different. But all praised both Julie and Victoria for their vitality and talent.

The show was described as 'a ragbag collection of gruesome "Living Newspaper" stories' by Michael Coveney for the *Financial Times*. He complimented the imagination of the sketches and the acting from, among others, Julie Walters. Also up for praise was Victoria Wood: 'There are some unguent songs and sketches by Victoria Wood, a performer new to me and a delightful discovery, mixing a direct earthy comedy style with a winning way at the keyboards.'

Victoria's requiem for Guy the Gorilla, who passed away at London Zoo, was noted, as was the song 'Road Blocks'. The latter, performed by Julie, was about the death of a teenage motorcyclist killed in a police chase through Surrey. 'Victoria Wood stands out in a vigorous company, for songs that successfully blend a gallows humour with an unexpected touch of humanity,' wrote John Barber for the *Daily Telegraph*.

The whole cast were involved in two sketches: 'Compensation' by Ron Hutchinson, about a Belfast family's eponymous scam; and 'Ghouls' by Dusty Hughes. 'The compiler and director contributes a capital sketch,' enthused Barber, 'satirising ghouls who drive up in hordes to the scene of fatal accidents. He features a nasty family eagerly taking snapshots for their scrapbook of horrors.'

Julie also appeared as the middle-aged widow in Snoo's sketch 'The Language of the Dead is Tongued with Fire, Etcetera'. 'By some inner osmosis, she instantly became competently narrow and middle-aged, to play the woman whose excavations destroy the foundation of the bungalow in which she lives following the glimmerings of a descending light that is, we discover, her dead husband in the Underworld,' recalls Snoo. 'You would give her these things to perform and, if the structure was right, she would do them, just like that, without any discussion about how weird they were. And some of them were certainly stretchers . . .'

Victoria was brought in primarily for her songwriting skills and performance, but, when the revue turned out to be lacking in length, she seized the opportunity. Unable to find any more inspiration on the given theme, she asked Dusty if she could write a comedy sketch instead. She had never tried this genre before, but there was an old typewriter on the set and Dusty needed some more material. During one lunchtime she produced 'Sex'.

'It was the first thing I'd written with proper jokes,' she remembers. 'I thought, Aha, I've suddenly found something I could do. It was a blinding flash, like learning a new language.'

'Sex' was triggered by a *Daily Express* article about a woman desperate to have a test-tube baby against medical advice. Victoria relocated the saga to a library in Manchester and cast Julie as a panicky teenage girl who thinks she might be pregnant.

'The thing that brought the house down every night,' says Julie, 'was her asking me, "Where are you in the menstrual cycle?" And me mouthing, "Taurus"!' The sketch was a breath of fresh air in the heavy second half, and was heralded as 'fifteen minutes of sheer delight' by the *West London Observer*.

The laughs weren't all on stage, though, and the two friends were always getting into mischief. 'In those days, all the actors and actresses shared a dressing room and they were rather thrown in together,' explains Simon Stokes, who ran the Bush Theatre at the time. 'Victoria and Julie got on very well – they were both rather lively.'

Julie related the scenario to *Woman's Own*: 'There wasn't a dressing room – backstage was just a set of stairs leading to the street through a fire door. There was no toilet and, although you could go to the one at the back of the pub, we used beer glasses! People would come in and we'd shout, "Argh! Don't drink that!"'

Clearly having established a unique rapport, Julie says today, 'Victoria was like a cold drink in the desert.' Victoria repays the compliment: 'I've never met anyone who didn't like her, which is remarkable really because she isn't bland at all!'

Mike Bradwell, an employee at the theatre, remembers one incident in particular. 'Some time during the run of the show, everyone was sitting on the windowsill,' he says. 'They thought they saw Harold Pinter down below on Shepherd's Bush Green. Julie shouted out, "Is that Harold Pinter? Are you a writer, because we could use one up here!"'

During rehearsals, Julie would serenade the cast and crew with her old favourites. 'She had tremendous ability as a singer and impersonator of singers,' marvels Dusty. 'She was doing an exact Shirley Bassey long before Jane Horrocks – as soon as she finished they would ask her to do it again. Julie is naturally very, very funny, in quite an original way. She doesn't try to be funny, she's not a show-off.'

Julie, who was evidently still living it up in the capital – Simon Stokes says, 'She had a reputation for being something of a party girl in those days' – looks back fondly: 'We had some mad times!'

7. TALENT

'As a result of *In at the Death*, Victoria Wood was asked to write a play for the Crucible Theatre in Sheffield by David Leland, who was the director that season,' says Mike Bradwell of the Bush Theatre. In fact, David had wanted Victoria to collaborate with Ron Hutchinson but, when the latter was busy, he went out on a limb and commissioned Victoria on her own. 'She wrote *Talent*, specifically for her and Julie,' continues Mike, 'but Julie couldn't do it.' The increasingly popular actress was already signed up for some television work, so Hazel Clyne co-starred with Victoria instead.

Julie had in fact jumped at the chance to work with Alan Bennett, one of the greatest playwrights of the time. Finding fame in the satirical review *Beyond the Fringe* with Dudley Moore, Peter Cooke and Jonathan Miller in 1960, Bennett had garnered high regard for his ability to create detailed, memorable character sketches of complicated people. Hailing from Yorkshire, Bennett roots his characters in that particular social environment, but the issues they raise possess a more universal appeal, all told in a tone simultaneously ironic and tender.

When the BBC said they could produce only one of Bennett's plays a year, he was offended and ITV picked up the tab. Michael Grade, then up-and-coming in the business, commissioned a series simply titled *Six Plays by Alan Bennett*. The first programme, *Me! I'm Afraid of Virginia Woolf*, was aired on 2 December 1978. Bennett narrated the piece, which starred Neville Smith and Thora Hird, and, as fellow actor Hugh Lloyd recalls, 'That was very much a team show, all using Alan's magic words.' (Hird would be awarded an OBE in 1983 and be made a dame a decade later. She died in March 2003 after suffering a stroke.)

Julie had only a small part, but that was irrelevant. She was hooked on Bennett's 'magic words' and, like Hird, found herself regularly returning to his work.

Meanwhile, *Talent* was proving popular in Sheffield and warranted a London transfer. While Victoria was calculating the mechanics of such a move, however, she was approached with an even more exciting offer.

'I was a freelance director,' says Baz Taylor, 'and I'd worked for Granada a couple of times. One of their producers, Peter Eckersley, rang up one day and said, "I want you to come up to Sheffield and have a look at a play."

'I went to the Crucible Theatre and saw *Talent* on the stage. I thought it was very funny, very witty, and what was different about it was that this girl, Victoria Wood, could sing. It was a nice, silly story about dirty northern girls and I thought it would make fun television.' Baz relayed his thoughts to Peter, who felt the same and they set up a meeting with Victoria.

'We'd like to make this into a television play,' said Peter.

'OK,' she replied, 'but, if we're going to do that, can I do it with my great mate, Julie Walters?'

Peter hadn't heard of the actress, but compromised: 'We'll certainly have a look at her.'

'Of course we didn't know her,' continues Baz, 'so we all got together and they read a bit. Well, they were just a double act from the beginning – they were two people who absolutely clicked; they were on the same wavelength. So that was it!'

The stage cast travelled to London to perform an eighteen-night run at the ICA commencing 31 January 1979, and then Victoria and Julie went to Manchester to prepare for the television adaptation. (Peter Ellis, incidentally, was the only cast member, besides Victoria, to be in all three productions.)

Talent is a bittersweet musical comedy that deals with the lives, loves and dreams of two mismatched friends. Set backstage at a night-club, it shows Julie, an ambitious singer nervously waiting for the talent contest, accompanied by Maureen, her plump, dull, but loyal, companion.

One of the most refreshing things about Victoria's writing is its accessibility. She is able to communicate with the public on a very basic level, by distributing familiar monikers, be they famous television personalities such as Cilla Black and Paul Daniels or branded names such as Palmolive and Tunes, throughout her dialogue.

'What attracted me was that it had product names and English that people spoke,' enthuses Baz. 'It wasn't singing about love from a hilltop in an idealistic way: it was, "If I eat another bag of Maltesers, then I'll get fat and he won't fancy me." Julie's great song in it was "Fourteen Again". She sang something like, "I want to be fourteen again, when sex was just called number ten, and I was up to seven and a half." That was the one that caught everyone's imagination. There was no question about it – it was very funny and really original.'

Another quirk that would become one of Victoria's trademarks was a hilarious obsession with all things gynaecological. When accused of alienating men, Victoria simply replied, 'All my comedy is done from a woman's point of view, which doesn't mean that it's not accessible to men, just that it will always have a particular relevance for women.'

To achieve that raw humour, much of her language was frank and she certainly called a spade a spade. Unfortunately, that meant that some of the more colourful phrases and scenes that worked so well on stage were considered a little racy for television.

'The girls are in the dressing room and Julie's character is getting nervous,' says Baz of one such scene. 'She wants to go to the loo, but it's blocked, so she pees in one of the other artists' hats. We couldn't do that on television then: we felt it was a bit too crude.'

Similarly, while the word 'twat' and two references to 'cock' squeezed through the censors, the f-word did not make it, leaving Julie with the blander, 'I thought coq au vin was love in a lorry.'

Victoria hadn't deliberately put those terms in to shock her audience. The reason it was so funny was because it was natural, but not everyone expected to hear such blue language from two women, even in 1979.

'They were terrible together,' exclaims Baz of their off-stage behaviour. 'I think it was the first time that they had radio mikes put on – although it's not as good quality, it made life a bit easier and meant that they could run around and sing and dance. The first time they went to the loo [between rehearsals], they were sitting there chatting about the crew ...'

'What do you think of cameraman number three?' one asked.

'I don't think he's got a very big willy,' replied the other.

'They were like that in real life,' Baz continues, 'but this was going all around the gallery – we could hear exactly what they were talking about! Anyway, Vic, Jules and I went out to the pub that evening and I said, "Look, you've got to be a bit careful what you say when you go to the loo, because we can hear you." They were absolutely gobsmacked. So I told them what we had heard and said, "Just remember, we can hear you from the speakers all round the building."

'So, the next day, once they'd got their radio mikes on, they went down to the loo. This time they did *everybody*! From the managing director down. And the whole conversation was *littered* with rude words – certainly "clitoris" was mentioned, which was quite a shock back then ...'

'Oh my clit, it aches!' squealed one of the girls. 'I don't think I can jump on that bar stool again!'

'Do you fancy the German?' asked the other.

'Nah, he's too old for me,' came the response.

'Of course, they were doing it on purpose, knowing that everybody was listening,' says Baz. 'When they came back on the studio floor, everyone was looking at them. They just grinned.'

Another reason why *Talent* was so charming was its novel combination of script and song. It was one thing on stage, but it created a headache in the studio.

'It was hard, because to be honest none of us knew much about musicals,' admits Baz. 'I certainly had no experience of doing musicals and we were trying to be as innovative as we could.'

He wasn't the only one to be apprehensive about reproducing Victoria's successful piece in the studio.

'Obviously Vic knew Jules could sing, otherwise she wouldn't have written the songs for her,' he elaborates. 'Jules wasn't nervous in itself, because she was in a studio with only a few people around, but she was nervous about letting her friend down. She was so concerned that she should do it well. So she'd belt it out, then ask Vic if she was flat. Vic would just say, "Yes you were, you silly old tart," and they'd do it again!

'The funny thing was, because Vic had written it hearing Julie saying the words, Julie stuck rigidly to the script. But we had very free, jokey rehearsals – I'd sit there making comments, then they'd make comments and, if we came up with a new line or a new end to a scene, Vic would say, "Quick, has anyone written that down?" Then she would go off and write it overnight, we'd come back the next day and it would be different.

'It became a little factory in strange way. Occasionally Vic would say she couldn't judge something because she was acting in it. So they would do the new changes and I would have to say whether it worked or not. When it was really working we used to stop. Once they said they knew it, we'd leave it and save it for the studio, because if it gets overworked it becomes stale. But Vic and Jules were great fun, because they just loved what they were doing.'

They worked hard, so they played hard. The small cast and crew stayed in a hotel in Manchester during the few weeks of rehearsal and filming. 'We all went a bit mad,' recalls Baz. 'God knows what the other guests must have thought! There was a lot of socialising, because the Granada studios were quite small then and there were only a few pubs.'

The resulting piece was aired after the watershed at 9.30 p.m. on Sunday, 5 August to resounding praise. Both Julie and Victoria were fantastic in their roles, the script was sharp and witty and the direction slick. 'We got various awards abroad and nominations for BAFTAs and so on because it was very new at the time,' Baz remembers. 'It was very refreshing to have people burst into song.

'Vic suddenly became a household name the night after *Talent* went out. It was one of those rare things – because it was such an original idea, from a woman who writes her own songs and plays the piano, and is cheeky with it.'

In fact 1979 was truly an era of 'girl power' as Margaret Thatcher had just been elected as the first female prime minister of Great Britain. Although Victoria and Julie didn't agree with her politics, it was good to see women taking control at last.

The only criticism Victoria *had* anticipated was the predictable references to her size, not least because she had played up their differences in the film, but it still hurt. They were labelled 'the thin one' and 'the fat one' and were compared to Laurel and Hardy, Abbott and Costello and, God forbid, Little and Large. 'I was always very upset if they ever said I was fat, even though I was,' she says. 'I felt they shouldn't mention it, I felt it wasn't relevant, but of course it's a British obsession.' Which was why she felt obliged to mention it herself.

Granada organised a press viewing and conference in London, where they laid the pair open to the journalists. The girls were completely unfazed. Julie, in particular, just said what she thought and the reporters responded well to her open nature.

'Peter immediately asked me, "Shall we see if Vic can write some more?"' recalls Baz. 'So we did.'

Back in London in 1979, Julie revelled in being able to spread her wings, and her other projects of the year were no less exciting. In Liverpool she had achieved limited diversity by working with Vanload and taking on the occasional radio play – now she was working in all media with a variety of big names.

First on her list was the inimitable Mike Leigh. Hailing from Manchester, Leigh was rapidly gaining a solid reputation as a skilled writer and director, as his dramas wove humour and social commentary into ordinary working-class life. He had achieved critical acclaim with *Abigail's Party* at Hampstead Theatre and was subsequently commissioned for another, similar piece entitled *Ecstasy*.

At the start of any Mike Leigh project, the actors are obliged to launch themselves into lengthy improvisational work. Typically, this means the cast help the director to create the characters and then Leigh writes a play around the personalities that have evolved – his critics claim this is simply a ploy to make the actors produce the script, but it is his preferred method of working and it usually maximises the individual's potential.

'*Ecstasy* was blessed by a particularly inspired group of people: Jim Broadbent [who had just been in *Talent* at the ICA], Sheila Kelley,

Stephen Rea, Ron Cook, Rachel Davies and, of course, Julie Walters,' says Leigh. 'I had seen Julie in various shows around and about in theatres, including my friend Mike Stott's play *Funny Peculiar*, so I knew much of her work. We got together for an informal audition and I asked her to do it.

'The way I always work is by getting the actors to talk about lots of people that they know and then build their characters. Julie is wonderfully precise, articulate, perceptive and amusing about people. She is a great collaborator, and very creative. My stock in the trade is to be able to make plays *for* the actors, so if you read *Ecstasy* you will see Julie Walters in her character, Dawn. I also had the vaguely inspired notion of getting her and Sheila, who are both Brummies of a similar age, together and plugging into that.'

The group spent many weeks working on the background to the play before they even started rehearsals, which lasted another month or so. This approach was quite different for all involved as Leigh put the actors through a series of stages, liberating them to a level of creativity rarely available in the industry.

'With this kind of work there was always a lot of talking about work and *then* there was the acting. Julie would always say, "When are we going to do the *acting*?" She's an original,' laughs Leigh.

As the director, he worked his cast to the point of near exhaustion for this bedsit saga, inciting some critics to suggest that by the time they got the play onto the stage, the actors were close to breakdown.

Indeed, Jim Broadbent did not feel well one night and excused himself from the proceedings. When he got to the bathroom, he passed out. It was then up to Julie and Sheila to convince the audience that it was not part of the play and if there were any doctors in the house, could they please make their way backstage. Fortunately for Jim, the location of the theatre in the heart of Hampstead afforded no fewer than fourteen medical men on call. *Ecstasy* was forced to close for a few nights due to Jim's mystery illness.

'The previous play I had done was *Abigail's Party*, so it was generally assumed that *Ecstasy* would be just such a play,' comments Leigh. 'In fact, my natural instinct was to subvert that expectation and so it's nothing like *Abigail's Party*!'

Leigh told Sheila Kelley his reason for doing the play: 'for my sanity'. She confirms that the author writes best when he has reached the end of his tether. 'When he's comfortable and has money, I don't like the work so much,' she says. 'I don't think he pushes it hard enough.' However, Hampstead Theatre, who had hoped for another zingy comedy that might transfer to the West End, were surprised in *Ecstasy* to say the least.

Ecstasy turned out to be three hours of grimly unremitting, cheerless intensity. That is not to say it was bad, just heavy going. There is humour in the sarcastically named piece, but the overall mood is one of desperation.

Located in a bedsit on Kilburn High Road, the drama revolves around the four main characters: Jean (Sheila Kelley), an alcoholic, suicidal garage attendant who sleeps with unsuitable men; her trite friend Dawn (Julie Walters), who has three children; Dawn's husband Mick (Stephen Rea), an Irish labourer; and his uncommunicative friend Len (Jim Broadbent).

'The ensemble character study that went on between Julie, Sheila, Stephen and Jim was a relationship from the past, which is why we spent such a lot of time working on the ten years prior to the action,' Leigh explains. 'We were then able to plug into the present time and that's what you get in the play. A lot of the long second act is all about remembering the past, and that's the stuff that we'd experienced.

'It was a very in-depth and sustained kind of acting, but the nature of that work, not least that project, was such that everyone knew what they were doing. It was very solid.'

Two highlights of the play are an eerily hypnotic, dead-of-night boozy singalong, and one of the best – and gloomiest – party scenes in contemporary drama (bar, of course, *Abigail's Party*). Leigh appeared to be happy investigating this miserable reality that lay less than a mile from the affluent surrounds of the theatre. Reviewers, on the other hand, were hoping for another *Abigail's Party*, and *Ecstasy* was sadly overlooked when they realised it was so different.

Still, audiences flocked to see Mike Leigh's new play – which, by the way, was nearly called *One Mile Behind You*, due to the proximity of Kilburn High Road to Hampstead – and the theatre was packed every night of the run. 'It was a very successful play and it absolutely blew people away,' says Leigh. 'It should have gone into the West End, but it was too uncompromising and harsh a piece as the impresarios saw it.'

The cast definitely felt rewarded by the production. Sheila was thrilled to have such a complex character, especially as she and Leigh had moulded the extent of her misery from scratch. Jim Broadbent commented that is was, 'like going on a huge acting course, with a wonderful play at the end of it'. Stephen Rea was also praising of Leigh's method, labelling it as, 'a training that's required if you're going to get into all the corners of acting'.

For Julie's part, she simply said that it was, 'one of the happiest times of my career'. She not only made an impression on the audience but, like all her previous directors, Leigh was also enamoured with the actress.

'She was a generous, loving, funny person with a great take on life and a great open-mindedness about everything,' he says. 'She was great fun, full of beans and wise-cracking gags, endlessly entertaining.'

As always, Julie was up for serious socialising as Mike Leigh confirms, laughing, 'If there was a drink going on, you can bet your bottom dollar she was there.'

During the 1978–9 season at the Bristol Old Vic theatre, Julie continued to turn her hand to every genre, appearing in Shakespeare's *As You Like It*, directed by Richard Cottrell, and Thomas Middleton's *The Changeling*, directed by Adrian Noble. Pete Postlethwaite was also in *The Changeling*; their relationship was still going strong and, as always when they worked together, they had a lot of fun both on and off stage.

Julie's final project of 1979 was her third appearance in a Snoo Wilson play. This time it was *Flaming Bodies* at the ICA, directed by John Ashford. The three-hander (just a trio on stage) had originally been offered to the Royal Court, but, as Snoo recalls, 'they declined on the grounds that it was impossible to have a car come in through a window. The ICA was briefly in a period where they were able to embrace the impossible as well as the theatrical, and the Chevrolet coming in through the window with its twin headlights ablaze was accomplished with insolent, counterbalanced ease.

'*Flaming Bodies*, a play about a fat lesbian who had come down from an LA high-rise, came about more through my sister's antagonism to my mother. Julie played the English ingénue – though no one is ever quite ingénue in the play. Miriam Margolyes played the lead – a part that is longer than Hamlet's – and Hugh Thomas filled the male role.

'Julie had this speech at her entrance, when she announced she was somehow clean and ready for life, having just got off the plane from London. I thought she was electrifying, but people still didn't quite see how much she was doing. The fact that she did it so well is a fulfilment: she performs everything with a sharpshooter's precision, incredibly well, and I am so grateful.'

The play was undoubtedly a weird scenario, but it proved popular as queues formed around the block for 'the play where the car came through the window'. *Flaming Bodies* ran at the ICA for four weeks in December.

8. HER BIG CHANCE

Nineteen eighty was a very busy year for Julie Walters. It started back in Manchester with Victoria Wood's sequel to *Talent*, as commissioned by Peter Eckersley and again directed by Baz Taylor.

'The second one was much the same idea as the first,' says Baz. 'To be perfectly honest, I think Vic thought, What else can we do as two girls? *Talent* was about dreaming of the good life, falling in love and getting married and *Nearly a Happy Ending* was essentially all about getting boys, except [the girls] went to a slimming club.'

In *Nearly a Happy Ending* the characters are the same, but this time the roles are reversed. Julie is depressed because her boyfriend is dead and her mother is in a psychiatric hospital; Maureen, on the other hand, is experiencing one of life's upswings – she has slimmed down and passed her driving test. They plan a night out and needless to say the conversation turns to sex, specifically to Maureen's losing her virginity.

When their car breaks down, Julie and Maureen find themselves in a hotel with a bunch of randy businessmen. While Julie seriously considers teaming up with the comedian Les Dickey (Peter Martin), Maureen bluntly requests sex from Tony (Paul Seed). When Maureen returns, yet to be deflowered, Julie tells her that relations with men are overrated, but then swiftly arranges a liaison with Tony for herself.

The conclusion of the play leaves Julie bored and in despair over men, and Maureen, still a virgin, tucking into a box of chocolates. They sing a duet in which they describe how their life hasn't turned out the way they imagined, but how it is nearly happy. 'My real point,' says Victoria, 'is to show that people don't really know what they want.'

While the plot direction and theme were a little predictable, one thing was different: Victoria had clearly been hurt by previous comments on her size and had lost a considerable amount of weight. To keep trim while rehearsing and filming, she attended the local swimming pool in Salford, Manchester, regularly accompanied by Julie and sporadically joined by Baz, who confesses, 'I think they were better at it than I was.'

The girls may have achieved a modicum of fame, but it was their names people remembered, as their faces were not yet familiar. 'Even when we got a bus to the seedy end of Stockport to film outside a fish-and-chip shop, no one recognised them,' says Baz.

They were still working with a small budget, but at least the itinerary was more lenient, thanks to the benefit of hindsight. 'Previously, with *Talent*, the schedule had been based on a normal play where everybody came in, sat down and talked. But, as the film frequently burst into song, it was totally different. After *Talent* we were aware of just how difficult it had been to get the sound, technology and everything right. So we had more time for *Nearly a Happy Ending*, particularly because it was more ambitious.

'We did one shot where Julie's in the pub. The comic chats her up and she goes into this routine and sings, "I want to be a comedienne", and does a dance around the bar and ends up back where she started. We took a whole day to do that shot. Nowadays we could have probably done it in three-quarters of an hour, but then we were lumbering a five-foot-tall camera around on a three-foot-wide pedestal. We were all tied up with cables and, every time we went round a corner, someone had to unravel the cable so we could go back. But it was a new shot at the time, and it gave us impact.

'God knows how many times we did it – nine times out of ten, the camera would hit the bar, or fall over, or get tangled up. Poor Julie had to sing that song at least fifteen times, but she was young and keen and she just did it.'

There was also a dream sequence in the bathroom for Victoria, which entailed her standing on a revolving platform while a tight tube of mirrors was constructed around her, before filming began outside the tube. It may not sound like it now, but it was cutting-edge technology.

Rehearsals and filming for *Nearly a Happy Ending* were completed in February 1980 and the finished product aired on 1 June. Although the critics realised it was a little samey, they were still fascinated by the duo and wrote warm reviews. Indeed, when viewed today, the script is as slick as ever, the songs wry and the direction inventive. Moreover, both Julie and Victoria shine in their comfortable roles.

Having shed nearly three stone, Victoria Wood looked radiant at her wedding on 1 March to Geoffrey Durham, whom she had been dating for four years. Julie knew Geoffrey from living in the room above him during her Everyman Theatre days and was thrilled for the happy couple, although, strangely, Victoria insisted they keep it quiet for some time afterwards, as marriage was not a popular choice in the industry at the time.

Julie's relationship with Pete Postlethwaite, on the other hand, had run its natural course. 'We have to play so many roles in society, in work, with those we love. We have to compromise and you find you get further away from your real self,' explains Julie poetically. 'When I was in love with someone, we both compromised. I wasn't the only one making adjustments, though it'd be easy to think so!'

Julie moved on and out of the Soho flat she had shared with Pete, renting modest accommodation in Clapham for a while. She returned to her independent and carefree self. 'I never had a desire to be a brilliant cook, so it was always takeaways,' she told Roald Rynning. 'I was just not a home sort of person. I was happiest sleeping on other people's floors and hotel rooms. I liked the feeling that I was moving on.'

Never one to wallow in self-pity, she plunged straight back into work. She accepted another role with Victoria, this time on stage in a play called *Good Fun*. The main character is Liz, a community arts administrator who is manipulated by a geography teacher-cum-Punch and Judy man. Padding is provided by a number of oddball extras including Frank, an immature and horny librarian; Elsie, a cynical old friend; and Betty, a middle-aged cosmetics saleswoman who likes to boogie. The unlikely plot revolves around a reception for three hundred cystitis sufferers, which obviously opens the door for endless crude jokes focusing squarely on 'women's issues'.

Perhaps surprisingly, Julie turned down the lead in favour of the irresistibly comical Betty, thus marking the first time she played a bizarre, aged character for Victoria. Wood reluctantly created the small role of Elsie for herself when the producers insisted she also appear on stage.

Sadly, *Good Fun* did not live up to its name, or its two predecessors. The setting limited its appeal and the jokes seemed to fall between two stools. (Indeed, eight years later, when the play was published by Methuen, Victoria admitted that she knew she hadn't got it right.) Opening on Good Friday, 1980, in Sheffield, the show struggled through an unhappy run. Amazingly, there was talk of a West End transfer, but that fell through and Victoria felt her bubble had burst. Never one to concede defeat in the face of a challenge, she was determined the play would work and set about revising it. But, while Victoria fought a crisis of confidence, Julie was offered a part in Willy Russell's new play. She was torn. She didn't want to appear to be abandoning her friend in her hour of need, but the combination of the role, the play and the theatre was almost too good to be true. Despite the poor reception for *Breezeblock Park*, Julie chose Russell's new project over a struggling modification of *Good Fun*.

Originally, Russell had been commissioned by the Royal Court to write a new play. However, when he presented it to them, they changed their minds and instead the Royal Shakespeare Company acquired his latest offering: *Educating Rita*. But the RSC immediately ran into problems, because, although it was only a two-hander, the entire company were committed to the current production of *Nicholas Nickleby*.

At this point the author stepped in and recommended an actress whom he rated and who had featured in his previous plays: Julie Walters. She met the director, Mike Ockrent, and won the approval of all involved. The RSC then teamed her up with an actor they had earmarked for future work, Mark Kingston.

'I knew absolutely nothing of Julie – our paths had never crossed,' admits Mark. 'The first time we met was at the read-through and she was immensely likable. She was so warm, friendly and full of enthusiasm, it was made very easy. Then we sat down and talked with Willy and Mike, and we read the play. We were both appalled by our reading, but, even so, I could tell what a spectacular talent she was.'

The plot was intriguing: Julie plays Rita, a 26-year-old hairdresser who enrols on an Open University literature course. Mark portrays Frank, her alcoholic lecturer and dried-up poet, whose wife has left him. Rita's husband insists she drop her self-improvement, but, rebelling against his working-class aspirations, she abandons him. Meanwhile, Frank becomes obsessed with his student, cuts down his drinking and smartens himself up.

Rita realises the direction their relationship has taken but refuses to play Eliza Doolittle for his friends. Instead, she fine-tunes her skills at a summer school in London, and Frank sinks back into the bottle when she no longer needs him. The tutor likens her transformation to *Frankenstein*, rather than *Pygmalion* – to which she accuses him of wanting to 'keep the natives thick'. Regardless of the outcome, the crux of the story is that Rita takes her education into her own hands.

Interestingly, the play was semiautobiographical as Russell left school at fifteen, became a ladies' hairdresser and only in later life chose to return to college. 'All these strange, innocent, outrageous things that Rita would come out with, Willy would have done that,' thinks Mark. 'Like so many plays, it comes from one's own experience in life.'

Rehearsals started in the opera rooms in the East End of London and everything went smoothly during May. 'Willy was there at every rehearsal,' says Mark. 'He knew exactly what the play should be like and was invited to be vocal by Mike Ockrent. Mike had no pride about that: his sole concern was that the play should be done as well as possible. You couldn't find a nicer, more astute guy.

'So, it became a four-handed rehearsal [Julie, Mark, Mike and Willy] that was a joy throughout – painful on many occasions because it was a struggle to get there, but we were grateful for Willy's input. Whereas Mike was approaching it from a director's point of view, Willy could shortcut things, because he knew these people backwards. When you're standing there saying, "Why, why, why?" He'd say, "I'll tell you why." '

The quartet worked intensely from Monday to Saturday, every week for four and a half weeks. There wasn't much interaction after hours, not least because they were all so drained.

Come June, with the premiere less than a fortnight away, things became a little shaky. 'I remember growing more and more in awe of her skill,' continues Mark, 'but on the final rehearsal we said, "We cannot be opening next week." We walked back through the East End, thinking, Where can we get a plane to Rio and get out of this?

'It had just been a rehearsal that hadn't worked – all the work we had done seemed to have disappeared. But that's par for the course. It often happens that you think you've got it going and then, on the final run, you think, "God Almighty, this is ghastly!"

'What that means, in fact, is that you need an audience to respond. You forget how funny the play is, so depression sets in. All the things that made you laugh disappear during rehearsal, but suddenly an audience will do it for you.'

Indeed, Mark and Julie recovered from their atrocious final run-through and the opening night, 10 June 1980, was a triumph. The play was performed at the Donmar Warehouse, a particularly small theatre, which lent itself well to the intimacy of just the two actors on stage.

'Like me, Julie was very nervous,' says Mark, 'but there is an inner confidence in her that has proved very valuable – confidence is vital to an actor.'

The play, set entirely in Frank's study, consisted of several short scenes faded in and out. 'I never changed,' says Mark of his character's attire. 'I wore the same brown corduroy jacket, trousers, pullover and open-necked shirt.' Julie altered her outfit to represent her gradual metamorphosis, but the adjustments had to be very simple because she was off stage only briefly when the lights dimmed, coming straight back on again when they lifted. Her greatest change was during the interval, which represented the passage of the summer break.

While Julie provided comedy in her character's naïveté and blunt nature, Mark was concerned that the humour didn't eclipse Frank's deep-felt passions. 'We had to be careful that there wasn't such huge laughter that it spoilt the emotions that were going on,' he says. 'Her character didn't feel that way about Frank, but I had to come in from a different point of view, as Frank had obviously fallen for her in a big way and tried to change his life.'

The pair coped with all their trials and tribulations admirably and the play was generally considered a success. If there were any criticisms, they were usually, but not exclusively, aimed at Russell's script. Perhaps the most analytical appraisal came from the journalist Simon Howard:

> *Julie Walters's portrayal of Rita was utterly complete on the outside –*
> *wonderful nods, precarious balancings on her high heels, ear-piercing*
> *squeaks in her voice, producing moments like when, for some reason or*
> *other, she couldn't look Frank in the eye. One sometimes felt the inner*
> *work was not full, but never mind, it was an outrageous, dazzling*
> *performance.*
>
> *Rita's gains at Frank's expense were echoed in the acting and Mark*
> *Kingston usually refused to step out of Julie Walters's shadow. Many of*
> *his problems came from the writing. As with all of Willy Russell's work,*
> *there is an extraordinary imbalance in the quality of the writing.*

Howard couldn't resist a final dig: 'Educating Rita is undeniably flawed, but one certainly welcomes its having been written.'

'We thought it was just a four- or five-week job at the Donmar,' says Mark Kingston of Educating Rita, 'but towards the end of the run they said, "Would you be interested in continuing it in the West End for a while?" We both said yes and prayed for one of the smaller theatres!'

Julie and Mark were allowed a couple of weeks off before they relocated in September 1980. While Mark went abroad and relaxed, Julie squeezed in just a bit more work. On the strength of Talent and Nearly a Happy Ending, Peter Eckersley had offered Victoria Wood a solo pilot sketch show. Considering that she had written only one sketch previously ('Sex' for In at the Death), this was quite a leap of faith.

'It was his way of keeping the industry going,' explains Baz Taylor. 'Peter saw these two girls and realised they were great together and wanted them to do a variety show. That was very much his baby.'

While Peter had every confidence in Victoria, she was wary and leaned heavily on Julie's involvement. The sketches and songs in the half-hour programme favoured Victoria's familiar soap box subjects: relationships and keeping fit.

As for naming the show, they both had equal input. 'My dad Thomas was a builder,' says Julie, 'but he wasn't the owner of a giant organisation – there was simply him and Reg Wood up the road. It was amazing how history repeated itself.' Similarly, the show's prefix became Wood & Walters and, although Victoria hated snipes about her size, she perversely finished the title off with Two Creatures Great and Small.

Victoria felt the pilot was dire. However, it was nominated for a BAFTA award, alongside *The Kenny Everett Video Show*, *The Two Ronnies* and the eventual winner, *The Stanley Baxter Series*.

By the time *Wood & Walters: Two Creatures Great and Small* aired on 1 January 1981, however, Julie was receiving higher recognition.

After her brief interlude with Victoria, Julie was back with Mark Kingston, facing the prospect of a grandiose West End transfer of their intimate little play.

'When we were told of the move to the Piccadilly Theatre, we were aghast!' says Mark. 'It seemed absurd – it was just the most unlikely theatre to put it on.' But the management company dictated it and so *Educating Rita* jumped from a small setting with 250 seats to a large, lavish venue, steeped in history with the capacity of an additional 1,000 people.

'There we were, these two actors, plonked down on this vast stage,' says Mark. 'We transferred the set, and although it was flattened out a bit so it had less of an angle, it still couldn't take up the entire stage. But the difficulty is the extra projection that you have to use. In a small playhouse you can virtually speak as one does normally. In that theatre you simply couldn't do that: you *had* to project, and that made it slightly false to oneself. We thought, Can we really do this play to such a vast house?

'Well! All I can say is that for six months it was a total sellout; it was a huge success! It was quite draining to begin with, full of nerves and emotion, but once a play is up and running, and that dread of failure is gone, it becomes much more of a routine. *Then*, of course, you have to be careful to tell yourself that this audience have paid as much as the one that came the first night. Long runs can be very hard, particularly a two-hander where you're on stage the whole time.'

Julie was in her element.

She found live theatre frightening, but it also excited and satisfied her. It was during this time that she first felt the full force of stage acting. 'On a good night the audience were so captured by the play and the character that I sensed they were almost breathing with me. It felt as if I could manipulate them however I wanted, almost as if playing a giant musical instrument,' she wrote in *Julie Walters Is an Alien*.

The show went from strength to strength and attracted a lot of attention within the industry. Many actors couldn't resist the play that everyone was talking about, and Michael Angelis turned up to see the erstwhile *Liver Birds* cameo actress. 'I went backstage to congratulate her on a wonderful performance,' says Michael. 'It was a brilliant show –

Willy Russell at his best. She and Mark Kingston really hit off each other.'

Michael was just a small fish, though. 'A lot of starry people used to come backstage,' Mark remembers. 'One night one of the doormen came up to us with a message: "Mr Rusty Koffman, a short American actor, says, 'Please tell the actors I am loving it, but I've got to leave in the interval because my wife is about to give birth!'"'

The actor in question, Dustin Hoffman, was enjoying phenomenal success with *Kramer vs. Kramer*, and his second wife Lisa was in labour with their first child, Jacob.

Mark continues, 'He dashed off, but lots of other famous people came back – we knew it was a big success.'

Educating Rita was the perfect showcase for Julie's innate talent and she was nominated for a Laurence Olivier award for Best Comedy Performance of the Year, sadly losing to Beryl Reid. Instead she won two Best Newcomer awards, from the Variety Club and the London Critics.

Between her television career with Victoria and this acclaimed stage work, after a decade in the business, Julie was suddenly considered hot property. Still, she never let it go to her head, and one night, after one of the award events, she showed her true colours.

'We were coming back from a lovely evening ceremony where we all had dinner and Julie had won the prize,' remembers Mark's wife, Marigold. 'She was going to Fulham that night and asked us for a lift. We were driving in the car and suddenly we saw an old lady slip and literally fall into the gutter, right in front of us.

'Julie was out of the car in seconds and, of course, we followed her. She was so sweet and, because she had trained to be a nurse, she knew what she was doing – she felt the lady's heart and ribs and everything, and decided that she should take her to the hospital. She was insistent that we didn't do it because Mark had had a long day – just like Julie – and said if we could get her a taxi, she would take her. So Julie, still in her finery (although she wasn't one for glitter, so it was just a very nice black dress and jacket), and still holding her wonderful gold award, carried this old lady into the taxi and took her to hospital. Nobody ever mentioned the award, neither the taxi driver nor the old lady, who was beginning to come round.'

Julie even managed to keep her feet firmly on the ground when there was talk of a film tie-in.

'Although she was known within the profession, this was the play that put her on the map,' says Mark. 'I had to accept that, while for me it was a marvellous part, for Julie it was a triumph. But I was never jealous of that for one second, because I anticipated that from the word go.' Julie left the show when her six-month contract ran out, as she had a string of other projects lined up.

'Her understudy took over and we did a few more months,' continues Mark. However, he felt 'it was never the same because Julie's so electric and unique. Time flew by when she was in it, and dragged when she had gone. You can't replace the inner life that Julie brings to everything. I couldn't stand it any more, so I left.'

9. THE FURTHER EDUCATION OF RITA

Although Julie was in negotiations for a Hollywood version of *Educating Rita*, she didn't let the situation go to her head – she still needed bread-and-butter money and to build her career in case it turned out to be nothing more than a pipe dream.

During her hunt for more work, Julie had bumped into a fellow actress, Rosalind March, and the two women discovered they had much in common and soon became close. In lieu of a boyfriend, it was Ros with whom Julie had intended to celebrate after the awards ceremony for the play, when she had instead rescued the old woman. When the contract expired on Julie's place in Clapham, Ros offered the perfect solution – she needed a lodger in her flat in Fulham.

While developing an enduring friendship, both actresses enjoyed a raucous and carefree single life. 'We just got on and were often up all night long, talking about relationships – like you do!' Julie told *Woman's Own*. 'There's a sensitivity between friends. A desire to share. Ros and I got up to lots of naughty things. Some of the men ... aah!'

Returning to the job search, Julie teamed up with her former fellow Manchester Poly student, David Ross, for a new version of an Alan Bleasdale play in April and May 1981.

'I knew Alan from the Contact Theatre, where he was writer in residence,' explains David 'Having a Ball was written for Oldham Coliseum in Manchester. It's about a man, Lenny, who's at a crisis in his life and goes into a clinic to have a vasectomy. The female lead is also at crisis point: she's an alcoholic married to a very upright and stiff man. She comes to this vasectomy clinic drunk and meets up with Lenny. They form a bond between them: they have a connection because they're both looking for the same thing.

'It's basically a huge, great farcical comedy, because Lenny has to take his clothes off and is nude through quite a lot of the play.'

Ross and Bleasdale were not the only blasts from the past. The piece was to be revived at the Lyric Theatre, Hammersmith, with Alan Dossor directing. Unfortunately, given that Bleasdale likes to be hands-on with productions of his work, according to David Ross, the two Alans did not see eye to eye. Compounding the issue, the author was not particularly happy that the name was being changed: *Having a Ball* was considered too crude a title for a play about a vasectomy, so they chose the more discreet *Private Practices* for the London run.

David kept his distance from the author–director arguments, not least because he had his own problems to deal with. 'I had played the lead in the Oldham Coliseum, but when we did it in the Lyric I played a male nurse, which is actually a very good character, but Pip Donaghy played Lenny. I was trying to swallow the pill of not playing the lead, while finding the guy who was playing the lead wasn't as funny as I had been, through various reasons – he was heavier and more stolid than I was and [I felt] the character needed to be lightweight and feathery.'

To complicate matters further, adding to the Everyman Theatre reunion, Pete Postlethwaite was cast as Julie's husband. It was their first time together since splitting up.

'It was very difficult for Pete,' David continues, 'because he was confronted with working with Julie as his wife in the play. He was very cut up by the break-up of the relationship. It didn't work out so well at the beginning because Pete found it so hard.'

A consummate professional, Julie calmed the situation and eventually she and Pete were able to work together. Despite all the clashes of personality, *Private Practices* achieved a successful six-week run and received positive reviews; the leading lady, in particular, was praised for her fine tragicomic portrayal of a woman on the edge.

Delicate relations with Pete aside, Julie thoroughly enjoyed spending some time with her old crowd: Bill Nighy, Bernard Hill, George Costigan and Matthew Kelly. She lived up to her growing reputation as a lively girl about town. 'I came back to the theatre one day and the upper foyer was totally dishevelled,' says David. 'Somebody had taken the fire hose and doused everyone in the early hours of the morning. The Liverpool Everyman crowd were quite a wild bunch – our Manchester group felt like the quiet, mousy relations.'

Back on the small screen, Julie also appeared in a BBC made-for-television movie in 1981. Written and directed by Malcolm Mowbray, *Days at the Beach* was a period drama, set in 1920, about a trio of British soldiers who have to guard an unexploded mine that has washed up on the beach. Julie starred in the piece alongside Sam Kelly, Stephen Bill, Mark Aspinall, Charles McKeown and Kathryn Pogson.

Tellingly, *Days at the Beach* was reshown over a decade later as part of Alan Bennett's ideal night's viewing, *A Night In With Alan Bennett*, on

BBC2 in July 1992. His other chosen programmes were Mike Leigh's *Abigail's Party*, an episode of *Whatever Happened to the Likely Lads?*, a Melvyn Bragg profile of Sir John Barbirolli, and snippets of such comedy programmes as *Dad's Army*, Jimmy Edwards in *Whack-O* and John Cleese in *Fawlty Towers*.

Julie's next commitment was the third television play for Baz Taylor and Peter Eckersley. Victoria Wood realised she had exhausted the characters of Julie and Maureen, and instead opted to write a film for Julie alone, called *Happy Since I Met You*.

'It is always referred to as the final part of the trilogy, because it was Vic and Jules,' says Baz, 'but it wasn't really that at all. The other two were studio pieces and go together, they're the same style; but this was a straightforward television film, a vehicle for Julie.'

Once again the theme is affairs of the heart, namely the rocky course of true love for Frances Gordon, a straight-talking drama teacher, and Jim Smith, a struggling young actor. Fran, feisty and independent, studies the range of relationships around her: a neighbour, who faces a lonely Christmas; her sister, who's in the throes of a divorce; another sister, who's totally dependent on her boyfriend; Fran's friend, who promotes the convenience of a relationship; and a colleague, who demonstrates the material benefits of marriage.

With all these examples in mind, Fran is sure she is better off alone and tries to resist Jim when they are thrown together at a typically dreary dinner party. However, her heart rules her head and, against her better judgement, she enters into this new liaison. Soon, however, playful romance turns to mild irritation, followed by violent arguments and an inevitable break. Although the pair clearly love each other, they have much to learn about retaining independence while cohabiting. Back on form, Victoria was very perceptive about the nature of a relationship and wrote an authentic script.

Julie took the lead in *Happy Since I Met You*, but she and Victoria had to look for a suitable co-star: they chose Duncan Preston. Among many theatrical credits, he had also appeared in the 1973 television series *Hunter's Walk*. The girls went out on a fairly liquid lunch and then sat in on his audition. 'It was absolutely terrifying, but I read a couple of scenes,' recalls Duncan. 'They totally overwhelmed me with this torrent of good-natured banter. Then Julie said, "Ooh, I want him to do it because he's so big!" And she jumped up and gave me a playful punch.'

Baz, too, remembers the interview and says, 'They just took to Duncan, and that was it. Vic is very loyal: if she finds someone that she works with that she likes, that's it.'

As Victoria was not in the play, preparation was a little different this time around. 'We sat down and all read it, as we always did, and we talked about it,' says Baz. 'We had about a week of rehearsals, and Vic was only there for a couple of days. Then Jules and I went off and shot it. Vic didn't come along very often: she wasn't proprietorial because she knew us both very well and we talked about what we were going to do, and that was all right with her. Then Vic took a look at it and wrote some music for it.'

That was the last project from the successful triumvirate and the threesome bade farewell in high style. 'We *did* have a big wrap party, but it was like if you remember the sixties you weren't really there,' laughs Baz. 'We all got drunk and somehow found our way home!'

Happy Since I Met You first aired on 9 August 1981, receiving mixed reviews. The film was short, at just under an hour, and left the viewer hanging, slightly unsure of how the relationship between Fran and Jim was going to continue. However, Julie and Duncan are utterly convincing as a couple travelling the bumpy road of love: having fun together, slipping into comfortable companionship, then becoming annoyed by each other's presence. The fight scenes, too, are realistic, especially when one of Julie's slaps leaves Duncan with a swollen cheek.

While Victoria's writing was insightful about the characteristics of a modern relationship, she was still unable to convey deeper emotions in dialogue and relied heavily on the acting ability of the two leads. She also used the words of 'Living Together', which was sung over two time-passing montages, to sum up the couple's feelings. As a singer-songwriter, Victoria chose to perform the song herself, which unfortunately lent a misplaced strain of comedy to an otherwise successful piece.

On the whole the critics enjoyed it. The only criticism was to point out Victoria's novice status and limitations as a playwright. The film is also notable for a small role for the young Tracey Ullman. Ironically, as Tracey's fame grew over the next five years, she and Julie Walters would frequently be mistaken for each other.

The trilogy of films aside, Peter Eckersley had been thrilled by the success of his 'baby', *Wood & Walters: Two Creatures Great and Small*, and commissioned a full series. Sadly, Peter never saw the result of his faith, as he died of cancer shortly before work on the show commenced.

'He had lots of ideas,' recalls Victoria, 'but he never told me what they were. His value to me was inestimable. He had a marvellous eye for what was unnecessary and great attention to detail. He had liked the first material for the series but never saw any of the other stuff.'

Still, work had to continue and Brian Armstrong took over as producer. No one could live up to Peter in Victoria's eyes and she and Brian clashed. And there were other problems. She had not accounted for quite how much material would be needed – in fact her final line-up fell so short that they could produce only six half-hour shows, with the last one being a 'best of' compilation. Furthermore, Victoria complained that some of the extras were not up to the job and the live studio audience were pensioners who did not understand the humour.

By now, Victoria's low self-esteem had taken one too many knocks and she masochistically pursued attacks on herself for being 'the fat one'.

'I would set myself up as a victim and Julie would be the cruel one,' said Victoria. 'I think that was my own chip on my shoulder, and my own insecurity about being fat, or northern, or whatever I felt insecure about [that] I worked through in those sketches.'

One of the most savage assaults is in 'The Boutique'. Julie plays a snobbish assistant and, when Victoria asks her for a size 14, the reply is that it is a boutique, not the Elephant House. The insults fly about how depressing and sweaty overweight people are, before the assistant finally calls the customer 'Porky'. Julie was more comfortable playing the impossible Dotty, another middle-aged northern grotesque, akin to Betty from *Good Fun*.

Perhaps due to the personal vulnerabilities laid bare on screen, rehearsals and filming were miserable for all involved, but the series was aired in January and February 1982 to respectable ratings. 'A not always brilliant – but not far short of it – sketch series starring two fast-emerging talents,' wrote the *Radio Times*. 'At the very least, *Wood & Walters*, a fine blend of comedy sketches and comedy songs, showed a great promise.'

Victoria was offered a second series, but her confidence was so low she couldn't face another failure. She distanced herself from everything: the show, her husband, family and friends.

Even Julie felt enough was enough. 'I want to do something more serious than *Wood & Walters* now,' she told the *Daily Mail*. 'Comedy can get you down awfully after a while, and I have done so much that it becomes depressing.' It seemed that the famous friends were resigned to leave the female double act to the rising stars of Dawn French and Jennifer Saunders.

With all her other commitments completed, and with negotiations complete, Julie had to attend to one final detail prior to her first Hollywood movie. 'Before we started filming *Educating Rita*, I had a big boil on my face, so Willy Russell sent me off to a health farm to get it sorted,' she says.

The pipe dream project had indeed materialised and reunited the director Lewis Gilbert with the actor Michael Caine: the duo had made history with the garish sex comedy *Alfie* in 1966. Gilbert had optioned that work on his wife Hylda's recommendation, and had persuaded Paramount to cast Michael, then a relative unknown, in the lead.

With *Educating Rita*, it was again Hylda who had seen the play and suggested it to her husband. Gilbert was keen, but none of the studios would touch it – Columbia even said they would consider the film only with Dolly Parton in the lead. So it became a labour of love for the director. He recast the now-bankable Michael Caine, and went out on a limb with Julie as Rita, for, although she was respected in the theatre world, her screen appearances were generally overlooked as lightweight comedy.

'I knew the part inside bloody out,' laughed Julie, 'but the film was different. Lewis kept saying, "Too much, darling, too much."' Julie, who had last played Rita in the grand Piccadilly Theatre, toned down her portrayal of the hairdresser seeking self-improvement, and got on famously with her director.

'Wherever Julie is, there is fun and laughter,' says Lewis Gilbert. 'Julie is also a superb professional. She's never late, always knows her lines and always knows what she's doing.' He adds that no one else would dare to throw a divaesque tantrum while Julie's around as she's a calming influence on the cast.

Educating Rita's general story remained much the same, but there were some inevitable alterations for Hollywood, which saddened Mark Kingston, who had so loved the stage version. 'The film is so different,' he says. 'I was very disappointed in that script, because the whole point of the play is the growing thing between them – what's happening to Rita and what's happening to Frank, which is done episodically, tracing the definite route. It's a developing thing that is more poignant due to Rita returning each scene in a slightly different frame of her development, and the growth and then the decline of their friendship. You don't get that in the film so much.'

Still, for those who hadn't seen the play or who liked the big screen, it was no disappointment. The plot had to lose some of its intensity for mass-market appeal but, with the opening of the the script to incorporate new characters, the audience is treated to a lovely performance by Maureen Lipman as Rita's music-loving, hippie flatmate with upper-class pretensions. Michael Caine gives a brilliant performance, virtually unrecognisable when compared to his more recent caricature image in the *Austin Powers* series, and Julie is just magnificent as the straight-talking Rita; the pair spark off each other to produce a thoroughly believable relationship with easy banter.

The script is beautifully poignant and, by the addition of a few scenes where the leads are not together, the audience sees how Rita's fresh perspective on life has intoxicated Frank. The viewer understands that, as she develops, Rita outgrows Frank, but it is heartbreaking to watch the professor returning to his cynical drunken self. Thankfully, the climax of the film does not cave in for the sake of a Hollywood happy ending: it's satisfactory but not too neat.

The focus of *Educating Rita* remains on the two leads despite the embellishments and it is undoubtedly Michael's and Julie's honest performances that make the film. 'Julie's spot-on comic timing is, of course, very much in evidence as she delivers Russell's caustically witty lines, but she is equally accomplished in scenes of great dramatic and emotional impact,' raved Yvette Huddleston of the *Television Mail*, before going on to praise Michael Caine as a low-key foil giving 'one of his best performances'.

As in the relationship between Frank and Rita, Michael took Julie under his wing. He realised that she was receiving the same break he had over fifteen years earlier and tried to pass on the knowledge he had picked up along the way. He offered her two pieces of advice: first to enjoy the fame and glory while it lasted; second he gave her a camera to record her memories.

Julie was overwhelmed by the whole experience, gushing in interviews, saying, 'It's been such a happy film to make, with such a cheerful atmosphere on the set all the time. Rita's a great part. I've loved playing her. There's a lot of humour, as well as hard truth, in it.'

10. BOYS FROM THE BLACKSTUFF

Despite having just completed filming in Hollywood with an A-list actor, Julie returned to England with her feet firmly on the ground. During the summer of 1982 she worked on a project that couldn't have been further removed from that glitz and glamour.

She was reunited once again with Alan Bleasdale, this time for his seminal piece about the early 1980s: social unrest created by high unemployment, compounded by the miners' strike and the Falklands War.

The BBC had commissioned the writer to expand his 1980 play, *The Blackstuff*, into a suite of five individual tales, interwoven by linking themes and storylines. The result, *Boys from the Blackstuff*, was directed by Philip Saville and still stands as television's most complete and dramatic response to the Thatcher era.

'I had been in *The Blackstuff*, the film about a gang of tarmac layers,' recalls Michael Angelis, who played Chrissie. 'It was a road movie, building roads and moving off, and Alan wrote the spin-off for the four main characters. He uses the actors he knows as touchstones for the characters he creates – he says it helps him because he can hear the words coming out of their mouths. It's an interesting way to go about writing.'

As always with Bleasdale's work, the script produced intricately crafted personalities, with warm and humorous touches. Ultimately, though, the series revealed that the economy was killing the British male working-class culture, and the author denounced both monetarist politics and far-left revolutionary ideologies. This was a theme to which he would return.

Bleasdale reassembled the original cast and episodically explored the fortunes of the different families. Much of the background from the original play is covered in the first episode. The gang, comprising Chrissie (Michael Angelis), Loggo (Alan Igbon), Dixie (Tom Georgeson), Yosser (Bernard Hill) and Snowy (Chris Darwin), have all once worked in the construction trade but have been out of regular work for several years. The story tracks their resolute defiance of destitution, with equal doses of tragedy and comedy lying comfortably side by side.

Episode 3 was originally written as Loggo and Chrissie's story, but Philip Saville felt the series as a whole lacked a feminine touch.

'We really do need some female input,' he told Bleasdale. 'We don't have a storyline with a woman and I think we need a female element somewhere.'

Bleasdale took the suggestion on board and rewrote the third episode, introducing Chrissie's wife, Angie. Shifting the focus, this episode examined the effects of the men's pain and anguish in terms of repercussions on the family unit.

'We hadn't started filming,' says Michael Angelis, 'and I'd only seen a rough draft of the first script. Then along came the finished draft. Originally it was a knockabout comedy between Loggo and Chrissie, but it became more "kitchen sink" and the characters were so beautifully drawn, it became one of the best episodes.'

Bleasdale had written the role with Julie in mind, and the actress instantly empathised with Angie's vulnerability. When Chrissie asks, 'What's the point in getting up in the morning when it's all downhill from now on?', instead of pitying him, Angie explodes in anger: 'Why don't you cry? Why don't you scream? Why don't you fight back?' she yells. 'Fight back! Fight back!' It was this spirit that so appealed to Julie, who says, 'I think women like Angie are wonderful. Real survivors.'

For once Julie was the outsider, joining a cast who had already worked together, but she was great friends with Alan Bleasdale and had connections with many of the actors, too. She had worked with Michael Angelis previously on *The Liver Birds*; she knew Bernard Hill from the Everyman Theatre; and Tom Georgeson had appeared in *Fat Harold* at the Liverpool Playhouse when Julie had toured with *Scully*. Furthermore, the series was set and filmed in Liverpool, her old stomping ground.

'She had a good reputation,' says Tom Georgeson. 'When I met her she was relaxed, professional and had a great sense of fun, which she coupled with a self-deprecating attitude. I liked her.' Alan Igbon adds, 'Julie wasn't bothered about being the only lady amongst half a dozen men – we just regarded her as one of the boys.'

'She was great fun socially – she was an honorary boy, definitely part of the gang,' says Michael. 'She wanted to call it *Girls from the Pinkstuff*, but we held out against her!'

The cast and crew spent six months filming *Boys from the Blackstuff* that summer, but the shoot was not without problems.

'It wasn't a London production, it was a "little hick" production,' says Michael Angelis. 'The whole series, six hours of television, was made for less than nine hundred thousand pounds. We all did it for peanuts, nobody was on big money. The crew were from the sports department – they were used to filming *Match of the Day* and couldn't believe what they were doing. And, because we didn't have the money to make it on film, they shot it on tape, which is much cheaper but not as good quality.' Ironically this technique was later praised by reviewers for giving the piece an 'earthy authenticity'.

'If it hadn't been for the producer David Rose it wouldn't have happened,' Michael concludes. 'Basically he had made so much noise about the script that they said, "Let him do it, just give him as little money as possible." It was only when Episode Three went back to the powers-that-be in London that they suddenly realised what they had.'

In the meantime, the cast worked long hours and had to make their own entertainment. 'It was very intense, because you were very much in each other's pockets all the time,' continues Michael. 'I had an awful lot of scenes with Julie, so we spent a lot of time together, but it was an absolute joy. Afterwards, we'd go back to the hotel, have a shower and just hit the bars. We just got drunk wherever we could – the nearest pub would do!'

Alan Igbon remembers, 'There was a lot of horseplay on set. Mike usually instigated the high jinks, or Bernard Hill – but the things Bernard did are not printable! Julie was always in good spirits, and we all had a giggle.'

The script often provided set-ups for on and off-set comedy. 'There was a lot of very wry humour in it,' says Michael, 'and, as you can imagine, Julie was great fun anyway. The arguments within the drama were terrific, because we just went for it. We didn't really rehearse the scene where she beats me up: we just walked it through very briefly.

'So, when I came out of the kitchen looking for Julie, I didn't know where she was coming from, and all of a sudden she launched herself at me! It was a complete shock, and you can actually see that if you look at the tape. Also, I had said, "Look, just go for it, don't pull any punches" – and she didn't! I was black and blue by the time she finished with me. It was only one take, there was no editing, so what you see is what actually happened. There was no holding back at all.'

Obviously the serious side was not as much fun. 'Most of the cast had lived in Liverpool or the northwest,' recalls Alan Igbon, 'and, being actors, we spent most of our time in job centres, so we knew about unemployment and all the problems associated with it. It was quite sad at points, because we began to realise that there were people who were thirty-five and more or less on the scrap heap, after being made redundant in that climate. When we were on location, we were meeting the people of Liverpool who were actually living the life, and we were getting hints and tips from them. That was pretty sad but we couldn't linger on it.'

There were further problems, as Tom Georgeson recalls: 'The director was a little removed from the Liverpool feel. I believe that in some episodes, including Mike and Julie's, this caused some tension and perhaps lack of rapport.'

Still, Julie managed to pull all the aspects of her character together. 'I think her comedic background helped because, although the show was heavy, it was splattered with Liverpool humour,' says Igbon. 'Julie was the right choice – I don't think you could have cast anyone else in the part.'

Julie's ability to switch between the comedic and dramatic proved invaluable. Not only did she have a heavy workload, but much of it was shot out of sequence, so any spare time was spent ploughing through the script, rapidly learning the lines and channelling the right emotion. Far from swanning around like an actress hot off a Hollywood set, Julie was, says Michael, forgetful: 'All I can remember her saying was, "What are we doing now?"'

Of course, she could always turn to Alan Bleasdale for guidance. 'He is one of those writers who's on the set every day,' says Alan Igbon. 'He's always got his finger on the pulse and is involved in everything.' In fact the author was a little distracted at the time because of his mother's ill health, but as Michael remembers, 'Where we were filming Episode Three was only a couple of miles from where Alan lived, so it was quite easy for him to just pop along and see how we were doing.'

The wrap party for Boys from the Blackstuff was a gloriously messy affair, worthy of all their effort. 'I was so pissed I don't remember much about it at all!' admits Michael Angelis. 'We all were – we'd been working so hard for six months that we all fell over really quickly. I remember it being lots of fun.'

When Alan Bleasdale saw the finished series, he regathered his cast. 'He was just knocked out,' says Alan Igbon. 'He didn't envisage it to be as good as it was. He had expectations, but the whole cast and crew surpassed anything he'd imagined.'

This was not just an author's biased pride in his work: the BBC, too, were thrilled with the result. There were suddenly a lot of events surrounding the series. 'It was the first time I'd ever been invited up to the hospitality room at Wood Lane,' says Michael. 'We were taken up to one of the suites and served lunch, with wine and mailbags of letters from all over the country saying how wonderful it was. It had a hell of an impact on the public as a whole. There were 3.5 million unemployed at the time and it really struck the nail on the head.

'And the reviews were extraordinary – one paper said, "Every politician in the land should be tied to a chair and made to watch Boys from the Blackstuff." That's quite an accolade.'

Then there were the award ceremonies: the series itself received a

BAFTA award, as did Alan Bleasdale. 'It was up against *Brideshead Revisited*, which they had thrown a huge amount of money at and expected to win, and of course this little production from the north stole the day,' says Michael. 'It really was a feather in Alan's cap, but it was totally unexpected.'

Tom Georgeson sums up about Bleasdale's early work being based on his own experiences. It 'was about Liverpool and Liverpudlians, was honest, dramatic, moving, uplifting and shot through with Scouse humour ... His feel for these things was instinctive and his awareness sharp.'

Both Julie and Bernard Hill were nominated for Best Actress and Actor BAFTAs in 1983 respectively, but were beaten by Beryl Reid and Alec Guinness for their performances in *Smiley's People*. '[Julie's] talent is obvious, you cannot ignore it,' says Alan Igbon, despite this defeat. 'We just knew she was going places – if anyone was going to make it, it was Julie, and we were all very happy for her.'

While in Liverpool, Julie became involved in the BBC's *Access* series, made by the public in conjunction with their Community Programme Unit. First, she presented an episode of the series, *Open Door*, on Croxteth Comprehensive School. The staff and parents had staged a sit-in to prevent closure by local authorities and chose to tell their story to Julie in the programme. 'It's an unusual school,' said Julie at the time. 'The kids don't want to escape. They saunter out of school. Shutting it would have broken up the community.'

On the success of *Open Door*, the BBC launched a new series of *Access* programmes for 1983 called *Open Space*. The opening sequence used the scene from *Boys from the Blackstuff* where Julie screams to Michael Angelis to 'Fight back'. The clip illustrates that, for many people, speaking out *and* being heard is a novelty. Julie was chosen to host the first programme, 'Power In Your Hands', by one of the groups from the previous series.

She was very enthusiastic about the project and was endlessly obliging: from drawing eloquence out of the public caught between the cameras, to lying down on a dirty tenement courtyard for the fourteen-year-old *Art In Action* cameraman, Flynn (and narrowly missing the spray from a passing mongrel in the process). That she was so happy to be involved in everyday issues – when the following year she would be an international star – is testament to her down-to-earth nature.

When Julie had revealed to the press that she desired 'something more serious' after *Wood & Walters*, she had meant it. Her next project was also tough work, reuniting her with 'the other Alan', Alan Bennett, who had tentatively returned to the BBC fold.

She appeared in his one-off play, *Intensive Care*, which aired on 9 November as part of the *Play For Today* series. This hospital drama tells the tale of Midgley, a married schoolteacher who rushes to his father's deathbed and keeps a guilt-driven vigil by his side, waiting for the end. As his father persists in hanging on, Midgley becomes increasingly attracted to the night nurse, Valery Lightfoot. In the privacy of her room he asks her for sex and, while she is not averse to the idea, Valery is on duty. They agree to wait until the following day, provided his father hasn't died in the meantime. Now Midgley hopes his father will survive for his own lustful gains.

When Midgley meets his father's former lover, he sees it almost as permission to pursue Valery. Returning to Valery's room, he takes off his glasses, she takes the phone off the hook and the scene fades out. In the next scene Valery replaces the receiver and predictably it rings with the news that Midgley's father has died.

Intensive Care is one of Bennett's most celebrated plays, fraught with unspoken emotion. As it is also one of his most father-fixated plays (it was even filmed at the hospital in which his own father died), the author was keen to assure reporters, 'I never felt I let my dad down,' and show that the story's focus was that the death of a loved one can sometimes free an individual.

The director, Gavin Millar, cast Thora Hird as Midgley's interfering Aunt Kitty and Julie as the naughty nurse. The lead actor fell ill before production and, after an audition, Millar gave the role of Midgley to Alan Bennett himself.

Julie's favourite moment with Bennett was the scene where Midgley finally beds Valery. 'Once Alan had the part, all these changes started appearing in the script,' Julie told the *Observer*. 'Suddenly, we're getting undressed, and where I'd once had to rip his shirt off, now I was supposed to say, "That's a nice shirt – keep it on!"'

The cheeky actress never missed an opportunity. 'When the scene came round, he'd go out of the room while I got undressed and I'd shout, "Hold on, Alan, I'm just trying to put my cap in!" You could feel him blushing through the walls!' No matter how serious the work, Julie could always be relied on to lighten the atmosphere.

Relations between Alan Bennett and the BBC drama unit had been restored with the airing of *Intensive Care*. However, the BBC faced new competition with the launch of Channel 4 in November 1982, and counterattacked with a series of offbeat dramas by Alan Bennett, later published under the title *Object of Affection*.

Julie Walters was involved in Bennett's play, *Say Something Happened*, for this series. Directed by Giles Foster, the three-hander showcased a trio of great Bennett interpreters: Thora Hird (who died in spring 2003), Hugh Lloyd and Julie Walters.

Thora and Hugh played the elderly couple known merely as Mam and Dad, who are visited by June Potter from the Social Services Department (Julie). It is June's first day on the job and she has to complete a register of senior citizens with the aim of preventing any 'mishaps' involving 'old people who have become isolated from the community'. Mam and Dad are fiercely independent and feel their pride is being dented as they are considered old and in need of care. Besides, they insist their daughter will look after them.

'One of the things that struck me enormously about Julie was that she got to the awkwardness and embarrassment of the social worker very quickly,' says Giles Foster. 'She understood exactly what level to take that to, and how to pick up on and capitalise on Thora and Hugh's sharpness.

'Later in the play both of them become quite acerbic with her and say, almost in chorus, "That's not us: that's *old* people you're talking about." Julie's character is wrong-footed and she has that wonderful, physical awkwardness – her shoulders twist and she wants to hide back into herself, but she's got to persist with this absurd questioning.

'She's also totally oblivious to the subtext of what Thora and Hugh are saying, which is terribly moving. When she's quizzing them about, "Say something happened?" they say, "Well, we've got our daughter," and immediately become quite defensive. It's clear that the daughter is running a racy lifestyle around Europe (Brussels is one of Alan's shorthand places for the lunacy of the Euro dream), but one of them says, "She visits often," and the other says, "Whenever her schedule permits."

This is a popular theme in Bennett's plays, where the parents are sedentary and receive news about their wandering offspring only via postcards. 'Alan opens up the whole question of the guilt of children who don't visit their parents, and the void of the parents who pretend to their friends that they do,' continues Giles. 'There's a wonderful bemused understanding and learned judgement from Julie. She's very much the daughter they lost.

'Hugh was the perfect foil for the two actresses because he was so much less mobile, but very watchful.' Hugh was delighted with the opportunity. 'I felt honoured, coming from the more light-entertainment department, to work with two such lovely actresses,' he says. 'It was so well written, as is all of Alan's work. Thora and I were the sad old couple that the social worker was supposed to help, and in the end we were all right and she left completely distraught, worrying about *her* future! A real Alan Bennett twist.'

Say Something Happened was rehearsed and recorded in a fairly intense few weeks. 'When there's only three of you, you're involved all the time,' says Hugh, 'and when you're under pressure, under the cameras, you have to get to know each other very well. None of us are temperamental people and we got on like a house on fire.'

Like Alan Bleasdale, Alan Bennett likes to be involved in his work and was on hand at all times. 'It can be awkward to have the writer present at every rehearsal because they can slow things up,' says Hugh, 'but Alan is so helpful and every word is so carefully chosen, one relishes to try and do the script as written and not try and alter it.'

As the director, Giles worked closely with both the author and actors. 'Julie tries to make the truth of the performance seem effortless. It is apparently effortless, but actually costs her a great deal,' he comments. 'What was interesting was that she didn't lapse into sentimentality. Nobody can in Alan's work, because that's not what it's about, and Alan is very strict about that when he's judging the performances that are going on. He was in the control room, actively watching what was happening.'

Julie's performance was highly rated by all and she received another well-deserved BAFTA nomination for Best Actress in 1983.

11. WIDE-EYED AND LEGLESS

Educating Rita was finally released in cinemas in 1983 and 'Julie Walters' swiftly became a household name.

It must have been a strange scenario for the unpretentious actress from Birmingham to have to stop and sign autographs in the street – suddenly, she could no longer stroll the aisles of her local Sainsbury's without being interrupted by an excitable fan. Offers of work poured in and Julie was inundated by interview requests from newspapers, radio and television. Still, she took the extra attention in her stride, and soon became embroiled in her next project, the bizarre BBC film, *Unfair Exchanges*.

Directed by Gavin Millar, this uneven play falters between the suspense of a thriller and the absurdity of a farce. Julie, as Mavis, leaves her gay husband to live with her daughter, but she is stalked by an evil telephone company intent on controlling its customers' lives. Along the way, she has strange liaisons with a sexually charged dwarf who is well versed in conspiracy theories.

One can only assume that Julie accepted the part because of her colleagues-to-be – she was reunited with Gavin Millar and the writer and actor Ken Campbell, and worked with her best friend Rosalind March. Fortunately, better things were to come.

Her next piece was another BBC play in a series under the guidance of the established writer and director, Derek Lister. 'Love and Marriage was the generic title; *Family Man* was the individual play,' explains Derek. 'It's about a guy's attempts to form a relationship with a single mother, a dancer.'

Derek and the producer, Pat Sandys, were aware of Julie through the promotion for *Rita*, and so arranged a meeting. Derek's previous impressions of her were 'versatile and funny', but, after their discussion, he found the 'more serious underside to her personality. She was well grounded, despite her celebrity.'

'We had to discuss her dancing,' he says, 'which she was particularly keen to do. So, I hired a choreographer, Michael Moore, to coach her.' There were just two weeks of rehearsals, but things went smoothly as Julie and her co-star, John Duttine, became great friends. Derek also found Julie a delight to work with. 'She was open and responsive to direction, and was happy once she trusted you,' he says.

'Although she worked hard, she was always affable and friendly, but both John and I found her real personality a little bit elusive. She was single in those days, so maybe needed to protect herself.'

This is a far cry from the Julie described by the Bleasdale crew on *Boys from the Blackstuff*, but she was suffering from other demands on her time. 'Left to herself, I think she would have been sociable,' continues Derek, 'but there were lots of pressures from *Educating Rita* that she had to work through, too. The PR people were after her all the time – it was relentless. But she was always good to have around. She, John and I always had lunch together and that's where we socialised and unwound.'

When the shoot began in Leeds, life became increasingly difficult for the cast and crew. 'While filming was relaxed, the studio was in the grip of an Electrical Trades Union dispute, and general union activity at Yorkshire Television Studios was militant and surly. It was hard for the actors in that kind of atmosphere.'

Working in such a disagreeable climate and constantly being pulled away for promotion for *Rita* meant it was not long before Julie began physically to feel the strain. 'She had suspected gallstones in the middle of the production and was hospitalised,' recalls Derek. 'YTV took a decision, at my bidding, not to replace her and we rescheduled around the illness.'

Julie was crippled by severe back pain and was forced to go into hospital, but her newfound celebrity status prevented any valuable recuperation. She was taken to hospital by ambulance, 'ashen-faced in a pool of sweat and paralysing discomfort. I remember the trip only as a blur of my pain punctuated by one unforgettable event – the ambulance man, who was otherwise wonderful, *asked me for my autograph!*' she explained in *Baby Talk*.

'It *is* you, isn't it, Rita?' insisted the orderly as Julie writhed in agony. Despite barely clinging on to consciousness, the ever-polite Julie just about managed to oblige.

Her working-class roots dictated that she asked for a public ward. 'I don't believe in private medicine,' she said in an interview, but suddenly she found herself the centre of much unwanted attention: 'I'd wake to find any old person there offering a bunch of grapes in return for an autograph.

'Those who were up and about often grouped together to stare and talk loudly about me as though I were totally deaf or blind, or simply not there. As if I was there on TV.' The gaggle of onlookers discussed their considered opinions on her work, her comic ability and her current condition.

Julie sat, or rather lay, through the whole farce. It was not gallstones that were the problem: she had in fact torn a muscle in her back and was on strong painkillers, which helped pass the time at least. But even the pethidine couldn't blur one particularly persistent gentleman caller. A local lad named Dave read in the neighbourhood paper of Julie's incarceration and took it upon himself to keep her company. He visited for a couple of hours every day, and, rather than let her rest, barraged her with a multitude of questions.

'What's it like to work with Michael Caine?'

'How did you get into acting?'

'What are you doing next?'

With the patience of a saint, Julie grinned until she could bear it no more. The crunch came when Dave brought a friend along and insisted that the three of them be photographed together by one of the nurses. Julie finally snapped when the other patients innocently assumed Dave must be her boyfriend. 'I was boiling with rage inside, at which point Dave's dumb friend asked, "What will you be doing next?" I answered, eyes full of hatred, "I'll be strangling you, if you don't leave now."'

Julie loved acting, but was clearly less enamoured with the idea that fame made her public property.

Dave's antics aside, she generally understood the attitude of the other patients, who spoke about her as if she were invisible. 'It's difficult to behave normally towards a person you feel familiar with because of television and the media, and yet don't know personally,' she reasoned.

Equally, she dealt with those fans who were brave or savvy enough to approach her with considered respect, providing she was feeling well. 'But when you're ill, you realise how wonderfully private anonymity is, and how important,' she concludes.

Once Julie's back pain eased off, and she had finished *Family Man*, the real frenzy surrounding *Educating Rita* kicked off. The cinematic release instigated a deafening buzz. Hollywood was crazy about its latest find and the major studios clambered over each other to sign her up.

The executives loved the assertive role of Rita and felt Julie had great potential, but they were flummoxed as to what to offer her. Ironically, given the elocution torture she suffered as a child, part of Julie's charm was her plain speaking and broad accent. 'Well, my voice certainly gets me noticed,' she says, 'especially when I start laughing. I do love a good laugh.' That's laff, mind, not larf.

The little lady from Birmingham was flown to Los Angeles, and wined and dined by them all. She listened, but she didn't like what she heard. They pitched a plethora of what Julie considered to be unsuitable romances, followed by a stream of inappropriate action films.

'They smothered me with scripts, but you can't believe what crap they were. I would have felt too awful if I had been involved in that kind of rubbish,' she later recalled. 'They didn't know what to do with me. I don't know why, they just didn't. Meryl Streep gets all the roles you would want to play – who's going to ask an English person?' Streep was indeed hot property at the time with three Oscar nominations (*The Deer Hunter*, *The French Lieutenant's Woman* and *Silkwood*) and two Oscar wins (*Kramer vs. Kramer* and *Sophie's Choice*) in the previous five years.

For an actress used to working with the likes of Bleasdale, Bennett and Russell, Julie found the situation mildly funny, but mostly insulting. Unsurprisingly, she turned them all down – even a personal plea from the mustachioed heart-throb, Burt Reynolds. 'He got terribly keen that I appear in a film of his called *Stick*,' she said. 'He flew me to Miami to talk to me about the part, and he was very charming. It was playing a high-class New York stockbroker. Imagine that!'

'You should get Candice Bergen,' she told the producers.

'It will be more interesting if it's you,' they replied.

'It was a very classy, glamorous role – definitely not me! I was flattered, but no way could I accept,' she continued. 'I had just a couple of small reasons for saying no, namely that it was a terrible part and an awful script, but that seemed enough for me at that stage in my career. There were no bad feelings, though. He even flew me to the airport in his private helicopter.' (Burt Reynolds went on to direct and star in *Stick*, and his female co-star was indeed played by Candice Bergen.)

Throwing away that particular deal, Julie also waved goodbye to £500,000, but that wasn't even a consideration. 'I'd never do anything for money because it's the work that counts. At the end of the day I've got to live with myself. OK, I've done some bad things, but at least I did them for the right reason.'

Then something happened to change all that and she accepted one rather unlikely offer. Disney approached her and persuaded her to sign for a 'development' deal. This meant that the studio paid for her exclusivity while they searched for suitable projects. Unable to work for anyone else, Julie tried to enjoy the high life of Los Angeles, but found it 'dreary, violent and boring'.

Despite their best efforts, Disney were no luckier in tracking down that elusive role, and, with egg on the faces of both parties, they parted company. To Julie's mirth, however, she was allowed to keep the money.

Her head seemed to have been turned by the bright lights and the money, not to mention the formation of an American fan club, but she hadn't changed her overall impression of Hollywood. 'Those shoulder pads and shiny lips aren't me. And there was snobbery there like you've never seen.' She didn't think everyone should feel they had to look gorgeous continually. 'I'd hate to be an actress in LA: I couldn't stand the pressure.'

Julie returned to rainy old England, and expected life to continue as normal. But it had been in her own country that the *Educating Rita* star had first experienced the unwelcome demands of fame, and that had not diminished while she had been away. If anything, Julie had now proved herself in all media, and all the aspects of her career converged in overwhelming success.

She was recognised wherever she went, which was sometimes a little daunting. 'When I see a group of punks staring at me and muttering, I think, Oh Christ, I'm going to be mugged! Instead they come up and want my autograph,' she said at the time.

'My image is a bit of a pressure at times. People expect me to be funny and sometimes you don't feel very quick-witted. You feel depressed or tired. But I usually rise to the occasion. And I like talking and chatting. I don't mind people coming up as long as they're not completely mad.'

Her run-in with Dave et al. and subsequent escalation of recognition had not changed Julie into a media recluse. She was well aware that her earning power was due to her fame, and unfortunately her omnipresent face on screens and in magazines bred the feeling of familiarity. But she would never turn her fans away because, without them, she would be reduced to a struggling, out-of-work actress.

As her popularity increased, so she rose through the ranks of celebrity guest lists and was invited to every event imaginable. Always a party girl at heart, Julie positively thrived. 'I was single, so it didn't matter,' she says. 'I really embraced it like a mad dervish round London. I was at everything. Drinking, carousing. I was mad, going to absolutely everything. Anything you could do, I was doing it.'

Although she was not at a stage where she was dependent on alcohol, as befitting many a darling of the screen, drink had been a part of Julie's everyday life for some time. She was reliving her wild teenage years with no one to stop her or pull in the reins. 'I went through a period where I was always pissed,' she later admitted. 'Partying and working all the time . . . but you do get a bit fed up being photographed in the *Mail on Sunday* looking pissed and hideous!'

Away from the prying paparazzi, Julie and Ros March were even more reckless on their expeditions abroad. 'It's a wonder we didn't end up in a ditch on some of our holidays,' Julie told *Woman's Own*. 'We were wild. We went to Greece a lot and had some wild times on beaches in the middle of the night!'

Money certainly wasn't an issue. Although she was splashing her cash on boozy nights out and girly getaways, she didn't own a car because she couldn't drive and still rented her accommodation from Ros. Julie continued to accept work on its merit rather than pay cheque. 'I have no desire to be rich,' she said. 'I'm not greedy. Money isn't that important.' Evidently, Julie's only commitment was to her career.

During this social whirl, Julie became caught up in a little romance. While out in Hollywood, she had casually hooked up with an American scriptwriter, but their affair quickly acquired momentum of its own. 'It was a very passionate relationship,' she says, 'and we spent a lot of the time crossing the Atlantic to be with each other.'

He was so besotted that he asked her to marry him and move to Los Angeles. She quickly, but politely, declined his offer, aware that she still had a lot to accomplish. 'He couldn't understand why my work is so important, but it's what I am,' she explained to *Woman's Own* interviewer Jo Weedon.

'Somehow I find it hard to juggle career and men successfully. I could never have a full-time relationship with a man who has a fragile ego and who regards my career as a sort of threat. Acting doesn't always come first, but there are times when it must. It can be very stressful, all-consuming. So it's probably better to be alone.'

Another relationship that was suffering a little under the strain of her success was her association with Victoria Wood. While Julie was reaping fame and fortune, Victoria was still struggling to prove her worth as a stand-up

Victoria later admitted that she was envious of Julie's rise. 'I was pleased for her. But I was very insecure at the time and I felt I was being compared with her ... I could never explain to people that I was not an actress and my career didn't lie in that direction.'

Victoria was also concerned that, while Julie may have remained the same person inside, her circumstances had altered and the comedienne was 'nervous of bothering' the actress. Fortunately, Victoria found that the friendship was still intact when Julie happily accepted a role in the latest Wood film, about the seaside summer season.

It was not a sympathy gesture. The public didn't understand why Julie would choose a television programme over a film, but, according to Victoria, 'It's the acting equivalent of putting your feet up and having a fag and a good gossip. It's great to be able to make yourself look awful in a show like mine – it's such a relief from all the Hollywood stuff.'

Sadly, the film never saw the light of day, but Julie's loyalty meant a lot to Victoria and the alliance endured.

12. GIRLS FROM THE PINKSTUFF

After the initial furore surrounding *Educating Rita* had died down, Julie accepted more work at the end of 1983. The film *She'll Be Wearing Pink Pyjamas* was written by Eva Hardy and based on her own experiences. The story followed a group of women on an Outward Bound course.

John Goldschmidt, an experienced television director, was brought in to direct the predominantly female piece. 'The producer, Tara Pren, had formed a company with Eva Hardy, which was to be an all-women's company to do drama', he remembers. 'Eva had written this script and the film was being one hundred per cent funded by Channel 4. I had worked with Tara before and, when I was offered the job, I signed it very quickly.'

'It was a brilliant idea – telling an outdoors adventure, which was typically a male domain, from a group of women's perspective. The script was a little bit rough around the edges from my point of view, but I liked the concept.' However, Goldschmidt felt that Eva Hardy was not as flexible with developing the script as he would have wished. 'It wasn't dramatic enough in terms of the resolution of the story and we had a big row,' he explains.

'Climax is a male concept,' retorted Eva.

'I was flabbergasted!' says John.

There were still some unresolved issues when the production team approached Julie Walters, who was very keen to do it. 'Shortly afterwards, Julie got an Oscar nomination for *Educating Rita*,' continues Goldschmidt. 'Suddenly the film became even more attractive – to have Julie Walters and a story which was fresh and original.'

While John spent the beginning of 1984 sorting out a multitude of problems, Julie maintained her usual pace and plunged into a new play while waiting for the award ceremonies.

Disregarding her newfound A-list status, Julie accepted the role of Dotty in Tom Stoppard's play, *Jumpers*. The absurd comedy centres around a moral-philosophy professor who enquires about the existence of God, and encounters strange characters, including a retired actress, a group of gymnasts and a trained rabbit.

One impressionable and aspiring actor couldn't believe his luck at seeing the screen star on the stage. 'She played the female lead, opposite Tom Courtenay,' recalls Peter Whitfield, who would work with her himself on *Wide-Eyed and Legless*. 'The play was excellent and I thought she, in particular, was great. They had a four-week run in March at the Exchange Theatre in Manchester.'

Two days after finishing the play, Julie attended the 56th Academy Award ceremony. During promotion for *Educating Rita*, Michael Caine had hinted, 'I won my first Oscar nomination for *Alfie* and I've got a feeling that *Rita* could do the same for Julie.' Perhaps he was psychic, because a nomination was exactly what she received, losing out on the Best Actress Academy Award to Shirley MacLaine for *Terms of Endearment*. However, Julie picked up a BAFTA, a Golden Globe and a Variety Club Award for her portrayal of Rita, while the film also received awards, as well as solid critical and financial success both sides of the Atlantic.

From the glamour and glitz of Hollywood to the exposed mountainsides of Cumbria, Julie's world was full of contrasts. Work had already begun on *She'll Be Wearing Pink Pyjamas*, but she had been excused for her award-ceremony commitments.

Meanwhile John Goldschmidt felt he had reached an impasse with Eva Hardy and another producer, Adrian Hughes, was brought on board to team up with Tara Pren. 'I had already signed so I couldn't walk off,' recalls Goldschmidt. 'Besides the opportunity to work with Julie was too appealing.' In the meantime he was also trying to protect the actresses from any knowledge of all of this.

As well as conventional rehearsals, the eight women (Julie Walters, Jane Evers, Janet Henfrey, Paula Jacobs, Maureen O'Brien, Alyson Spiro, Jane Wood and Pauline Yates) had to learn to perform all the activities that would be required of them. 'They said from the beginning, "We're not having stunt people unless it's something very serious that you really feel you can't do, but we'd really rather not,"' recalls Alyson, one of the younger women in the group of mixed ages. 'You went in with your eyes wide open.'

Harder still, Penelope Nice was cast as the instructor, so it was vital that she looked as if she knew what she was doing. She recalled, 'We had to meet up at the Sobell Leisure Centre in north London to experiment with rock climbing. Julie wasn't there at that time because she was still in America. So we started belaying people up rock faces, then we went to the swimming pool and learned to canoe, including rolls. I had to look proficient, but I'd never been in a canoe before and it's not very easy!'

Julie had flown into the country just in time to catch the coach to the Lake District with everyone else. 'I remember she slept all the way there, because she was so tired. And she had this incredible long hair, which they chopped off for the film – I think it was quite upsetting for her, although she was good about it.'

After all the traumas prior to arriving on location, John Goldschmidt could not have hoped for better conditions once they got there. It was spring, lambing season, and the area was experiencing the best weather for some fifty years. The only downside was the proximity of the Eskdale Centre, where they were based, to a certain troubled nuclear-power plant.

'We were staying near Sellafield when it was constantly in the news,' recalls Alyson. 'It was at the time when everyone was saying there were much higher leukaemia rates et cetera. We were in a very privileged position, coming in and making this film, so you had to be careful what you said. But it's a fantastic part of the countryside.'

Julie caught up with the physical aspect of the job on site in the Lake District at break-neck speed. 'She threw herself into it when we got there and was as good, or as bad, as we all were!' says Alyson. 'In the face of a challenge she would just go for it.'

It was this unbreakable spirit that amazed and impressed everyone. 'There was a circuit of ropes, heights and drops at the Eskdale Centre. Everybody did it, but she would be the first round; she would be up there straightaway,' says Penelope Nice, but that was just for starters.

'She had to do a parachute drop from an extremely high tree, probably as high as the fourth floor of a block of flats. We went up a wooden ladder to a small platform at the top. Up there was the cameraman, the real trainer, me, the actress trainer, and Julie. She had the harness on and waited for the call: "Red light, green light, go!"

'But, by the time you get up the tree and you're waiting for the cameraman to be ready, you have time to think about what you're doing. It becomes more and more nerve-racking and you suddenly realise the drop is huge. Then you realise that something could go wrong. We were up there for a long time waiting for the cameras to be ready, but when they said, "Red light, green light, go," she just dropped. She had to do it about five or six times and she never complained or moaned. She loved it really – she's gutsy.'

Julie was not only brave enough to repeat the exercise several times herself, but she also provided support for her new friend.

'Then I had to do it,' continues Penelope, 'but I'd been up there for so long, about an hour and a half, so I started to climb down the ladder, only they wouldn't let me. Julie was at the bottom shouting, "Go on, Pen! You can do it!" So I did it.' Unfortunately, after all that effort, the scene wasn't even used in the final film.

'I had to cross a fast-flowing stream with a pack on my back,' says Alyson. 'I lost my footing and went into the water – suddenly I felt like I was drowning! It was a fairly serious panic and I found a strength within me that I never knew I had and got out of the water.

'But it was a real eye opener. Everyone had some sort of panic that they had to get through themselves, because we didn't have any stunt women. Maureen O'Brien had a crisis going up one of the rock faces; Pauline Yates was not a particularly strong swimmer and had to fall out of a canoe. Everybody had a moment they had to get through, but you felt so supported and helped by everybody there. It was a great personal learning experience.'

The unconditional succour offered by each of the actresses forged a strong alliance among the diverse crowd. 'We bonded as a group,' explains Penelope. 'That's how the course is supposed to work, and it did. All the people outside were having their own difficulties, and we were having to do all these gutsy things, so we supported each other in the way that these centres are supposed to make you work. It was very interesting.'

Another memorable scene was jumping off a high bridge into a deep pool, with icy-cold water and rocks underneath. Alyson was understandably nervous of this task. 'I was terrified and a couple of the crew members said, "Don't worry we'll do it first to show you it's OK." So the sparkies did it first. If you were nervous there was always somebody who would say, "Look, I'll do it first to help you."'

Neither Julie nor Penelope was involved in this particular stunt, but they wanted to show solidarity to the others. 'At the end of the day Julie grabbed my hand and said, "Let's do it!" She just jumped in – she didn't have to but she wanted to!' recalls Penelope.

Although Julie was brought in as the 'big name', she didn't ask for any special treatment and proved that she was just one of the gang. 'At the beginning everybody thought, Oh God, Julie Walters, she's a star,' says Alyson. 'But everybody was very much on a par, and there was none of that attitude. We all peed in our wetsuits and she did too! She was absolutely lovely to work with, very easy and giving.'

The schedule for *Pink Pyjamas* was relentless, including a few tough overnight sessions. 'We did one endless night shoot trudging through a bloody forest,' says Alyson. 'That was a really awful night. We were all tied up with rope and the task was to tramp through the forest in the middle of the night, tied together. It took a long time to film and it was not a particularly pleasant experience, but somebody would always produce a hip flask and keep us going!'

The actresses were allowed one day off a week for some much-needed relaxation. 'On Sundays, Julie would spend the day on her own in private,' says Penelope. 'I think that was to gather her thoughts and have a little space, take time for herself and re-energise. That's something you normally learn later in life, but she was doing it even then.'

The rest of the time, Monday to Saturday, the cast and crew would get up early, travel to the location, put in a long, hard day filming, and return exhausted. This intensive routine lasted for six weeks. 'We used to go to work in the morning in a jeep,' says Penelope. 'We had so much fun. Julie did brilliant baby voices and I had done a play where I had to record my own baby voice, so we used to be two babies together! She was very funny, but there was also a serious side to her. She used to talk about her nursing a lot, like the first time she ever saw a dead body.

'Then we'd be singing all the way home, like the scene in the film where we'd come back covered in mud and soaked through, just singing away and enjoying ourselves, so proud of what we'd accomplished that day. We'd get back, pile into one of the bedrooms and get the gin and tonics out! Then we'd be at the bar in the hotel and get the wine out. Everyone looked so healthy, all windswept and tanned, and we just had the best time.'

Indeed, the girls really let their hair down and, fuelled by the G&Ts and wine, ran riot every night.

'We took over this hotel,' laughs Alyson. 'I'm sure the poor people there didn't know what had hit them. We made our own entertainment. We were always joking, laughing, dressing up and so on – it was that kind of atmosphere. Julie created this character, the "Birmingham Bar Lady", and she used to go behind the bar and serve drinks. It was wonderful, they loved it! We were loud, it was just a continuous party. It was a laugh a minute, absolutely high all the time. We drank a lot – there wasn't much else to do – and we often had to drag ourselves out with horrendous hangovers.'

Director John Goldschmidt marvels, 'The thing about Julie was that she was able to hang out and have a few drinks with everyone in the bar of an evening, have a great time, and then be perfectly professional in the meeting the next day. She was the driving force amongst the cast – she was so willing to do everything. She's such a good person to have on board. Unfortunately, because of the time problems, I was usually out looking for the next location.'

For John, the movie became more complicated daily. 'It was a logistically difficult film to shoot,' he continues. 'For example, we had to shoot on a rock face, which meant that we had to build a platform for the camera crane, all on a tight budget and timescale. That kind of work needed very thorough preparation, and I would have liked to have been able to prepare in more detail.

'Several scenes were tricky and rather time-consuming to film, and there were film locations which were rather inaccessible. When we filmed on top of the mountains, you couldn't drive there by jeep and we hadn't got the time in the schedule to walk to the top. So we got two helicopters on a shuttle service to fly the film crew and actors up there. Every day, filming costs a lot of money, so to save two or three days by using helicopter becomes a cost-effective way to operate.'

Overcoming these difficulties, John was faced with more inconveniences. 'We had a problem with the camera, so we had to replace it. Then we projected the rushes at the local cinema and it was out of focus. We thought there was a problem with the laboratory and it would have to be reshot. Subsequently we discovered that it was the cinema's projection equipment that was at fault and everything was fine!

'We were all so punch drunk from the catalogue of mishaps that I thought, What else can go wrong?'

Against this backdrop of high spirits and production difficulties, one morning the girls discovered that the next day's filming was a nude shower scene, and so planned a great ruse.

'It was one of those things that came out of a conversation at lunchtime,' smirks Alyson. 'In those days every set had to have an Equity representative, and I had volunteered my services. We'd already had various Equity issues that had been brought up and I was the go-between to the producers. So we wrote a letter to the producer, Adrian Hughes, and snuck it in his pigeonhole: he had to call the general secretary of Equity, Peter Plouviez.'

Pauline Yates's husband, Donald Church, had kindly agreed to assist the girls and played the part of Plouviez.

'I've had a message to call,' said Adrian. 'What's the problem?'

'I'm afraid there is a new ruling,' replied Donald, as Plouviez. 'If the girls have to take their clothes off for a scene, the crew also have to take their clothes off.'

'What?' said Adrian in disbelief.

'I'm terribly sorry,' said 'Plouviez' calmly. 'I know it sounds ridiculous but that's the motion that's been passed and I advise you to go along with it.'

'We were in the bar,' continues Penelope. 'We knew that at some point one of the producers was going to ring 'Plouviez', but we didn't know when it was going to happen – until we saw Adrian come in, looking so hassled. He was panicking and we were wetting ourselves!'

The following morning, events escalated out of control. 'It was six thirty a.m. and it had to look steamy in the shower,' recalls John. 'But we had problems with the machines that morning.'

Alyson well remembers the situation. 'The first shot of that scene the steam-making machine went wrong,' she says. 'Everybody was fraught and worried. We did think maybe we shouldn't go through with it as everybody was in such a tense mood, but we thought, No, to hell with it: we've set it up, so we're going to do it!'

Adrian approached Alyson in her capacity as Equity rep.

'Are the girls *really* going to insist on this? he asked.

'Yes they are,' she replied. 'I'm sorry but that's the deal. We have to go with our union's ruling.'

John was baffled. 'I was told by the producers that there was a problem. Apparently Equity had recently had an annual conference and passed a motion that, if women had to be naked in a film scene, then the film technicians should be naked as well. I just couldn't believe it. We were in this ridiculous situation where we were standing around with seminaked actresses, just trying to get this thing done and this was sprung on us . . . So I took my shirt off.'

'The sound guys got down to their underpants,' laughs Penelope, 'saying that if they took their underpants off they'd get an electric shock!'

'Oh, come on,' said Clive Tickner, the cameraman, 'don't be stupid.' And he stripped off, climbed on to the dolly stark-naked and said, 'Let's shoot this damn scene!'

It is impossible to imagine how the actresses kept straight faces.

Only after filming finished did they admit that it was a hoax and Penelope produced the bottles of champagne they had bought for whoever accepted the challenge. Clive won the lot.

'But we fell for it, assuming that this was just another obstacle in the filming, just another mishap,' says John. 'They conned everyone!'

'Afterwards, the guys were absolutely thrilled,' says Alyson. 'Adrian was delighted – he thought it was a great wheeze! And the publicity they got from that stunt for the film was enormous. It hit the *New Yorker* magazine the following week, which was pretty unprecedented.'

Several months later, everyone gathered at the Haymarket in Leicester Square for the first cinema showing. 'We felt a little disappointed by the outcome of the film,' says Alyson. 'It was very unusual to have so many women in one cast and just one man, and it made for a very special atmosphere, but the film just didn't have the feel of the camaraderie. I think everybody thought it was going to come out better than it did.'

Unfortunately, the general public picked up on this shortcoming and the film did not fare well at the box office, being pulled from cinemas very quickly. The bonding on set was not seen until the final scene, which is the ultimate test, but, to be fair, that was the intended plot. However, *She'll Be Wearing Pink Pyjamas* is a little hard to get into: although the characters introduce themselves around a table, explaining who they are and why they're on the course, the scenes are short and abrupt, and tend to show events rather than depth of character.

It certainly isn't a film for a prude because the women discuss all elements of sex, the language is best described as raw and there are two extended nude scenes, not just the shower sensation.

However, *Pink Pyjamas* achieved one of the highest viewing figures for films shown on Channel 4. 'I think that the huge ratings were due to Julie Walters,' says John, 'and the fact that it was something that women wanted to watch – it was very well promoted on Channel 4.' Julie's performance was accomplished and polished. 'I think people who have a comedic talent make for the best dramatic actors,' John summarises. 'Comedy is so much more difficult to do, that if you can do that, you have the ability to play real tragedy successfully.'

The reviews were generally complimentary, all singling Julie out as the highlight of the film. 'An excellent emotive outdoor drama,' raved the *TV Times*. 'Julie Walters is the only star name and indeed comes over as the most clearly defined character.' However, the review acknowledged the ability of Julie's co-stars, and praised the relaxed use of frank language, summing it all up as: 'An unusual film that is, by its own standards, right on target.'

13. WOBBLY SETS

In 1984 Julie drifted from one extreme to another. After the emotional outpourings of *She'll Be Wearing Pink Pyjamas*, her next project was the inane comedy *Car Trouble*. Julie is paired up with Ian Charleson as Jacqueline and Gerald Spong, a couple enduring a fractious marriage. 'She is the type that desperately wants to look like the women from *Dynasty* or *Dallas*,' says Julie.

While Gerald eyes his new prized possession, a shiny E-type Jaguar, his wife sets her sights on the hunky car salesman, Kevin (Vincenzo Ricotta). Jacqueline is banned from driving the car, but finds Gerald's keys one day and sneaks out. She accidentally bumps into Kevin and picks him up, and they end up parked in the woods, getting intimate.

'It was so funny,' Julie told the *Star*. 'There's one scene where I've got my head underneath the dashboard, and he's on top of me with his face squashed up against the window and I say, "I have to go in a minute."'

Jacqueline is so preoccupied with getting home before her husband that she doesn't think twice about moving the handbrake that's digging into her side. The car rolls down the hill and crashes straight into a tree. In their panic to get out, the lovers become trapped in a compromising position. Eventually, the fire brigade have to cut the entangled pair free from the wreckage, much to the amusement of onlookers, including neighbours and news reporters. After such a humiliating debacle, Gerald's intentions towards his wife become increasingly murderous, continuing the farce.

That the script is based on a real-life experience truly appealed to Julie's wicked sense of humour. Although Julie and Ian got on famously, the filming wasn't always a pleasant experience. 'E-types are very phallic with their long noses, but, ooh, they are uncomfortable,' laughed Julie. 'We had padding and anti-cramp tablets, but we were still covered in bruises by the time we'd finished those scenes. You would have to be really desperate to do that.'

However, in the publicity for the film, the actress revealed she had tried it for real. 'We were in love and had nowhere else to go,' she continued, referring to an ancient affair. 'It was a long time ago and we only did it once. It wasn't a sports car. He had a Rover, there was lots of room in it, so it was easy!'

While the cramped conditions filming in the Jaguar proved painful for Julie, she caused the producers just as much agony. She still couldn't drive, so, when she made a motoring gaffe in the film, she wasn't pretending. 'They wanted me to make a mistake in the car lot,' she said. 'Easy, I thought. Vincenzo told me to rev it up, put it in reverse, then let the clutch out. The car shot backwards at sixty miles an hour; I'm not joking. The producers thought I was going to wreck it. You should have seen their faces!'

After a six-month heavy schedule, Julie took some time off and escaped to Barbados over the summer of 1984. 'Everyone needs contrasts in life,' she said. 'Like the contrast of working and going on holiday.'

The idea was to escape her celebrity. Julie never imagined that her fame would stretch to the small Caribbean island and looked forward to some much-needed peace and quiet. But, one day, she awoke from a deep sleep on the beach to find a portly fellow Brummie staring down at her through the lens of a camera.

'I've been waiting for you to open your eyes' he said, clicking away furiously.

'Then he told everyone who I was,' says Julie, 'and I spent the next two days answering people's questions about Hollywood.' All the same, the easy-going actress swore she didn't mind too much. She always said, 'Fame's too short-lived,' and did as Michael Caine had instructed: enjoyed it while it lasted.

As Julie was getting used to being recognised, a few other hardened aspects of her personality were slowly thawing. Still a fun-loving, independent woman, she appreciated her financial security and tentatively began to put down roots.

'I don't need much to keep me happy,' she said at the time. 'I'm glad I was able to afford to buy my own house last year, but it's very sparsely furnished. Just the basics: a TV, stereo and video. I like space, room to breathe.' For one who always used to love hotels, Julie was becoming a self-confessed home bird.

One of her greatest extravagances was being able to fly first class wherever she went. However, Julie had been mortified on her most recent transatlantic flight to find that the movie being shown was *Educating Rita*. She spent the majority of the trip hiding under a blanket. 'It was quite embarrassing peeping out and seeing all those people nodding off during my film,' she told interviewer Jo Weedon.

'I don't think I've changed much over the years. Despite what people believe, actors are only ordinary people. You have to be a right berk to believe all the crap you read about us.'

Despite the brave exterior, Julie remained vulnerable underneath. 'I have my moments of despair,' she continued. 'I'm not saying I'm a manic depressive, but I have been unhappy. I have anxieties about work, my ability, about relationships and responsibilities towards other people.'

Finding and nurturing a romantic partner was a tough prospect. Although Julie wasn't necessarily looking for a high level of involvement or commitment, she knew what she liked: her ideal man was usually dark haired, tall and, above all, he had to possess a sense of humour. Owing to the chaotic nature of show business, Julie was always attracted by a calm bloke who could put some order in her life.

While she claimed not to be interested in a long-term relationship, Julie was concerned that her career kept her away from her family. 'I talk to my mum on the phone a lot but I don't see her that often,' she said. 'My personal life is sometimes nonexistent. It's a vicious circle. You have to work and have no time to play. Then the job is finished and, because you have nobody to play with, you work. In the end you don't need a private life.'

Being an actress and moving from job to job makes it very difficult to maintain a circle of friends. When a set wraps, everyone promises to keep in touch, and they do for a while, but eventually life moves on. Even when Julie had formed solid friendships, as in *Boys from the Blackstuff* or *She'll Be Wearing Pink Pyjamas*, she found it hard to sustain those ties while working on the next job.

Fortunately, Julie had a small core of people who were always there for her. Her family were supportive and she viewed Tommy and Kevin Walters as, 'friends as well as brothers – there's nothing like a sibling'. In friends, Julie sought a similar nature. 'I love being with people who make me laugh,' she said. 'Women are much funnier than men. I was a guest at a posh party at the National Portrait Gallery once and I spent most of the time huddled in a corner having a giggle with the waitresses.'

While Julie's best friend Ros could always be relied on, her old pal Victoria Wood was also never far away. 'She's the funniest person I know,' says Julie. 'She just makes me laugh. Her comments on life are absolutely hilarious. She sends me funny postcards, like, "Here I am, brown as a tennis sock," and letters addressed to: Junie Waters, c/o The Box Office.'

Victoria reciprocated the feeling, 'I've only had a tiny bit of the exposure [Julie's] had and I've seen the pressure it puts on you. Julie's come out of it with flying colours.' She feels their working relationship works in the long term because, though they do a lot on their own, and 'whenever we come together we have such a good time.'

Julie was disappointed that the seaside film Victoria had planned the previous year had fallen through, and, keen to work with her again, agreed to appear in her new series, *Victoria Wood As Seen On TV*. Compared to the time before, the filming was a happier experience. Since the death of Peter Eckersley, Victoria had teamed up with a like-minded director, Geoff Posner, and built up her own repertory of players who would be constants in her work: Celia Imrie, Susie Blake, Duncan Preston and Julie Walters.

Additionally, Victoria knew what was expected of her and devised a format that she followed to a certain extent for each programme. She would start with a stand-up routine, followed by a mickey-taking TV commercial, and a lengthy sketch with either Julie or Celia. Susie provided sarcasm as the continuity presenter, and there were some traditional gags, a song from Victoria and various character monologues. Every episode was rounded off with a slice of 'Acorn Antiques', a spoof soap opera.

Victoria created a collection of wonderfully outrageous characters, some of whom became regulars, and was honoured with some marvellous performances from a highbrow cast including Jim Broadbent, Thora Hird and Patricia Routledge. Julie was given some prime material such as a monologue as Alma, the director of the Piecrust Players' hysterically crass version of *Hamlet*, and the daytime television host, Margery, opposite Victoria's Joan.

Rehearsals and filming spanned from July through to September 1984 and the series was a solid success when it aired the following January and February. By far the most popular piece of the whole show was 'Acorn Antiques'.

Victoria had always loved her soaps, and a parody was inevitable. Thus the complicated relationships between the characters were far more confusing than the plot, and Victoria cashed in on the farcical goings on of a regular soap opera including shock deaths, a disease of the week, corruption and an unprofessional lack of continuity. 'I remember when I first wrote "Acorn Antiques",' she recalls, 'Geoffrey said, "I don't think people will ever get that." I said, "I think they will."' And they did.

The *Radio Times* heralded it, 'The screamingly funny continuing TV soap spoof *Acorn Antiques*, with its wobbly sets, sensationalist plots, appalling acting, crude camerawork and dopey dialogue, uncannily reminiscent of bad soaps in general and *Crossroads* in particular.'

Through the enduring appeal of 'Acorn Antiques', Julie remains in everyone's heart as the hunchbacked old charwoman, Mrs Overall. 'Victoria knows I like playing old women,' says Julie, 'Why? Because I am one! I love the shape of them.'

Celia Imrie admits she cannot even look Julie in the eye when they work together as she invariably bursts into fits of giggles. 'When she appeared in "Acorn Antiques" as Mrs Overall in a lime-green leotard, the inside of my mouth was bleeding from biting it so hard to stop laughing!' she says.

'Acorn Antiques' undoubtedly struck a chord with viewers: a fanzine was launched and appreciation gatherings were held at which devotees dressed up and recited lines. The episodes even found their way on to a solo video, as opposed to being part of a *Victoria Wood As Seen On TV* compilation. The phenomenal popularity of this segment of the show increased ratings to 4.5 million by the penultimate episode, thereby pushing it into the top ten programmes on BBC2.

14. HAPPY SINCE I MET YOU

As was common practice, Julie was out drinking at a wine bar in Fulham with Ros March one day at the beginning of December 1984. By the late evening, they were both decidedly the worse for wear.

'I bet there's no one in here who votes Labour, is there?' yelled Julie in her harsh Brummie accent.

'I do, actually,' said a tall, dark and handsome man.

Taken aback by this response, Julie felt obliged to talk to the good-looking stranger. His name was Grant Roffey. He was a 28-year-old sociology student and was probably the only man in the bar not to know that he was chatting up an award-winning actress. A true gentleman, Grant offered to walk the tipsy ladies home and when he reached their place, Julie invited him in for a nightcap.

'I had some Beaujolais Nouveau – it was the eighties, after all – so I opened that,' said Julie. 'I'd told him on the way home that I couldn't get the water out of my washing machine, and he said he'd have a look.'

Grant was on all fours with his head craned round the back of the misbehaving machine when he told Julie she would need a pump.

'At the time I mistook his meaning and, instantly filled with mischief and glee, I took a running jump and sprang several feet in the air, landing on his back like a bareback rider in a circus,' she continued. Grant did not know what to make of the turn of events and, fearing he was being attacked, stood up and tried his best to remove her. Julie refused to dismount, roared with laughter and declared, 'I want you to have my children! It's right! I feel it in my ovaries.'

By morning her prey had disappeared and Julie, racked with embarrassment at her behaviour, was thankful that she would not bump into him looking so hung over. Grant, however, was intrigued by the drunken banshee and called around to her house later that day. When she opened the door she realised that, without looking and if a little unconventionally, she had stumbled across her soul mate.

'Grant was so nice and so solid with his feet on the ground, so un-neurotic and everything that actors aren't,' she told reporters. 'He's very responsible, totally reliable, strong, gentle, kind and unutterably practical.' Although seven years her junior, Grant was mature and domesticated. He provided the stability that Julie wasn't aware she lacked.

The fact that Grant didn't know she was an actress was a bonus – it meant that his head wasn't turned by fame or money. Although he had held a succession of down-to-earth jobs including those as a police constable, a lorry driver and an AA man, Julie was pleased that he was able to mix with her friends so easily. 'It wasn't hard for him to come into my life. My actor friends at the time were people like Ian Charleson, not showbizzy plonkers.'

Julie's friend Alan Bleasdale remembers his feelings after first meeting Grant: 'I [was] almost singing in the rain, because they seemed so right together. He was the perfectly timed full stop at the end of that particular sentence in her life, if you like.'

Julie enjoyed what was probably her happiest Christmas and New Year up to then. In an article promoting *Car Trouble*, she frankly revealed *just* how good it was: 'When I'm working really hard, sex is put to the back of my mind ... You get out of practice. Mind you, I've got plenty of practice over Christmas – I had a lot of catching up to do!'

In the New Year, she started her next project. Working again with Ian Charleson, she affected an American accent for her theatrical portrayal of May in Sam Shepherd's *Fool For Love*. Directed by the highly acclaimed Peter Gill, it was an emotionally draining role in the complex four-handed psychodrama set in a motel room on the edge of the Mojave Desert. The play, ninety minutes without an interval, opened on 4 February 1985 at the Lyric on Shaftsbury Avenue and earned Julie a Laurence Olivier Award for Best Actress.

During this time, Julie was also on the small screen in *Victoria Wood As Seen On TV*. And, as if to prove her diversity, she was in talks for a feature film.

Alan Bleasdale had written *No Surrender* with his usual cast in mind. It is a dark comedy set in a dilapidated nightclub on the outskirts of Liverpool, chronicling the rivalry between Irish Catholic and Protestant attendees to a New Year's Eve party.

No Surrender was directed by Peter Smith, and, although he was offered the script with the idea of using the Bleasdale troupe, for some reason he did not want to cast Julie. Bernard Hill, Michael Angelis and Tom Georgeson were so appalled that Peter would not only go against Bleasdale's wishes, but also didn't consider Julie for the role, that they all pulled out.

Bleasdale in turn was absolutely incensed and threatened to cancel the whole film and sack the director. The roles were swiftly reoffered to the original cast. Sadly, in the meantime, Julie had signed up for another project. She was not an easy person to replace, but eventually Joanne Whalley stepped in.

Julie had not waited for the *No Surrender* disputes to be resolved and had instead agreed to appear in a new BBC comedy series based on Sue Townsend's immensely popular book, *The Secret Diary of Adrian Mole Aged 13¾*. The hero, Adrian, is bewildered by his adolescence, battles against acne, lusts after the unattainable Pandora and worries about his parents, who in turn embarrass him and argue with each other.

'I was given a copy of the book by the producers David Elstein and Lloyd Shirley, with two questions: did I see this story as something I'd like to develop, and in my opinion would it make a feasible TV series?' recalls the Hungarian director Peter Sasdy. 'My answers were positive and they arranged a lunch meeting with Townsend, to see how we'd get on. Soon after, we bought the TV rights and the rest is history.'

Peter chose two newcomers, Gian Sammarco and Lindsay Stagg, as the awkward teenagers in the series and selected their parents accordingly. 'It was my idea to cast Julie as Pauline Mole. Before the offer was made I had a nice Hungarian lunch with her at the Gay Hussar restaurant in Soho and, once the parts of Adrian and Pandora were firmly cast, she was next in line to be contracted.'

Pauline's husband, George Mole, was played by Stephen Moore, with whom Julie had worked briefly in *Soldiers Talking Cleanly*. 'I had read the book and thought highly of it,' says Stephen. 'Everyone thought it was extremely funny, but I found it desperately sad too. So, I went to meet Peter and Sue Townsend. I said, "I think I should do this, don't you?" I was much more pushy in those days, but they said yes anyway!'

Considering their poor relationship on screen, Julie and Stephen had a great rapport off screen. 'She is the warmest and friendliest of people, and a fine actress both in comedy and drama,' he says, 'extremely quick-witted and intelligent. How she came to be mixed up in this acting lark I can't begin to imagine!' Julie also mixed well with the rest of the cast, including the youngsters, and became great friends with Beryl Reid, who played Grandma Mole.

Filming for *Adrian Mole* got under way in Harrow, Middlesex. 'It was one of those estates with lots of cul-de-sacs,' says Stephen, 'and the house we used was rented to Thames Television because the owner wanted to have his living room wall knocked down, two rooms made into one and redecorated for free while he was away! The estate was rather posher than the estate in Leicester which Sue showed us when we filmed a scene there.'

Other shots were completed on location in Leicester, Birmingham, Skegness and Hull and, despite Grant Roffey's grounding influence, Julie was up to her old tricks after hours. 'We had a modest party at the end of the location shoot at our hotel in Leicester,' recalls Peter Sasdy. 'I believe Julie must have enjoyed herself, as in the early hours she used a fire extinguisher to spray foam under various doors on the hotel corridor.'

The shoot was quite strenuous, with early wake-up calls to allow for time in the make-up chair before the 8 a.m. start. They continued through to 6 p.m. at the earliest, six days a week. 'There were lots and lots of short scenes,' recalls Stephen. 'Sometimes you could be in twelve or so in a day, which made the script difficult to learn.' Julie was used to the demands of such a tight schedule, but she found it much harder now that she was also juggling a relationship.

'The set was busy, but happy,' says Peter. 'On location the atmosphere was more relaxed than inside the house, where we were very much on top of each other. Sue Townsend visited a couple of times and she enjoyed her first experience on a film set.

'I always thought of Julie as someone with a very special strong personality, a great sense of humour and a very direct approach in her communication. We had good communication. She was always ready to try anything I suggested and of course she made the character very much her own.'

The series was aired in September 1985 to a great response. The audience could identify with all the characters and cringed in sympathy for Adrian during every episode. 'I was very pleased with the result and it's still one of my favourite productions,' says Peter. 'It meant a lot for me as a Hungarian-born director, coming from such a different background, to have a hit film dealing with British working-class life!'

The success of *Adrian Mole* led to second series, but once again Julie ran into problems and could not return as Pauline Mole not least because she had accepted work on a new movie.

The film that Julie was tied up with was a new departure, as she was not acting as such, but providing a voiceover. The movie was called *Dreamchild* and was directed by her old colleague Gavin Millar.

Written by the darkly controversial Dennis Potter, it is set in 1932 at the hundredth anniversary of the birth of the *Alice's Adventures in Wonderland* creator, Lewis Carroll. The guest of honour at the New York-based celebration is eighty-year-old Alice Liddell (Coral Browne), who as a child inspired Carroll's whimsical novels. Here, Potter voices an issue on which previous literary historians have only ruminated: Alice harbours a secret concerning her 'very special relationship' with Carroll. Flashback sequences tastefully reveal the true association of the young Alice (Amelia Shankley) and the virginal, child-obsessed clergyman Charles Dodgson, known as Lewis Carroll (Ian Holm).

The unpalatability of the story is lifted by Jim (*The Muppets*) Henson's re-creations of Carroll's characters, and, while Julie spoke for the dormouse, Alan Bennett was the voice of the mock turtle.

Julie was experimenting with new ventures, while being in a settled relationship with Grant was an exciting challenge in itself.

The couple had become serious very quickly and suddenly it was clear to Julie that she was ready for a change: she could picture herself with this man for ever. She was busy with interviews in the spring and summer of 1985, promoting *Car Trouble* and then *Adrian Mole*. Alongside assessing her career, she continued to talk openly about her personal life.

'I used to live in fear of failure,' she says of the former. 'A lot of that's gone. I realise I just have to do my best and I am less tense about things.' She remained very coy about the identity of her new beau, not least because he was not in the world of show business, yet she spoke freely about marriage and children.

'I don't know if I'll ever marry,' she told the *Star*, maintaining her previous stance of 'Why bother?' 'Maybe I'll be prepared to make a commitment when I'm forty or fifty. I certainly haven't talked about it with my present boyfriend; we've only been together for a few months.'

More pressing was that, at 35, her biological clock was ticking with vigour. 'I'm getting on a bit in years, but my mum reminded me the other day that my grandmother had her first child at 37 and ended up having four! So, who knows?' She certainly found herself unexpectedly broody. 'It comes and goes; it depends on what I'm doing,' she said acknowledging that the filming of *Adrian Mole* had triggered a maternal pull.

'I'll let you know if I'm going to have a baby. I've been talking about it with the new bloke actually. When it happens I'm going to be a good mother, I've decided.' By making the last comment flippant, Julie brushed over the fact that although she and Grant had been together only a very short while and had not spoken about marriage, they were already thinking about children. This probably seemed perfectly natural for Julie, seeing that she had announced this to him on their very first encounter.

Nancy Meckler, a pioneering female director, was the associate director of the Leicester Haymarket in 1985. *Macbeth* was one of her first productions in this new role and she chose Julie to play Lady Macbeth. The actress helped modernise the classic by basing her character on Margaret Thatcher.

'I loved doing that,' says Julie. 'It was a real act of bottle. I was very nervous about it. I did it while Mrs Mole was on the telly. I had visions of all these A-level students shouting derogatory things about Adrian's mum.' Fortunately, that was not the case and, playing opposite her old friend Bernard Hill, Julie received glowing reviews. One paper suggested that she was the best Lady Macbeth since Judi Dench – acclamation indeed!

Playing that role did give her some confidence. She says, 'Sometimes, in this business, you wonder if what you've done before was just a whim. So you have to keep testing yourself and the theatre is the best testing ground of all.'

During the 1985–6 season at the London Old Vic, a host of actors and actresses gathered for a special *Tribute To Sir Michael Redgrave*. Julie was among those directed by Anthony Page and was joined by Ian Charleson, Sir John Gielgud, Jonathan Pryce and many of the Redgrave dynasty.

After this, Julie toyed with two abortive projects. Victoria Wood had been trying to write a screenplay for herself and Julie, tentatively called *The Natural Order*. Julie was always interested in Victoria's work – 'I've never had a script from her that isn't funny' – but this particular project never got off the ground and Victoria was left yet to make her mark on the big screen.

Then, in the spring of 1986, the director Mike Leigh gathered 26 actors together in Blackburn, Lancashire, with the hope of making a feature film with the working title of *Rhubarb*. Julie, who had worked with Leigh in *Ecstasy*, was keen to be among the cast, including Jim Broadbent, Jane Horrocks and David Thewlis. Sadly, after seven weeks of rehearsals, Leigh withdrew from the project and it collapsed.

The accolades for *Macbeth* felt far removed by the summer and Julie felt the need to return to work. She was delighted to be contacted by Simon Stokes. 'I first met her briefly in Liverpool at the Everyman back in 1974, then I met her at the Bush Theatre during *In at the Death*,' he explains. 'Much later, I did a play, *When I Was a Girl I Used To Scream and Shout*, at the Bush Theatre.

'I was asked to revive it for the Edinburgh Festival at the Lyceum, which was a success. Then, the producer Howard Panter from the Ambassador Group wanted to put it on in the West End, providing the circumstances were right – that meant with the right actors. Sheila Reid and John Gordon Sinclair were two of the original Bush Theatre actors, so we asked them to do it. We also cast Geraldine James and Julie – it was just a four-hander. Julie was the lead, Sheila played her friend, Geraldine the mother and John was her sixteen-year-old boyfriend in flashback. It was a very pleasant company, everybody got on extremely well. I like to choose people who are going to get on well.'

The play is a comedy by Sharman McDonald, analysing the changing relationships of mothers and daughters. 'It is very funny and rude,' says Simon – right up Julie's street. 'A lot of the content was about girls growing up. It was the first play in a way to talk about boys' bits, sex, rudeness and swearing unashamedly. It is based on Sharman's background and set outside Edinburgh on the coast, in a place she knew.'

As with many of the playwrights with whom Julie had previously worked, Sharman was on hand to help the actors understand her work. The women also required the services of a voice coach to help perfect the Scottish accent; Glaswegian John needed only a bit of tweaking.

'It was quite a technical play in terms of lighting and movement, so the rehearsal time was tight,' says Simon, although they had the standard four weeks. 'It was done in just one set, but it was peculiar because there were time differences and they had to play a number of different ages. We weren't trying to depict all the different ages realistically, just get a feel for them, so we kept it incredibly simple – Julie just wore a black leotard and long skirt.'

Simon was very excited about the play, as he hoped to attract a new generation of theatregoers. 'It had a big female appeal for the audience – mothers and daughters used to come together, which was actually a bad idea. They would have liked it separately, but, as it's about the alienation between them, I don't think they should have seen it together!

'We thought the play was good and had already been proven, but we didn't know if it would work in a commercial sense. But it became very successful and won the *Evening Standard* awards at the time.'

When I Was a Girl I Used To Scream and Shout ran for a total of ten months at the Whitehall Theatre in the West End, but Julie signed up only for a six-month contract, which was the norm. 'It's quite boring to take six months on one play as an actor, so you have to be very attracted by the part,' says Simon. 'On the other hand it's six months' security both financially and in your career.'

This was the closest Julie had come to a regular job for a long time and, particularly given the two months needlessly devoted to *Rhubarb*, it suited her rapidly developing relationship. 'Grant would be waiting on his motorbike to pick her up,' Simon remembers. 'She used to do the curtain call, come off stage and, because her costume was so simple, she was out of the theatre and on the motorbike before the audience had even left the auditorium! Grant was very good for her, that was clear.'

Being so bankable, Julie was in demand for brand sponsorship. Given that it was easy money, Julie once joked, 'I'm such an old tart, I'd be quite happy just doing commercials.' While she did find herself signing up for numerous television adverts, Julie relishes the challenge and thrill of a role far too much to give it up.

Her worst experience occurred when she was asked to promote cars. Julie responded politely, saying that, while she was flattered by the offer, she couldn't drive. Amazingly, this didn't bother the company. She had to drive the car across the studio keeping its speed constant. She says, 'Well, that's not so easy for me, but the really tricky bit was these dancers jumping in and out round the car. I almost killed the lot of them. That was the day my acne came back!'

Far more suitable were the Asda supermarket adverts she filmed with Victoria Wood. It was highly appropriate casting, as many of their comedy routines referred to common household goods. The pair pushed their shopping trolleys, chatting away about mindless topics, oblivious of the glorious backdrops of the Austrian Alps, France and Spain. Julie received £60,000 for her brief stint of filming and went on to become the voice of Typhoo tea and rival supermarket, Sainsbury's.

The extra money came in handy, as Grant moved in with Julie over the summer. 'When we started living together he helped furnish my home,' she told the *Sun*, although Grant maintained his own flat for his studying.

'Suddenly, I found myself in a domestic situation, because he's very domestic. We often joke that he's my toy boy, but in reality he's more mature. I could never have tolerated a man who was inept on the home front,' she said. Grant was very handy around the home, not only at the traditional masculine hobbies, but he could also cook, sew and wash – 'probably better than me,' admitted Julie. Ever practical, Grant taught Julie to drive and she finally passed her test in 1987 after years of avoiding the issue.

15. A RIGHT PROPER MADAM

In the autumn of 1986, Julie appeared with a terrific cast in the television adaptation of Harold Pinter's first play, *The Birthday Party*. The author appeared alongside Colin Blakely, Joan Plowright, Robert Lang, Kenneth Cranham and Julie in this BBC production.

The original version at the Lyric Hammersmith back in May 1958 was cancelled after just one week, slated by the critics as a disaster. Trends change and now *The Birthday Party* is considered a modern classic. 'It's a typical Harold Pinter play,' says Robert Lang. 'It's eerie, with undertones of violence, sex, power games, long pauses and comic dialogue, if you appreciate that kind of humour. It's not as obscure as some of the plays he wrote later.

'It's set in a seaside town. The house it all happens in belongs to a couple called Meg and Petey Boles [Joan Plowright and Lang himself], who take in lodgers. One of the permanent lodgers is Stanley [Kenneth Cranham], a nice lad aged between twenty and thirty, who seems to be hiding in this house, taking refuge there. Two other characters appear in the very first act and stay for a couple of nights and they are obviously part of Stanley's background. You don't quite know who they are, but they're obviously up to no good – they are evil. Harold Pinter played the Jewish chap and Colin Blakely was the Irish chap.

'Julie's part was the girl next door. You guess that she works in Marks & Spencers or Woolworth's, she's of that intelligence and class, and she also becomes a victim of these two no-gooders. In the end they destroy Stanley and take him away. It's a very difficult play to describe.' Pinter plays with the audience, frustrating them by denying them logical answers to the myriad questions thrown up within the first act, thus making *The Birthday Party* so indefinable.

The director Kenneth Ives was fortunate that he had chosen a band of actors who had known each other for years. 'Colin Blakely, Joan Plowright and I were all at the National Theatre when it opened in 1963,' says Robert Lang, 'so had worked together for quite a long time. Kenneth Cranham was also a regular actor working with us. So it was Harold Pinter and Julie who were the new faces in the group.' Although he didn't realise it at the time, Robert later discovered that he had worked with Julie on the Edward Bond radio plays *Bingo* and *Week Ending* some eleven years earlier.

Rehearsals for *The Birthday Party* got under way at the BBC building in north Acton. 'I remember the room next to us had a rock group practising,' says Robert. 'Harold Pinter has very sensitive ears and doesn't like any interruption at all, and he found the rock group next door an enormous burden. He couldn't rehearse when there was a noise like that.' Still, they carried on for two weeks and spent a further week filming.

'Julie is impressive,' he continues. 'She doesn't have troubles, her acting comes easily to her. She's very instinctive and it comes quickly. She doesn't find or make problems. She always looks at ease when rehearsing and you never see her fretting too much about what the text means.

'The trouble with Harold Pinter plays is that they are so deep that if you start to plunge into them you could spend hours and hours finding out exactly what it means. And, if it means anything at all, it won't be of any help to you! She seemed to know that instinctively.'

In contrast with her previous work, Julie was surprised to find that having the author on hand was not that productive. 'It isn't always cosy with the author around,' explains Robert. 'We all knew not to ask questions with Harold Pinter, because he had the reputation of saying, "Well I don't know what it means, you must find out what it means!" Of course, he was also struggling with the problems of being an actor, because he hadn't done any acting for some twenty years.'

The play's atmosphere is of ordinary lower-middle-class life, except that it has a twist that makes it unnerving. *The Birthday Party* is essentially about people cracking up but the cast were obviously extremely experienced and refused to take the dark subject matter home with them. A challenging piece, and excellent for her CV though it was, this was not Julie's most raucous set. 'We were recording until about ten or eleven p.m., which was a long day,' says Robert. 'But there was a wrap party with a plentiful supply of wine or champagne, so we enjoyed each other's company for an hour or so and then went home to bed – it wasn't a young person's play!'

The Birthday Party proved a critical success, with the sterling cast all receiving glowing reviews – not least the author's return to acting: 'Pinter, as the menacing Goldberg, wrapped his Yiddish accent around his lines with a terrifying, chilly relish,' wrote Saskia Baron for the *Independent*, while Sue Summers from the *London Daily News* said, 'Pinter reveals the talent for playing villains on which he capitalised in his repertory days.'

It was time again for some light relief and Julie enjoyed a second series of *Victoria Wood As Seen On TV* in December 1986. Having tapped into the nation's funny bone, Victoria scored a smash hit with the follow-up. By the third week the viewing figure was 8.5 million, putting the programme at the top of BBC2's listings.

The format had been altered a little, but remained much the same. 'Acorn Antiques' returned by popular demand and was still very much a favourite spot. Julie and Victoria excelled as two lower-middle-class women in the sketches 'Spaghetti' and 'No Gossip'. Simply, they were placed in a restaurant and tearoom, and capitalised on the banalities of everyday chatter. 'I still think her elderly waitress in the second series was one of the funniest things I've ever seen,' says actress Susie Blake.

In March 1987 *Victoria Wood As Seen On TV* won the Best Light Entertainment Programme BAFTA, and both Victoria and Julie were nominated for the Best Light Entertainment Performance. However, Victoria decided to call it a day and pulled the plug on her series. She stressed that it wasn't because she felt 'burned out' but she believed she should always give her best 'and I think – so far as TV sketches go – I've given all I've got for a while. Now I need some fresh challenges.'

Victoria wasn't the only one seeking fresh challenges: soon after, Julie sought and found a new vehicle to get her back on the big screen. This was *Prick Up Your Ears* – an Alan Bennett adaptation of John Lahr's biography about the brilliant playwright Joe Orton. Julie was cast in the small role of Joe's mother.

Joe – strikingly portrayed by the star of *Sid and Nancy*, Gary Oldman – led a vibrant, if short, existence, flaunting his homosexuality in the face of 1950s society until he was violently bludgeoned to death by his long-term lover, Kenneth Halliwell, played by Alfred Molina. Bennett's script carefully balances the anarchic humour of Orton's plays with the bleakness of his tortured life.

Such a scandalous story would be easy to sensationalise, but the movie was in safe hands with the experienced Bennett director, Stephen Frears (who later went on to direct *Dangerous Liaisons* and *High Fidelity* among other films). The destructive relationship between Joe and Kenneth is sensitively told through flashbacks from the vantage point of Joe's agent (Vanessa Redgrave) and his biographer (Wallace Shawn). It is fascinating to look back on the ten-year relationship and witness Kenneth's descent into depression and jealousy. The film also highlights Kenneth's involvement in Joe's career and how Joe's six-month prison sentence freed him from his lover, enabling him to write properly. These scenes also allow a wonderful appearance from Richard Wilson as the prison psychiatrist.

The stellar cast excelled themselves with the two leads taking much of the praise for their performances: Gary Oldman was sexy, dangerous and utterly compelling compared with Alfred Molina's needy gloom of an unwanted lover. On its release in April 1987, *Prick Up Your Ears* became cult viewing and the other cast members were praised for their supporting roles: Vanessa Redgrave received Best Supporting Actress awards as the agent, and Julie and Frances Barber (as Joe's sister) were both picked out in reviews.

Unfortunately Alan Bennett succumbed to the stereotype of Julie in the role of Joe's toothless old mother in a floral housecoat: she could have easily challenged Vanessa Redgrave for the female lead. Still, to be involved in such a fine production was testament to Julie's versatility.

'There was a great meeting ground of talent in a lot of Alan's work,' says a previous Bennett producer, Giles Foster. 'It owes a lot to all genres and traditions: classic drama, music hall, soliloquy et cetera. I think he is delighted when big performers tailor their performance to accommodate the size he writes for.'

After such intensity on *Prick Up Your Ears*, Julie landed herself a fun, juicy role in another feature film. David Leland, the British actor, director and screenwriter, scored his first significant cinema success in 1986 with the script for *Mona Lisa*. He was keen to cement this achievement with his next piece, and so wrote *Personal Services*, a wry comedy about prostitution.

The film states, very clearly, that it is inspired by the book about Cynthia Payne, a former waitress who achieved notoriety as Britain's best-known and best-loved madam. However, as the issue was *sub judice*, the credits stress that it is not her life story and that the events and characters are entirely fictitious – even though Cynthia was credited as a consultant.

Julie plays the lead role, the carefully named Christine Painter, a working-class single mother struggling to send her child to private school. To subsidise her wages, she illegally sublets cheap flats to prostitutes. One of her ladies, Shirley (Shirley Stelfox), is always flush with money and pays on time, while another walks out owing eight weeks' rent.

Christine, in turn, owes the landlord and is forced to sell her own body to make up the difference. Although she likes to think she is liberated, she is actually quite naïve, so needs Shirley's help to 'service' retired Wing Commander Morten (Alec McCowen). The three are caught by the police, and, though Christine receives a slap on the wrist for soliciting, Shirley suggests they all work together. Morten confirms there is a market for elderly businessmen who like to indulge in transvestism, role playing and S&M, so Shirley instructs Christine how to act out a fantasy as a naughty schoolgirl or a strict nanny.

While Christine succumbs to the easy money of prostitution, we see that she aspires to much more. She was cast out of the family when she fell pregnant as a teenager, but is desperate to be welcomed back. Unfortunately, when her sister's wedding presents an opportunity for a reunion, she causes a scene and is disowned by her father once again. Julie is wonderful as the common tart with posh pretensions and a dirty mouth, but mention should also be made of Shirley and Christine's maid, Dolly, who steals the scene here.

Business is booming and they expand, with the wing commander helping Christine to buy a large detached house. She creates a safe haven for her sexually deviant clients, hosting lavish erotic parties and a brothel three times a week. They are one big, perverse, happy family. Life couldn't be better for Christine, as she can at last afford the luxury she dreamed of, and is thrilled to welcome her father into her home – quite literally.

A police raid at Christmas disrupts her charmed existence, yet Christine retains her sharp tongue and dignity, refusing to go in the police van and agreeing to travel only with the operation leader. With several charges against her and enough evidence to sink a ship, it seems she will spend the rest of her days in prison, unless a judge with a penchant for a certain strict headmistress has his way.

Personal Services was directed by Terry Jones, best known as a member of the Monty Python troupe, and contains its fair share of blue language and call-girl humour. It can be described as good, clean, dirty fun and is a fabulous film, worthy of Julie's talent.

'Cynthia fascinated me, but it was difficult at first playing someone who's alive,' says Julie, belying the fact that Christine was supposed to be a fictional character. 'One day, she turned up on the set.'

'Have you done that bit yet when I was in the garden shed and my dad caught me?' Cynthia asked. (This was a scene Emily Lloyd re-enacted in *Wish You Were Here*, a film based on Cynthia Payne's childhood.)

'No, that's not in it,' replied Julie. 'You were only fourteen!'

'I could never have done Cynthia's job though,' Julie continues. 'I couldn't have been a madam, I just couldn't do the organising!'

As Christine, Julie achieved the ideal balance of innocence, smut, desire and survival, and not only gained critical kudos for her gritty realisation of Cynthia, but also received a BAFTA nomination for Best Actress.

She was required to provide some heavy-duty promotion for *Personal Services* and a round-the-world tour was organised. Her first port of call was New York, but, as the publicity company kept her onward-travel documents for safety, Julie and her single ticket aroused suspicion at passport control. 'The man with the steely gaze asked where the rest of my ticket was and I immediately panicked, imagined I had just committed a series of terrible crimes and prepared to face the full wrath of the American judicial system,' she explains in *Julie Walters Is an Alien*

As she couldn't instantly prove the continuation of her journey, Julie was ushered into a nondescript office for further questioning by a grim-faced official. Flustered, she found to her dismay that she couldn't remember any of the most basic details, such as the name of the trip co-ordinators.

'This really did not impress old Granite Features and, when I told him that I was in fact an actress publicising a film about prostitution in which I played a madam, it sort of went downhill from that point,' she later relayed. 'It took a long time for me to find that company name, and he made me suffer until I could prove my innocence and be a free woman again.'

When she was finally allowed into America, Julie toured the circuit of chat shows, obliging her hosts with reams of anecdotes and gags. She captivated the audience on *Late Night with David Letterman* and then again on *Jay Leno*. She also enamoured rival host Johnny Carson so much that he immediately invited her back. 'He said, "Do you wanna come back Thursday?"' mimicked Julie to a reporter, in a perfect Carson impersonation. 'Apparently he'd never done that before.'

Strangely, though it wasn't written with her last role in mind, Alan Bennett's next creation was a piece for Julie that led on neatly from *Personal Services*. In *Her Big Chance*, Julie plays Lesley, a naïve, aspiring actress who unwittingly accepts the lead in a soft-porn movie. She agrees to strip for a scene with her boyfriend only because she is told, and believes, it shows her contempt for his whole way of life. And of course she ends up sleeping with the director.

But what makes *Her Big Chance* so different is that the whole scenario is portrayed solely by Julie, in a monologue. This was not the first time such an idea had been tackled by Bennett.

'Around the time of *Say Something Happened* [1982], Alan said, "I've got this script, it's just for Pat [Routledge], see what you think,"' recalls the director Giles Foster. 'I read it and thought it was exceptional. I was impressed by the fact that he could sustain what turned out to be a forty-minute monologue just with his words. He had some trepidation as to whether it would work or not, so we started rehearsing it and putting some movement in it, but it wasn't really working.

'Alan came in and said, "Be brave, just keep it still. These really are 'talking heads'." So we tried with Pat just talking to a video camera – it wasn't even turned on but just gave her a focus. And that really worked and it was popular.

'So, when Alan said he had written a series of monologues for specific people and one of them was Julie, I was delighted, because I'd discovered how funny and how skilful she was doing the three-hander, *Say Something Happened*. Julie is an enormously articulate, part gifted actress, part crazy comedienne from an almost vaudeville tradition, and part postgraduate English literature student. She approached her work from all those angles.'

Her Big Chance was recorded on 29 March 1987 and aired shortly thereafter as one of six monologues in Bennett's BBC series, *Talking Heads*. As always, Bennett was present during rehearsals and filming.

'You wanted it to be close to a theatrical production, but also to have precision,' says Giles. 'Alan is very precise, not just in terms of the actual words, but also the pronunciation, because he writes from experience. So he would stop you and say, "That's not how it was meant." It's such a close personal text that he writes, so, when he does talk about it, it's illuminating. It has a great deal more authority if Alan, rather than the director, advises an actor.'

Character development and vocal inflection aside, the concept of a monologue proved as hard for the actors as the directors. 'The technical thing about doing monologues is that there's nowhere to cut to,' explains Giles. 'There are no other characters to focus on, so you have to cut smoothly. At the start we ambitiously thought it could be done in one take, but twenty-five closely written pages of A4 is a memory feat beyond anyone. Besides, things go wrong technically – for instance the camera may not hit its mark, and editing wasn't as sophisticated in those days and drop-ins weren't so easy to achieve, so you would do your best to cut well during the filming.

'It's also very different just working with one actor – quite intense. It was very daunting for Julie and there was a big time pressure. Towards the end of recording we began to run out of time. We did it more or less in order, which helped, but it was a challenge. Something that doesn't work is to have an autocue, so she had to take the text and *really* learn it. One of the things I learned very early on, to sustain somebody for that length of time, is that the actor or actress has to look away and then come back to you. It was a huge challenge and she pulled it off magnificently.'

Although Julie was a big star at this point, she was not averse to taking on small roles, and during this period she also undertook a cameo in *Help*. The two-series sitcom, written by Joe Boyle, followed the stories of three unemployed Liverpool youths. *Help* ran from 1986 to 1988 and starred David Albany, Stephen McGann (the youngest of the four acting brothers), Jake Abraham and Sheila Fay.

16. BUSTED

After Julie and Grant had been living together for a couple of years, they decided to have a baby. 'To us it was much more of a commitment than getting married, which is just a legality,' said Julie in *Woman's Own*. 'We planned it properly, although people told us you can't plan that sort of thing, but we did.'

Indeed, Julie and Grant had been holidaying in Corsica when they came to this conclusion, and, as Julie was 37, they realised that time was not on their side. Shortly afterwards, in June 1987, Julie stopped using contraception and amazingly conceived the following month. At the end of August, when she was violently sick, she took a pregnancy test and was thrilled to find it was positive.

'Having worked out the approximate date of conception, it seems it happened on holiday – this means it was made in Hong Kong!' joked Julie. 'We ... had to stay in bed for four days to get over our jetlag.' There was no doubt in Julie's mind that Grant had all the right qualities to make an excellent father. Whereas many women have to persuade their partners to start a family, Julie knew that Grant wanted children as much as she did, and that he would take his responsibilities very seriously.

The decision to have a baby would traditionally prompt the question of marriage. The subject certainly came up in the Walters–Roffey relationship fairly often, but somehow never got off the ground. Julie was still a nonbeliever. 'When we decided to have a child, I thought we *ought* to get married to signify a proper commitment,' she said. 'But then we decided that having a child *was* a proper commitment and so we put it off.' She argued that marriage vows were supposed to be sacred, and yet the divorce rate indicated otherwise. So long as she and Grant were secure and their child was happy, that was enough for her.

Coming back down to earth with a bump, Julie realised that she would have to admit to her mother that she was going to be an unmarried mother, which would mean that her child would be 'illegitimate'. Feeling like an irresponsible teenager rather than a mature mother-to-be, Julie chickened out of speaking to Mary directly and instead wrote a letter. The reply came on 10 September: 'I opened it with a racing heart. She was pleased, and concerned for my health,' said Julie, relieved that the correspondence did not contain the lecture she had predicted.

Although Julie says the pregnancy was preplanned, she had not accounted for the problems she would face with her next film. In September 1987, she reported to the set of *Buster*, David Green's movie glamorising the Great Train Robbery as told through the eyes of the junior thief, Buster Edwards. The starring role of June, opposite the singer-songwriter Phil Collins, would be the crowning glory on her work over the last year, cementing her big-screen career.

This was Phil Collins's first adult foray into film and he said he was attracted to the script primarily because it was a love story, but also because he would be co-starring with Julie Walters, of whom he was a big fan.

Julie was reluctant to announce her baby news until she was safely past the first trimester, particularly as the risks for older women, known medically as *elderly primigravida*, are higher. Her secrecy presented Julie with a few awkward situations. The first issue was her nausea.

'I thought morning sickness was a little mild queasiness experienced first thing in the morning,' Julie relayed to *Woman's Own*. 'For some women, yes. For me, not a bit of it. In fact, I have renamed it "vile, unrelenting, morning, noon and night sickness."'

She was so sick that she spent much of her time rushing to the loo – she laughed about the fact that the cast and crew must have thought she was on drugs.

As embarrassing as that was, Julie was far more concerned by a miscarriage requirement in the script. 'I didn't know what a miscarriage was like, so they got the midwife in to talk to me,' she says. 'The midwife was pinching me and explaining this is what a contraction feels like. And she taught me the panting women do to cope with the pains.' Julie was naturally upset by the experience but, as only the producer and director knew she was pregnant, she couldn't say anything.

'If somebody happened to be pregnant and they did this breathing they wouldn't have a miscarriage, would they?' Julie asked, as casually as she could.

'No,' replied the midwife, 'but you're not pregnant, are you?'

'No, just checking, I just wondered,' muttered Julie.

As they talked further, it transpired that the midwife looked after a number of actresses, including the *Not The Nine O'Clock News* comedienne, Pamela Stephenson. Julie finally admitted the truth and promptly hired the midwife.

The next person who really had to be aware of Julie's condition was the costume designer. Julie wrote in her diary at the time: 'Having only fitted me a couple of weeks ago, she visibly blanched when she saw that the 1960s bra that she had brought, and which had fitted me perfectly when first tried on, was now bulging.'

Julie felt the wardrobe lady's eyes peering at her, searching for signs of weight gain, silicone implants, or any other feasible explanation to her ballooning breasts. She couldn't bear the scrutiny any longer and blurted out the sole word 'pregnant'. The women stood staring at each other and Julie finally elaborated; both parties were grateful that the awkward situation could finally be explained.

In mid-October Julie passed the first trimester and was not only happy, but also relieved to tell Phil Collins, and the rest of the cast and crew, that her strange behaviour and increasing size was due to her pregnancy. Julie chose a quiet time, when her co-star was sitting in his car with his chauffeur, to break the news.

'Phil, I've got something to tell you,' she said, leaning through the window. 'I'm pregnant.' Julie realised that, to Danny the chauffeur, it must have sounded as if a paternity suit was looming and, thinking quickly on her feet, acted the part. 'It's OK, I'm not a greedy girl,' she added. 'I'm sure we can come to some reasonable financial arrangement.'

Phil and Danny both offered their congratulations, and Danny joked, 'If the press find out, you'll think I'm the grass.' By the time Julie got home that evening, the media had indeed uncovered her secret. One reporter had staked out the house and another, who knew Julie, had left a cheerful message on her answer machine saying that she had heard the news. Lo and behold, the following day, articles and pictures adorned the front page of one of the tabloids. 'Just to set the story straight,' says Julie, 'Danny was not the grass – but he was ribbed heavily about it for the rest of the film!'

Finally, Julie was able to concentrate on filming *Buster* without sneaking around. In fact, the set encouraged a family atmosphere as Ellie Beavan (who played June and Buster's daughter Nicky) was only seven years old and David Green had a child of a similar age. 'He had a little girl called Jessica,' says an older Ellie. 'When she came on set with him, she'd come into my dressing room and we used to spend hours playing together. David was really sweet, patient and gentle. Obviously, having a daughter of his own, he knew how to deal with me.'

This was Ellie's first job, but the fact that she was working with a chart-topping singer and an award-winning actress was lost on her. 'I knew Phil Collins sang but I didn't know on what scale – I wasn't into pop stars. I don't think I was aware of who Julie Walters was, either. My mum said to me, "You do realise who you are working with?" But it probably went right over my head! When I met Julie, she was so lovely and down to earth – you don't feel you're in the presence of a big star.'

Ellie's character was meant to grow up through the film, but, shortly after shooting commenced, all four of her front teeth fell out. 'I had to go to a Harley Street dentist to have false teeth made,' she laughs, 'which is why I sound and look like I'm having trouble talking, because I was getting used to these false teeth!'

And then there were the accents, both cockney and Spanish. Having played the Artful Dodger in a London production of *Oliver!*, Phil had no problems with the London twang, but all the actors benefited from the assistance of a dialect coach. The trainer in question was Joan Washington, who had recently married the hot new actor, Richard E Grant, flushed with the success of *Withnail & I*. Joan, like Julie, is eight years older than her husband; the women hit it off immediately and the two couples began to socialise together.

The story shows Buster as a petty criminal, frequently robbing Mothercare to provide for his unborn child. Pregnant June is fed up of living without security and, although she loves her husband, is equally despairing of his eternal quest for a 'dream come true'. Buster becomes embroiled in the infamous train heist, which he sees as his passport to heaven, but the gang are careless after the event, leaving fingerprints and clues. Within one month four of the perpetrators are picked up and the heat is on for the remaining criminals.

Meanwhile, June has a miscarriage, poignantly portrayed by Julie. When Buster and June spend six months in hiding, they manage to enjoy themselves, despite the fraught conditions, but Buster eventually has to fly to Zurich to organise his funds, leaving June alone with their four-year-old daughter, Nicky. Frightened, and seeing her photograph in the papers, she follows him.

Finally, the trio escape to the relaxed paradise of Acapulco. Buster and June have never been abroad before and are typical of uncultured Brits of the era. They frequently comment that it's not like Clacton, Brighton or Southend, yet they act as though it were: sitting on the beach fully clothed, not applying suntan lotion and wanting steak and chips for dinner.

The cast and crew of *Buster* were lucky to be required to spend the month of October in Mexico, filming on location. Grant accompanied his pregnant partner and learned a lot about his impending fatherhood. 'When we were in Acapulco, Julie and Phil were off filming quite a lot,' says Ellie, 'so Grant and I spent a lot of time playing in the pool when I wasn't working. He was really good fun, I probably pestered him, but he was brilliant.

'When we were shooting we laughed a lot, like the scenes on the beach – I don't think I ever really distinguished when we were filming and when we weren't because we were just messing about in the sand the whole time.' Phil was obviously also affected by the family atmosphere, as he announced that he was keen to have children with his second wife, Jill, who accompanied him to Mexico.

Julie had begun to feel much better in her second trimester, but the combination of the heat and foreign food was playing havoc with her unsettled insides. 'My mother had taken [the snack food] Hula Hoops out for me,' remembers Ellie, 'and Julie used to nick my Hula Hoops as it was the only thing that she could keep down, and they reminded her of home.'

However, there were further implications of Julie's condition: the long flight was difficult, as were some of the more physical scenes. June and Buster become homesick and the final straw comes when they have to take Nicky to an unsavoury local hospital after she swallows thirty pesetas hidden in the Christmas pudding – another English tradition on which the couple insisted. 'The scene in the hospital was filmed towards the end,' continues Ellie. 'I felt awful because she had to pick me up, but I wasn't this little four-year-old, I was a seven-year-old, and I wasn't particularly slight. I was really scared that I was going to hurt her or the baby.'

Worse still, during an argument afterwards, Buster hits June. 'I specifically remember when she got slapped, because I was trailing behind her, but just out of shot,' says Ellie. 'When he slapped her, I was really quite taken aback – it was just so real.'

Although the real Buster Edwards was a technical adviser on the film, just as Cynthia Payne had been for *Personal Services*, the slapping scene was dramatised for the big screen. Phil, who later became friendly with Buster, comments, 'I didn't ask questions about the script because I didn't know what questions to ask. I made the part my own but I said pretty much what was on the paper.' When Buster saw the scene where Phil slapped Julie, he said that he would never have hit his wife June, but Phil had simply followed the script.

Phil had studied the era and because many people smoked in the 1960s he felt Buster would also have done; he lit up throughout the film. The real Buster corrected that misconception too. Overall, though, Buster was honoured by the film and told Phil, 'You've got me down, apart from the clothes: I was a nattier dresser than you are!' (When Buster died in

December 1994, mourners entered the chapel to Phil Collins's 'A Groovy Kind of Love', which appeared on the film soundtrack.)

By all accounts, everyone thoroughly enjoyed their month in paradise and the celebrations heralding the wrap proved the icing on the cake. 'We were in this fabulous villa overlooking the Bay of Acapulco,' describes Julie, 'and nobody went home and got changed: they just burst into a party.' Apparently the producer supplied cases of champagne and a band. 'Everybody went absolutely mad, because it was spontaneous, and there was a real "goodbye" to it,' says Julie, laughing that everyone jumped into the pool still in full costume.

Pregnancy aside, Julie thoroughly enjoyed working on *Buster*, not least because of her co-star, with whom she became great friends. 'I would love to do another film with Phil because he's so easy and good – he really is an actor,' said Julie at the time, adding that although he was a rock star he was 'unpretentious and not at all posy'. She finished the shoot fit and healthy, if a few pounds heavier. In the final cut, the naturally slim actress has clearly filled out but looks positively radiant.

Buster received mixed reviews when it was released in November 1988. 'The robbery itself is handled in low-key fashion, and the film glosses over the less savoury aspects of the £2 million crime,' wrote the *TV Times*, commenting that the plot wasn't dramatic enough to sustain the film's length, but the sharp dialogue helped to carry it.

Just before they had gone to Mexico, Julie was required to have an amniocentesis, a normal precautionary procedure for pregnant women over the age of 35. She had fretted about the results anxiously while they were away.

Although Mexico was wonderful, the cast and crew had been away for long enough filming *Buster* and couldn't wait to return home. Julie couldn't wait to be in her own house, in control of her own laundry and cooking, and relax with her feet up. 'But above all, I couldn't wait for the result of the amniocentesis,' she wrote in her diary of the time.

The test was fine and, choosing to be told the sex of the child, Julie and Grant found out that they were expecting a little girl. They had previously chosen a female name and, now they knew the sex of their child, it stuck.

Apparently Grant had been reading a Dickens novel when he came across the name Maisie and, although they had never agreed on a name before, they both fell in love with the derivative of Margaret, meaning 'pearl'. 'It wasn't a character in the novel: it was just the name Maisie in a Victorian poster stuck in the back of the book, says Julie. 'And from then on we vowed that if we ever had a baby daughter, she would be called Maisie.'

At the end of 1987, Julie had squeezed in one more brief stint with Victoria Wood, appearing on her *As Seen On TV Christmas Special*. Although Victoria had hung up her sketch-show shoes after the second series, she couldn't resist a final festive instalment. The usual crowd all took part and the highlights included Julie and Celia Imrie conversing solely in advertising jargon, Julie and Victoria as gossips in a snack queue and also as unhelpful hotel receptionists.

To top off her spoof of soap operas, Victoria had taken 'Acorn Antiques' a step further. The BBC had recently shown a documentary about the making of *EastEnders*, so she plagiarised it superbly. Maggie Steed portrayed the scary executive producer Marion Clune, and was a direct parody of *EastEnders*' intimidating Julia Smith as she debated the future of the flagging show. Once again, Victoria cut right to the heart of the programme and effortlessly captured the lack of chemistry between the actors, the inaccessible cliques, the bitching, the prima donnas and the egos.

In 1988, with a baby on the way, the only tasks Julie undertook were two brief stints with Victoria. The first was an appearance in Comic Relief in February. The charity had been launched from the Safawa refugee camp in Sudan on Christmas Day 1985, as a response to the famine in Ethiopia, akin to the pop phenomenon Band Aid earlier in that year, and has been an annual event ever since.

The difference with Comic Relief is that it is more diverse in its focus. Two-thirds of all money raised is spent in Africa on projects dealing with HIV and AIDS, children forced to become soldiers of war, loans to people in city slums, and loans for women to start their own small businesses, while the remaining money is spent in the UK helping teenagers living with HIV and AIDS, victims of domestic abuse, elderly people living below the poverty line and children forced into prostitution.

February 1988 witnessed the first studio-based Comic Relief Red Nose Day, and Julie and Victoria performed a short Margery and Joan sketch (from the first series of *Victoria Wood As Seen On TV*), in which they helpfully demonstrated how to turn a leather jacket into a bookmark. The overall event raised more than £13 million, and both the actress and comedienne would become more involved as the years passed.

Julie's other appearance took place in August, after the birth of her daughter, when she attended Victoria's *An Audience With* night and was

Above At Holly Lodge Grammar School for Girls in Smethwick Julie quickly became known as an exuberant character

Right In the summer of 1962 Julie and other first years were cast in the school play *A Midsummer Night's Dream*

Below During her time at the Everyman, Julie appeared in *The Pig and the Junkle* – as the polite elephant who always forgets but who likes a song and a dance

Julie Walters has been lucky to have parts written specifically for her by a number of writers, including Alan Bennett (*right*) and Alan Bleasdale (*below*)

Above right Julie Walters's breakthrough was a play that was transferred to the big screen: *Educating Rita*. She starred opposite Michael Caine, who gave her a camera to record her memories

Below right Stars together at the premiere for *Educating Rita*: Sean Connery and Jackie Collins join Julie and Michael Caine to celebrate

Above Julie Walters is best known in the UK for her work with comedienne Victoria Wood, including *Wood & Walters*, *Pat and Margaret* and *dinnerladies*

Right As Christine Painter, Julie appeared in *Personal Services*, a programme inspired by the story of brothel madam Cynthia Payne

Top In another Hollywood film, *Buster*, Julie appeared with singer Phil Collins in the story of Great Train Robber Buster Edwards. During filming Julie was pregnant with her daughter Maisie

Above While appearing on film and television, Julie still continued to show her talent on the stage – here in *The Rose Tattoo*

Right *Wide-Eyed and Legless*, in which Julie appeared as Diana Longden, was one of her most challenging roles. The piece was renamed *The Wedding Gift* for its release in the USA

Above The epitome of 1950s motherhood in a very black comedy – Julie Walters as Marjorie Beasley in *Intimate Relations* with Matthew Walker and Laura Sadler

Below Brenda Blethyn and Julie Walters enjoy a *Girl's Night* in Las Vegas

Left In another stage play to become a film, Julie appeared in *Before You Go* as the eldest of three sisters bonding at their mother's funeral, with Joanne Whalley and Victoria Hamilton

Below For *Billy Elliot* Julie received her second Academy Award nomination, having appeared alongside newcomer Jamie Bell

Right A cause close to Julie's heart: *Calendar Girls* tells the story of Angela Baker (*right*) and Tricia Stewart (*left*), members of the Rylstone WI who put together a calendar to raise money for leukaemia and lymphoma research. Helen Mirren (*second left*) and Julie are just two of the famous cast members who appear

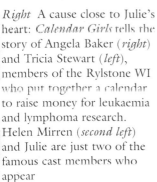

Left Julie met her husband-to-be Grant Roffey in a Fulham bar in 1984 and knew then that he was the man with whom she wanted to have children. They finally married on 2 July 1997

Right Julie Walters has become well known to a whole new generation of fans as Mrs Weasley in the *Harry Potter* films – a role she was persuaded to take by her daughter Maisie. She arrived at the London premiere for *Harry Potter and the Chamber of Secrets* with her family planted in said audience with a comment. This staging of 'spontaneous' questions is often awkward, but Victoria was on fine form and made fun of her interviewees. 'It was very nerve-racking because I could see their faces all lit up, with the cameras on *them*. Thank God they put Julie in the front row, so I could see a friendly face,' recalls Victoria, who promptly introduced her friend as 'the star of *Educating Rita* and Typhoo One Cup – and she only got that because Meryl Streep turned it down!'

Victoria performed the whole hour and a half without a single break, particularly amazing given that she herself was six months pregnant. She had managed to keep this news a secret, helped by the fact that she had actually lost weight through her own morning sickness. After the show she confided in a few friends, including Julie, Dawn French and Jennifer Saunders. Perhaps for the first time in years, she and Julie had something in common other than their shared history.

17. BAMBINO MIO

For the rest of 1988, Julie concentrated on her progressing pregnancy and she began to suffer from a few common complaints. She felt that her breasts, which had undoubtedly enlarged during the fittings for *Buster*, had now increased to 'mammoth proportions – men stare at them in the street, they sway in a matronly way and cause looks of awe and lust'.

When she finally stopped being sick wherever she went, frequently in the back of black cabs, much to the drivers' disgust, she suffered flatulence and incontinence. Or as straight-talking Julie would say, 'wind and peeing myself'.

In February, a routine appointment showed that Julie's baby was positioned upside down. 'I thought it was extremely sensible of her to want to come out feet first, but he said it would mean a Caesarean,' she wrote in her diary.

'He then tried to move her himself. Without going into too much detail, it made me feel like a bizarre glove puppet!'

Maisie refused to move, so a Caesarean was required. Furthermore, the baby didn't kick and Julie became quite concerned because her friends had complained about how much their children wriggled. However, this was normal for a breech baby. More worrying was the fact that her weight soared suddenly and she began to suffer from high blood pressure and gestational diabetes.

Julie, a staunch believer in the NHS, made the difficult decision to go private. Although the actress disapproved of Margaret Thatcher's policies on privatisation, she didn't want a repeat performance of the uninvited-guests debacle of 1983. She was registered at London's exclusive, and expensive, Portland Hospital.

In April her glucose test came back abnormal and her blood pressure was dangerously high. She was immediately admitted to the Portland with strict instructions to relax.

This was easier said than done, as the staff were always tickled to have a famous actress in their ward. Julie, who was usually recognised but, more often than not, mistaken for Tracey Ullman, was perturbed by one particular orderly. She preserved the incident in her diary:

A man in a green gown, wearing a J-cloth on his head, came in to take blood. He said he was very excited at meeting me. I was flattered until he responded to a little joke I made with, 'Oh, Tracey, you are funny.' I, of course, put him straight, much to his embarrassment. 'Oh yes,' he said. 'You work with that other girl. Marvellous!'

The 'other girl' – that is, Victoria Wood – came to visit me this afternoon, during which time the young leech returned for more blood. On seeing us both, he said 'Oh, I've got you both here!' and went out humming the theme tune to French and Saunders.

Interfering nurses and medical complications aside, Julie's Caesarean was scheduled for 26 April. She spent the evening prior to Maisie's birth talking to her and preparing her for the upcoming upheaval. By pure coincidence, Julie's waters broke that night.

'I was thrilled,' said Julie. 'I felt that Maisie and I really *had* had a chat in the bath and that we were in tune with one another and had synchronised our watches for the forthcoming event.'

Grant arrived at the hospital at 6.30 a.m. and half an hour later they were taken down to the anteroom where Julie was fitted with a drip and an epidural. At 8 a.m. they were taken into theatre and the operation began. The obstetrician accompanied the procedure with a running commentary:

'Here she comes, here she comes, here's her bottom. Oh, she looks just like her mother, she's as bald as a coot!'

Maisie Roffey entered the world upside down, healthy and weighing exactly six pounds. 'Grant and I just sat there while they got her out,' Julie told *Woman's Own*. 'It was extraordinary, like watching someone else give birth, not me. We just looked as they got out this little person and I wondered, "Who is *that*?" They brought her over to me and my first thought was, "Gee, she doesn't look like anyone I know."'

The baby was given straight to Julie, wrapped in a J-cloth, and the proud parents felt an instant bond with their daughter. 'She was looking at us all the time as though she recognised our voices. When other people talked she didn't look at them, just at us when we talked,' the new mum told reporters.

Julie recalled catching the love in her partner's eyes, and an emotional about-turn. 'Someone once said to me that a baby was the best present a man could ever give you. And at that time I'd said, "Puh-leaze, that's the last thing I want." But it's absolutely right. So I looked at Grant and I just said, "Thanks."

'What followed is a wonderful hazy blur, dominated by a single image – a tiny, perfect face with a cupid's bow for a mouth and a smattering of spun gold for hair. We thought her entirely beautiful.'

Just under a week later, on 2 May, Grant took Julie and Maisie home. 'It was terribly emotional,' says Julie. 'I couldn't stop crying, looking at this tiny little thing, with a teeny little face in a little hat. And then the first night at home, I thought, How am I ever going to be responsible for another human being? I spent hours in the middle of the night just wondering how I'd cope. And I kept checking to see if she was still breathing.'

This is, of course, a perfectly normal reaction for first-time mothers, and Julie received great support from her partner. 'Because I've got Grant I don't need a nanny,' boasted Julie in her first interview just a week later. 'Anyway, we couldn't have a good row, walk around the house with no clothes on or anything like that with a nanny on the premises. As for my career, well I'm planning time off to enjoy Maisie. Babies should have both their parents around, and Grant, being a student, can be at home with her a lot. In September, when the film *Buster* with Phil Collins is released, I'll be doing some publicity work, but that's all.' Julie was adamant that she would give her daughter all the love she never felt from her own parents.

Grant was in his element. He had always been the domestic half of the couple, and now looked after and cared for his little family. The only thing he couldn't help with was breastfeeding. 'I didn't know what I was letting myself in for when the milk came,' Julie said later in the *Sun*. 'Ouch! Suddenly I'm like Dolly Parton. It's all right when I'm lying down, but when I stand up they stick out like buzz bombs.

'It was so painful at first that I burst into tears. It hurts so much and nobody ever tells you about that before you have a baby. I look at Maisie sometimes and say to her, "It's a good job I love you." But it's lovely because it makes her so contented. Her little face afterwards is a picture.'

Julie was pleased to tell Mary, her own mother, of Maisie's safe arrival. Mindful of Julie's age and having had difficult experiences herself, Mary had been particularly concerned and was consequently very emotional on hearing the good news.

Julie, who had never previously felt maternal, was surprised by her own emotions. 'I'm a late developer, really,' she told the *Sun*. 'I never felt ready for motherhood until I met Grant. My career meant everything. Now I'm rather overwhelmed by the birth experience.'

She remembered being amazed during the casting for *When I Was a Girl I Used To Scream and Shout*, when the director had insisted that Geraldine James's character was a parent in real life. 'I thought any actress worth her salt could act motherhood,' said Julie, who fairly pointed out that you didn't have to be a drunk to play one. 'But now I realise that something psychological happens when you have a baby.

You acquire a sort of depth. For me it's been such an ultimate production that it's knocked my acting perspective. It adds another emotional dimension.'

Whereas she had once felt that other people's offspring were a nuisance, suddenly her compassion extended beyond her own child and she found herself looking forward to seeing all children.

'As soon as I gave birth, it was as if something happened,' she explained to the *Guardian*. 'It was not that I didn't like them. You understand them, they become people, not kids. You start to identify with them ... It's extraordinary. You can't watch anything to do with kids being harmed.' This she took to an extreme: 'I couldn't watch *Tom and Jerry*. The cruelty was too much. I had all these strange images, of tiny animals, all mixed up. All sorts of things touch you, that wouldn't normally.'

Through May and June, Julie and Grant were besotted with their daughter and let the world pass them by, until they received an official letter requesting them to register her birth within 48 hours. So, on 3 June 1988, the happy trio walked down to Fulham Town Hall to fill out the forms.

'All I do is dote on my baby,' confessed Julie later that month. 'Life isn't so selfish any more. It isn't just about me, and pleasure, and work any more. Now, with Maisie, it seems totally the opposite: everything I do is for somebody else.

'If Maisie wants to be an actress too, one day, well, that's fine. I hope Maisie will be strong enough to do whatever she wants. I hope she will inherit her father's looks and my sense of humour. I think enjoying a good laugh is vital. But it doesn't bother me whether she has talent or not. I just want her to be a happy person and one day to find a nice man, just like I did.'

These meaningful outpourings were quite a change from someone who used to run away from commitment and any dependence on men.

Julie may have altered her perspective on family life, but she remained the level-headed woman she had always been. Despite pressure on all celebrities to look slim and glamorous, she was remarkably comfortable with her post-baby figure. 'I love the fact that my body has changed. I am not worried about counting calories,' she said confidently.

At five foot three and a half, with impish features, Julie was the first to admit that she was not usually picked for languid, sex-goddess roles. 'If you're an actor, then vanity is incredibly boring and it holds you back so much,' she said in the *Sunday Mirror*. 'If you were really worried about the way you looked then there'd be a whole range of parts you'd be unable to play.' Julie felt that beautiful characters were usually two-dimensional, whereas the uglier characters – those who allowed their wicked ways to be seen – were the meatier, more interesting roles. 'It's that dark side that makes characters interesting to play.'

For someone unconcerned with outward appearances, Julie was fortunate in that she could eat what she liked and rarely put on weight. 'I don't exercise either,' she admitted. 'I haven't done any for fifteen years. I felt so guilty about it that I went out and bought an exercise bike recently. But I doubt if I will ever use it!' In an interview years later in 2002 she disclosed that, as with thousands of other people with good intentions, the bike had indeed become little more than a clothes horse.

'We haven't felt we needed a nanny yet because Grant does everything for me,' said Julie that summer. They had a weekly cleaner, an Italian Catholic woman, Benita, who spoke very little English, but Julie was aware that their needs might change when she returned to work.

Come the autumn, however, matters were different as Julie returned to her professional life. She started off with the promotion for *Buster*, before moving on to a new film. *Buster* received a royal premiere at the Leicester Square Odeon on 15 September 1988 in aid of the Prince's Trust. The soundtrack album garnered Phil Collins several hit singles and an Oscar nomination for 'Two Hearts', and both their performances were praised.

Julie undertook some of the publicity, but Phil shouldered the lion's share, travelling to America, Europe and Australia. Still, as she was back on the road, assistance was required at home. 'I was lucky,' says Julie. 'My first nanny started when Maisie was five months [old] and she wasn't a nymphomaniac and wasn't passionate about drink and, most importantly, Maisie adored her.'

During this time, Julie told her mother how wonderful Maisie was.

'Yes, but you're not with her twenty-four hours a day, seven days a week,' came the reply.

That put Julie in her place. She confided to her diary:

Now that Maisie is well and truly here, my relationship with my mother seems to have changed, simply because I have some idea of what being a mother entails. When I think of how much those early weeks took out of me – I never knew what real tiredness was before – and compare it with what my mother must have experienced having my two brothers during the war, with no washing-machine, no disposable nappies, no help and little money, it's heartbreaking.

These memories humbled Julie and she was eternally grateful for the luxury of support not only from her husband, but also the nanny.

With the house and family under control, the actress chose to ease herself back into work by playing one of her favourite stereotypes: an ageing, desperate, drunken tart. The feature film, *Killing Dad (Or How To Love Your Mother)*, was written and directed by Michael Austin and is best described as a surreal black comedy. Most characters are distinctly awry, the plot is just sinister. Alistair, a failed hair-tonic salesman, is a mummy's boy who lives at home. His father, Monty, left them 27 years earlier, but his mother, Edith, still holds a torch for him. Monty writes out of the blue one day asking for forgiveness and hoping to return. Alistair tells his mother no, three's a crowd.

From the beginning it is clear that Alistair has an unhealthy relationship with his mother, but he reluctantly agrees to go to Southend to bring his father back to the fold. En route he resolves to kill him instead.

First, we meet Monty's current girlfriend, Judith, played by Julie. She's a permanently pissed, bleached-blonde floozy looking for a good time. Always arguing with Monty, she throws herself at Alistair, thrusting her cleavage in his face, staring at his groin and dropping innuendoes in every sentence. She has a simple outlook on life and only wants to be loved and have a man to look after.

Monty however, a former ventriloquist, is a vomiting drunk. During the course of the film, two animals are killed, but Alistair's attempts to dispose of his father are less successful. Monty is determined to reconcile with Edith so that he can live out his days in comfort, which only angers his son further. The Spanish maid points out the obvious Oedipus complex, but Alistair puts that down to the fact that she's a foreigner.

After a farcical chase involving Monty's stolen dummy, Monty goes missing and Alistair finds himself firmly in the clutches of Judith. Reluctantly, he takes her home to meet his mother, where the shock of seeing his parents in bed together forces him to follow the Spanish maid to exotic Broadstairs, Kent.

The main characters were extremely well cast. The then rising star Richard E Grant plays the geeky, disturbed son; the much-loved character actor, Denholm Elliott, portrays the rumpled father; but it is Julie who steals the show as his glitzy, middle-aged seaside belle. She is a breath of fresh air in an otherwise bizarre and surprisingly drab piece.

Julie felt compassion for the 'tart with a heart' and, as Judith was permanently pissed, the actress went to great lengths to study people's actions when drunk. 'Acting drunk's good fun, but it's very hard to do,' she explained. 'I love the way drunk people behave as if everything's normal even though they can't focus. They're always one step behind, physically.'

Everyone was thrilled with her performance. The producer, Iain Smith, said at the time, 'Julie's ability to bring her personality to a part makes her a pleasure to work with.' However, her usual on-set tomfoolery sometimes got out of hand when she was playing such an outrageous part, opposite Richard, with whom she was great friends.

'We just laughed all the time,' she admits. 'We couldn't do some of the scenes for laughing.' The director, Michael Austin, would try and restore the calm saying that, if they didn't stop laughing he wouldn't be able to do a close-up. Quite often it was to no avail and he would have to push on to film the next scene.

Overall, the film was a little slow in parts, but worth the trip (if only to see Richard E Grant looking so young and gormless), and it received reasonable reviews upon its release in 1989. Julie, not normally interested in her looks, retained a legacy from the role for a while: instead of wearing a blonde wig, she jumped in feet first with a bottle of hair dye. 'Every girl should be blonde once in her life. I love it,' raved Julie, convinced she was attracting more attention than she had as a brunette.

'The first night I came home, Grant could not believe it. He said that it was fantastic, and that it was like going to bed with another woman!' Of course the neighbours were a little confused, some possibly thinking Grant was having an affair with a mystery woman.

18. WE TURNED EACH OTHER'S LIFE UPSIDE DOWN

Julie enjoyed a very special first Christmas with her new family at the end of 1988 and was thrilled to be successfully juggling her home life with a career. She had realised some of the trials her mother had faced, and felt much closer to her. Tragically, Julie was never able to voice this connection.

After the children left home and Thomas died, Mary moved out of the family abode in Bishopton Road into 37 Hickory Drive. Aged 74, she was in reasonable health and the small cul-de-sac in Bearwood was near to Kevin and his wife, Gillian, in case she needed anything. Kevin had trained as a physiotherapist and, after a while with Birmingham City and Wolverhampton Wanderers Football Clubs, taught physiotherapy. He was on hand when his mother was taken seriously ill.

Mary was admitted to Dudley Road Hospital, where she slipped into a coma. Shortly afterwards, she suffered a stroke which affected the life-support areas of the brain. This in turn triggered low blood pressure and a heart attack. She died on 13 April 1989.

Julie was devastated.

'My mother died before I had the chance to tell her that, "Now I Understand",' she wrote in her diary.

There were so many things Julie wanted to say. 'It wasn't until after her death that I appreciated just how close we were,' she says. 'She and I were quite alike and that meant that sometimes we couldn't get on and it could be pretty volatile.' As Julie's perspective changed when she had Maisie, she learnt a lot about being a mother and the intricate relationships mothers have with their daughters. She also realised that although Mary hadn't been demonstrative, she had still loved Julie.

Julie's pain only increased when she visited her mother's house to sort through her belongings with her siblings. In the process she found a box containing every newspaper article she'd ever appeared in. 'She pushed and pushed her children to do well and never actually said she was proud of me – God bless her, she'd really been proud of me all those years.'

Her discovery opened a floodgate of new emotions, which she would never be able to resolve with her mother. 'I think I've managed to process my feelings about her death but still, not a day goes by without my thinking, Oh God, I wish she was still here. I do miss her very much,' said Julie a decade later.

The tragedy forced Julie to think about her own mortality, particularly now that she had a dependant. 'When you lose both your parents, it does make you think about the fact that life is not for ever,' she remarked. Seeing the difference between her grandmother's slow and confusing demise and her parents' relatively quick passing, Julie concluded that she would rather die while she was still reasonably healthy, rather than hanging on as an infirm old lady. She particularly didn't want to be kept alive artificially and hated the fact that, while in a coma, Mary could hear her surroundings but could not communicate.

'I couldn't bear that, but I'm not worrying about it just yet. I'm still looking forward to a full life before I croak.'

Julie had to concentrate on the future, and, shortly after Maisie's first birthday, the family went through some major changes to their lifestyle.

Clearly Julie was the main breadwinner and would continue to keep the family in the style to which they were accustomed, but Grant was beginning to crave something more to life than his studies. Together, they hatched a plan that seemed to suit, with advantages all round.

The trio moved out of the smog of London, to a rambling farmhouse near Billingshurst, West Sussex. 'It's great not hearing traffic all the time or pneumatic drills,' commented Julie when they first moved. In fact, the property was perfectly placed, equidistant from London in the north and the coast to the south.

It was originally a fruit farm, but Grant gave the place an overhaul and transformed the seventy acres into a thriving organic farm. 'I'm surrounded by animals at our wonderful home,' said Julie in the summer of 1989. 'It's an old farm with sheep, pigs, chickens, cats and a dog.' She jokes that they even had some Vietnamese pot-bellied pigs who wouldn't eat, despite the tempting Chinese takeaway delights she offered them. 'Grant does most of the work, but I put the chickens out sometimes,' she adds. In fact, Julie became quite an expert at whizzing around the land on a squat quad bike, carrying food and hay out to the pigs and sheep.

'Grant and I certainly turned each other's lives upside down,' she elaborated to the *Sunday Mirror*. 'Within three years of meeting we had a child, moved to the country and were dealing with all that role-reversal stuff.' She admitted that it wasn't always plain sailing but was confident that their goal was the same.

Julie loved the fact that, as macho as Grant was, he wasn't afraid to be a househusband and homemaker. As all children copy their carers, so

Maisie began to toddle around the house with a dust cloth in her hand, aged just sixteen months. 'She takes after her father thankfully,' laughs Julie.

Although she had returned to work, Julie was mindful not to over-commit herself, because she couldn't bear to be apart from her daughter. To that end, and in her usual style of maintaining her image in all genres, in 1989 she appeared in a dark film, a light television comedy and a stage play.

The movie was *Mack the Knife*, an adaptation of Kurt Weill and Bertolt Brecht's musical play, *The Threepenny Opera*. The ambitious project was undertaken by the leading Israeli filmmaker, Menahem Golan. He had collaborated with his cousin, Yoram Globus, since the early 1960s to produce more than 150 movies. Nineteen eighty-nine was a monumental year, as the pair parted company: Globus became the head of Pathé International, while Golan took over the 21st Century Film Corporation.

Mack the Knife stars Raul Julia, Julia Migenes, Roger Daltrey, Richard Harris and Julie Walters, and is based on Joseph Papp's 1976 stage revival. The musical tells the tale of a motley group of beggars, thieves, killers and informants who, through their violent interactions and witty songs, provide an insight into the Victorian London underworld. Raul Julia plays MacHeath, the king of gangsters, who is engaged to an innocent young girl, Polly Peachum (Rachel Robertson). The eminent actor Richard Harris, who died in October 2002, teams up with Julie as Polly's parents and together they attempt to thwart the marriage by catching the thief in the act.

Unfortunately the film remained just a remake of a dark tale, unusual only in its musical leanings, and slipped out on video unnoticed by many.

Next, Julie appeared on stage with Brian Cox in *Frankie and Johnny in the Clair de Lune*. Scottish actor Cox had recently achieved fame as Hannibal Lecter in Michael Mann's 1986 film *Manhunter*, and proved Julie's perfect converse. Written by Terrence McNally, the play marked the writer's breakthrough in 1987 and was later adapted for the big screen, starring Al Pacino and Michelle Pfeiffer as Johnny and Frankie. Directed by Paul Benedict, this version was performed at the Comedy Theatre in London.

The two-hander is rich with emotion. Frankie, a waitress, and Johnny, a cook, work together in a restaurant. Throughout the two-act play, the star-crossed lovers are faced with trying to salvage something that ought to last, and not self-destruct.

The lighter side of Julie's work was fulfilled by a reunion with Victoria for a new series, known simply as *Victoria Wood*. The comedienne was bored by the routine sketch-show format, but had been unable to recapture the wit and charm of her plays a decade earlier. As a compromise, she presented the BBC with six individual half-hour playlets. This new system was designed to sustain characters and material without her being judged as a serious dramatist.

The unusual episode titles were 'Mens Sana In Thingummy Doodah', 'The Library', 'Over To Pam', 'We'd Quite Like To Apologise', 'Val De Ree (Ha Ha Ha Ha Ha)' and 'Staying In', but the subject matter was predictable enough: the diet industry, daytime television, bad customer service, country living and plain rudeness. Victoria was nervous about returning to the screen in this capacity, having opted out of appearing in *Happy Since I Met You*, and chose to ease gently back into it by playing herself: Victoria Wood – comedienne and television celebrity. Somewhat confusingly, Celia Imrie, Lill Roughley, Julie Walters and others from her repertory donned a variety of guises.

Julie appeared in only two of the episodes, 'Over To Pam' and 'We'd Quite Like To Apologise'. In the first half-hour scenario, Victoria takes her friend Lorraine on a behind-the-scenes tour of the television studios, highlighting the recognisable stereotypes within the industry. The climax of the visit is meeting Pam, an egocentric star of daytime drivel, superbly played by Julie.

Victoria takes Lorraine's place in the interview, posing as a dense northern tart who has led an extraordinary life; Pam laps up the sordid tale of endless babies left in skips, sexual abuse, and drink and drug addictions. The salacious interviewer gets her comeuppance when Victoria reveals her true identity, demonstrating on live television that Pam is 'the most patronising old cow to hit the airwaves since Mrs Bridges caught Ruby with her corsets on back to front'. A borderline hyperglycaemic, Pam collapses and her career is over.

The other playlet, 'We'd Quite Like To Apologise', was less personal to Wood's profession and vastly more accessible: Victoria, caught up in a package holiday nightmare. Again stereotyping the worst travellers imaginable, the banal banter between strangers is cringe-makingly accurate. Victoria is adopted by a lovey-dovey couple (Jane Horrocks and Richard Hope), moaned to by the graphic hypochondriac (Una Stubbs) and the miserable housewife (Lill Roughley), and taken under the wing of a serial slut (Julie Walters). While the other characters can feel boring and glum, Julie sparkles as the professional man-eater.

Although the material of the series was essentially funny, the format seemed to lack a crucial something. This awkwardness was exacerbated by the awful canned laughter, crudely indicating what was supposed to be funny, and Victoria's stilted aside confessions to the camera, as if in stand-up.

The programmes were aired from 16 November to 21 December 1989 and, although the ratings began well, interest soon waned. The reviews were less than favourable and the *Daily Express* branded the show as 'tiresome stuff'. Again, Victoria was forced to admit that she hadn't quite hit the mark. 'It wasn't as well written by me as it could have been,' she says, 'and I shouldn't have been in all of the sketches.'

After her little burst of work, Julie took a break at the beginning of 1990 to be at home with Grant and Maisie. It was particularly important for her to surround herself with friends and family as sadly, in January, her great friend and colleague, Ian Charleson, died of AIDS at the age of forty. He was deeply missed in the acting world and, the following year, the annual Ian Charleson Awards were first presented 'for outstanding performances anywhere in the UK by actors under the age of thirty in a classical role'.

Reeling a little from the news, Julie realised that, since Maisie's birth, she had been wrapped up in her own little world. Now, with time on her hands, she made a point of visiting her nearest and dearest. 'Some old friends have been frightened to keep in touch,' she sighed. 'It upsets me when people from the past think I might be grand now.' Far from airs and graces, Julie lived a normal life in a run-down cottage.

'Our place always looks as if a bomb has hit it,' she said. 'Drivers come to pick me up for films and you see them drive past, obviously thinking, No, it can't be that house.' The outside appears completely neglected; it's overgrown, untidy, the windows haven't been cleaned for years, the back garden is full of junk and the garage is old and crumbling.

The friends that Julie referred to are those whom she met during her early days as an actress, or even before. During a piece of work, they would find out that she was a wonderfully warm human being and bond, but when they went their separate ways Julie would suddenly become Julie Walters: star of Hollywood films, award-winning plays and television work. That was when each relationship would drift apart.

The circle with which Julie maintained contact were the group who continued to work with her and were in constant contact with the real Julie, not the image. 'People recognise that she's one of us and always will be,' comments Alan Bleasdale of Julie's audience appeal. 'She's not going to have a grand manner – or a grand manor – and we love her because of that.' It's a shame that more of her one-time acquaintances didn't feel the same way.

Still, Julie was surrounded by a kernel of companions, including the two Alans – Bleasdale and Bennett – Willy Russell, many of her original Liverpool crowd, Ros March, Victoria Wood, and her siblings. Along with Richard E Grant and his wife Joan, Julie and Grant also socialised with Phil Collins, who was now a relative neighbour of Julie's, living in Shalford, Surrey.

'I have some lovely friends. I don't think any one of them has ever let me down badly,' she said at the time. 'I appreciate them and, if they ever need me, I'll always try to be there. I hope I'm a good friend.'

Julie says she is more comfortable with the fairer sex. That is not to say that she doesn't get on with men, and indeed she has some very close male friends, but that she understands and relates better with women. 'Grant admits that he has much more fun with women, too,' she adds. 'He can talk to women more easily than he can talk to men.' This was fortunate, because, in time, Grant would be the one to attend mother-and-toddler groups.

Julie, once a reliable party animal, had even changed her views on alcohol with motherhood. 'I never thought I'd hear myself saying this, but I very rarely drink these days,' she said, 'because I never want to put myself in a situation where I might not behave responsibly towards my daughter Maisie.' She explained that she had lost the desire for alcohol, not through a change in her taste buds but because she didn't want to be out of control in case Maisie needed her. She doesn't bother with drink other than indulging in a glass or two of wine when her family visits.

David Ross had known Julie for many years and witnessed the effect having a child had on her. 'When I first knew her, she was a great socialiser,' he says, 'a drinker, a smoker and always out late. But, once Maisie was born, things changed in her social habits. She drank very little and ate very sensibly. She was certainly a very wild woman and has transformed into a very sensible woman.' Now, Julie and Maisie enjoyed getting together with Victoria Wood, who had had her daughter, Grace, on 1 October 1988.

And so 1990 saw the extension of Julie's domestic bliss into her career. She took the diary she had been writing throughout her pregnancy and turned it into a book called *Baby Talk*, printed by Guild Publishing. Julie's account of all the woes that torment an expectant mother is an entertaining read, as well as a small insight into her world. Unusually, the text is humorously illustrated by Maurice Dodd, which adds a very personal touch to some of the hilarious stories, recounting her numerous anecdotes.

19. THE ESCAPE OF BEING SOMEONE ELSE

After a quiet first half of 1990, Julie started work on an exciting new project. She was reunited with Lewis Gilbert, the man who put her face on the big screen with *Educating Rita*, and joined a dazzling cast including Liza Minnelli, daughter of the legendary Judy Garland, and the fabulous Oscar-winning Shelley Winters.

This was Gilbert's third go at adapting a popular play into a film. This time it was the musical, *Stepping Out*. The premise was textbook cliché with a side serving of feel-good factor: Liza Minnelli, a Broadway wannabe, runs a dance class in a church hall attended by a motley group of no-hopers with two left feet. Each dancer has his or her individual foible: Julie is a tactless upper-class Brit; Bill Irwin, the only man, is neat and shy and doesn't like to be noticed; Sheila McCarthy is the plain Jane with a crush on Bill; Andrea Martin is a caring librarian with hayfever; Carol Woods is a mother escaping her household chores; Shelley Winters is the pessimistic pianist and busybody. It's like a group-therapy session in tap-dancing.

Liza Minnelli's character has to teach the class to dance for a charity fundraiser organised by a snooty socialite and, rather predictably, they overcome their problems to produce a performance with only a few hiccups. Fast-forward to the following year, when they return by popular demand as a well-oiled dance machine.

Stepping Out is as cringe-making as it sounds and, worse still, it is overly indulgent of the star, Liza Minnelli. The storyline outside the dance class is slow and boring, simply because the viewer has no sympathy for the characters, and the lame romance occurs between the dullest pair possible. Yet, thanks to a few solid performances from Liza, the cantankerous Shelley Winters and some of the oddball chorus line – particularly the superbly brittle Julie – *Stepping Out* proves passable, if a little dated.

From the start, Julie Walters is a hoot. She is Vera, whose first plummy utterance elicits Robyn Stevan as Sylvia to say, 'Oh my God, it's Princess Di.' Given Julie's upbringing at St Paul's, it must have amused them that she had to pronounce 'because' as 'becawse'. Sporting a fantastic array of stretchy, sparkly catsuits, Vera is topped off with a Margaret Thatcher blonde 'do' and an ever-present string of pearls.

It was her character's sharp exterior that appealed most. 'Vera is a pain in the bottom, basically,' says Julie. 'She's completely and utterly insensitive, constantly putting her foot in it and leaving trails of devastated people behind her, never knowing she's done anything wrong.' Vera is also impossibly hygienic and ever critical. As Liza says in the film, she's 'got the sensitivity of linoleum'.

Although always one who enjoyed singing, Julie found the prospect of dancing, her first time since *Family Man*, a challenge. She appears competent – perhaps not the natural dancer of Liza's ability, but certainly proficient for such a show with some complex routines. What is hard to miss, given her Lycra outfits, is that she is extremely trim, particularly for a forty-year-old with a toddler. Although she is just one of a team, her performance is sterling and stands out from the crowd – it garnered her a BAFTA award nomination and Variety Club award for Best Supporting Actress.

The film was released in 1991 to poor reviews, not least because it is very cheesy and there are too many disparate characters for the audience to get truly involved; the audience is left nonchalant. Still, *Stepping Out* succeeded in showcasing Liza's abilities as both a singer and dancer, and her concert series based around the show broke box office records, spawning performances at London's Royal Albert Hall.

Although *Stepping Out* is set in New York, filming took place in Canada and the cast relocated over the summer of 1990. Julie couldn't bear to be apart from Grant and Maisie, so the family moved as a unit.

Through the excitement of moving, Julie and Grant couldn't help but notice that Maisie wasn't her usual bubbly self. At two and a half, she was a regular mischievous toddler, but, since their arrival in Canada, she had seemed off colour. 'Maisie had just banged her head on a swing,' says Julie, 'so she was X-rayed at a local hospital but they couldn't find anything wrong.'

Then she began to feel very tired and became unsociable and miserable. There was nothing specific that her parents could identify, so they put her change down to a combination of jet lag, homesickness and the recent bump. 'We were reading Penelope Leach [child psychologist and best-selling author] to see what it could be,' Julie continues, 'although I said to Grant that, if it was an emotional problem, it had to be a really big one.'

Julie was tied up with rehearsals, so, when Maisie failed to improve, Grant took her to a paediatrician. On seeing the listless child, the doctor ordered a blood test. Grant assumed this was routine but when he got home he received a phone call from the surgery. He was told to take Maisie to hospital immediately. It was an emergency: her white blood cell count was dangerously high. Grant did not have time to phone

Julie, so, when she arrived home after a hard day's work, she was concerned that they weren't there. Instead, she found Maisie's nanny, looking very pale. The nanny told her that Maisie had been taken to the hospital because she had a high white blood count.

'God – it makes you think of leukaemia,' replied Julie, 'but then you always think of the worst thing, don't you?'

Julie tried to remain calm as she rushed to the emergency room, where she found Maisie with a frightened Grant. 'Maisie looked absolutely terrible,' recalls Julie, 'completely waxy-faced, as if she needed a blood transfusion.'

Unfortunately, further tests confirmed the couple's worst fears – Maisie had acute lymphoblastic leukaemia.

'She has got leukaemia, and that is the very worst you're going to hear,' said the forthright consultant.

'From the start they were very straight with us,' says Julie. 'It's obviously a policy and it was very comforting.'

Still, it didn't hide the fact that their daughter had a potentially life-threatening disease.

'The doctor took me outside and said, "Leukaemia isn't what it used to be,"' recalls Julie. Of course, one of Julie's lasting memories from her days as a nurse was of the man who was given a death sentence when he was diagnosed with leukaemia. Although the doctor had told her that leukaemia wasn't as fatal nowadays, Julie could not shake the image from her mind and thought she had to prepare herself for the worst.

According to the charity, Children with Leukaemia, the disease is:

a cancer of the tissues which produce blood. In a leukaemic child, large numbers of abnormal white cells are produced, which are unable to carry out their normal function of fighting infection. In addition, these abnormal cells displace the normal production of red cells and platelets, which are vital in supplying oxygen and stopping bleeding respectively. If leukaemia is not effectively treated, the child will ultimately die.

Amazingly, there were some positives. 'The fact that Maisie is a girl, and for some reason girls do better than boys; that she's got the "best" type of leukaemia; and that we caught it early,' explained Julie at the time. Indeed, the most common type, and the easiest to treat, is acute lymphoblastic leukaemia, with a 70 per cent survival rate. Treatment involves a course of chemotherapy, which is a series of drugs and injections to destroy the abnormal blood cells. Some cases require a bone-marrow transplant, following chemotherapy. It is only three years after completing the course that a healthy patient is declared cured.

Patently, those rays of hope did nothing to deaden the pain. As Grant was Maisie's primary carer and only one parent could stay overnight, Julie had to leave them at the hospital and go home, alone. That cab ride, after she'd said goodbye to her seriously sick child, was the most painful moment of her life.

'I cried like I'd never known,' she remembers. 'It sounded like somebody else, as if it were outside me. It was like the Niagara Falls.' Filled with British reserve and politeness, Julie at first thought she couldn't cry in a cab but, on reflection of the situation, thought, 'My daughter's in hospital with leukaemia – what the hell do I care what this taxi driver thinks?'

The next few days passed in a blur. Grant and Julie tormented themselves by thinking there was something they could have done to help their daughter, by blaming themselves for not having noticed how ill she was earlier. 'It's hard not to feel guilty for having been impatient with a sick child,' says Julie. 'I'm convinced that Maisie was extremely relieved when people finally realised there was something wrong.' After her diagnosis, Maisie turned to Julie and said, 'Mummy, I've been very, very poorly,' part question and part reassurance.

Maisie's chemotherapy started straight away and it seemed like a miracle cure. 'As soon as she started treatment, out came this child we'd hardly seen,' marvels Julie. 'She was suddenly full of energy, laughing and joking, which made us realise just how ill she'd been.'

However, the phrase 'no pain, no gain' rang a little too true. Watching their daughter suffer the procedures was unbearable. 'In Canada they take bone-marrow samples without an anaesthetic,' she told *Chat*. 'They thought it was quicker and less traumatic that way. And she had six lumbar punctures without help, too. Six people would have to hold her down.'

Julie could hardly bear it. Maisie would be shouting for help at the top of her lungs but there was nothing she or Grant could do. They tried to calm her down saying that, while it was painful, it was making her better, but such reasoning was lost on one so young.

'There's one tablet she had to take which is obviously highly toxic. It used to make her feel really nauseous, but somehow she came to terms with it,' marvels Julie, particularly as many of the other children she saw in the hospital couldn't take it because it made them so sick. 'But not Maisie. She'd swallow the pill and hold it down. It used to break my heart.'

The true daughter of feisty Julie, little Maisie gave as good as she got. When one Canadian doctor was doing nose swabs, Maisie informed him, in her poshest voice, 'Doctor, I really don't think it would be a good plan to poke cotton wool up my nose!' The cheeky madam also once asked for a hammer – to quieten a baby who wouldn't stop crying.

While Maisie was being treated by the doctors, Grant took it upon himself to become an expert on the subject. 'He knows absolutely everything there is to know about leukaemia now from reading, reading, reading,' said Julie in 1991. 'Every time I came home from work, he'd be there reading *You And Leukaemia* in a corner.' Understanding as much as he could was his way of coping with the threat of the illness.

Of course, they couldn't ignore the reason they were in Canada in the first place – Julie's work. When she phoned Lewis Gilbert to tell him what had happened, he told her to forget about the film. It didn't matter, he said, compared with what they were going through. 'He was so lovely, and terribly upset, which touched me, too,' says Julie.

'Don't worry,' said Gilbert, 'any bills will be picked up by Paramount Studios. We're all behind you.'

He says he reacted as anyone would have and indeed, Julie received encouragement from all the cast. Liza Minnelli may have been the star of the show, but she couldn't do enough to help.

'She was very supportive and became terribly involved,' Julie told reporters. 'She had a lovely quilt made for Maisie, with little pockets in it all full of different toys.' Liza also realised that the worried parents wouldn't have any time to look after themselves and so took the time to send them food parcels. Furthermore, Liza made regular trips to the hospital herself, which is not that easy for someone so famous.

'She was fantastic and very, very sensitive,' says Julie. The actor Andrew Lancel worked with Julie four years later and recalls her saying that the whole cast of *Stepping Out* rallied round them: 'Julie was talking about Liza Minnelli and Shelley Winters, when Maisie was ill, and Shelley Winters, in a dramatic southern drawl, had said, "We're gonna pray for that child!"'

Of course, Julie and Grant were inundated with offers of assistance too from their closest friends and family. 'Ros March immediately said that she'd come over to Canada, although we told her not to. Alan Bleasdale asked us to stay with him when we got back to England,' says Julie. Willy Russell wrote a lovely long letter to the family offering his best wishes when he heard the news. 'That's the thing about friendship,' says the actress. 'Almost twenty years can go by and you don't feel like strangers.'

Victoria Wood also wrote Julie a supportive letter and called to check they were all right. 'There's nothing anyone else can do and often it's intrusive to be too sympathetic or make too many enquiries,' said Victoria, 'because that can drain what energy they have got that they need for dealing with the situation.'

Julie and Grant were overwhelmed by the encouragement they received. 'Although in the end Grant and I had to cope with it, everybody wanted to help. There was a great wave of warmth,' she says.

Conscientious about her commitments, Julie eventually returned to the film set and finished *Stepping Out*. 'I was terrified of going back,' she recalls. 'We'd been going between the hospital and home and I didn't want to go back to work in case all those intense emotions came out.' Julie managed to get through the first number, called 'Happy Feet', when she was back on set but straight afterwards all her pent-up emotions came flooding out.

As time went on, Julie settled into a gruelling routine: she'd rush to the hospital first thing in the morning, where the driver would get her a cappuccino while she sat with Maisie, then she would go to work and hurry back to the hospital for a goodnight kiss. 'Work became a fantastic diversion,' she says. 'It was something to escape to.'

Lewis Gilbert was in awe of the actress's resolute frame of mind under the circumstances. 'She is a true professional,' he says. 'Through all that terrible trauma she never gave less than her best on the film set.'

Coincidentally, Julie and Grant's next-door neighbours' son had also recently finished a course of cancer treatment. 'We'd only just been saying, "How do people cope with that?" and then we were in the thick of it ourselves,' says Julie. 'But we had these people who'd been through it and they were like counsellors to us.'

As soon as Julie finished filming *Stepping Out*, the trio returned to England and registered Maisie at London's Royal Marsden Hospital for the completion of her chemotherapy course.

The doctors were a little less brutal than they had been in Canada. 'Here they would first freeze her hand or give her a general anaesthetic for the lumbar puncture – which we preferred,' said Julie. However, the three of them were in for a long haul, as this was only the start of a two-year course. Julie and Grant took it in turns to sleep on a camp bed in the crowded unit whenever Maisie was admitted. After a few hiccups, they quickly fitted into the children's cancer ward 'family'.

During one of the first visits, someone said, 'You look like Julie W—'

The actress automatically denied it. 'I suddenly thought, I can't face being Julie Walters, because I was worried that a side of me was going to be needed that I couldn't give. Afterwards I felt really stupid.'

Instead, they learned that there is solidarity to be gained from other parents struggling through the same hell. 'We were virtually living at the hospital,' she relayed to *Woman's Own*. 'You get very close to the other families there, and want to know how their kids are doing ...

'A lot of nurses have told me that parents who lose children keep coming back to the ward to see everybody – and I can understand that. You're sort of all in it together.'

When a tabloid reporter sat in the waiting room at the Marsden, pretending to be a concerned mother of a patient, rather than become angry, Julie only had empathy for the woman. 'What a nasty job,' she said. 'Imagine having to do that on a children's cancer ward.'

As the treatment lasted for two years, the parents also got to know the doctors and nurses individually. Julie remains full of praise for the Marsden staff, for their care and attention – they even buy cartoon plasters for the children out of their own salaries, because such 'luxuries' are not part of the budget-conscious NHS stocks. Most importantly, they made Maisie feel at home and it got to the stage where she would instruct the doctors on the injections she should receive that day!

That Maisie was old enough to understand a little of what was happening, but young enough to be able to forget in time, made Julie feel that she was at a good age to deal with such a debilitating disease. Furthermore, Julie and Grant passed on the same honesty they received from the doctors telling Maisie that, although the medicine tasted nasty, it would be better to take it quickly, rather than trying to fool her into thinking it was alright.

'We always told Maisie to cry and scream – to let the pain out – because I think often that's what causes cancer, holding pain in. She's a very bright, positive child and she coped, bless her. Although she won't remember this, it'll be part of her make-up and give her strength.'

The reality of living with a longterm illness puts an incredible strain on a family, no matter what their background. Julie and Grant dealt with the trauma in different ways, but both coped admirably. She felt he was her rock, someone to lean on at all times. 'He is very protective towards Maisie and me,' she elaborates. 'When we were told she had leukaemia, it became the most natural thing in the world for him to say, "Don't worry, I'll take care of everything."'

Grant, however, simply felt that their 'emotions met in the middle'. While he read all there was to know about leukaemia and handled practical affairs, Julie helped him to deal with the expressive side. 'It's one of those things that could easily drive you apart, especially if you don't share your private feelings,' she says.

'We had a few cries together, but I think women find it simpler: all our conditioning is in our favour.' Grant found it hard at first to let his feelings out, but Julie suggested that he used some photos of Maisie to release the pain he was withholding. Arranging a selection of early pictures of his daughter on the bed did the trick and soon he too experienced the relief crying can provide.

No matter how careful they were to temper their emotions, both parents naturally had their ups and downs. Grant once turned to Julie and said, 'Oh, God, I'm just saturated in her illness,' and so Julie took over Maisie's care for a while. They supported each other and took it in turns to be strong.

They proved a powerful team, working together to fight the leukaemia. 'Basically, our salvation was that we were able to talk to each other and to look at the worst possible scenarios together,' said Julie. They promised each other that, no matter what happened, they would be there for Maisie to ensure she had the best life she could for as long as she was able. 'If you have come close to losing a child then there is a special dimension to the love you feel for them, obviously.'

A life-threatening situation such as Maisie's illness usually makes couples think about their own mortality and the future. Reporters half expected Grant and Julie to feel that this was an appropriate time to finally get married, but they were far too busy worrying to focus on such celebrations. Moreover, pulling through such an ordeal tested their strength enough; they were secure in their relationship and did not feel the need to legalise it.

'I know Grant is always there for me, just as I hope I am for him,' explained Julie in interviews. 'When your child is ill, it can drive couples apart because it brings with it massive strain and anxiety. But it actually brought Grant and me even closer together.'

While the pairing proved powerful, Julie was aware that it was in no small part due to her partner. 'There aren't many big-hearted men around like Grant,' she elaborated. 'He's looked after Maisie and me, and made our lives a joy. It is no coincidence that I didn't choose an obsessively career-minded man to have a child with.'

20. THE MERSEY MAFIA

The hospital bills piled up alongside the regular household outgoings. First of all, Grant and Julie let the nanny go, because it seemed pointless to employ someone when Grant was at home looking after Maisie during her recuperation. Then, at the beginning of 1991, Julie had no choice – they still needed to pay the mortgage.

She found it very hard. 'When she was ill, it was her daddy she called for, which was heartbreaking for me. But I've come to terms with it because that is the way things are.'

To make the transition a little more bearable, Julie chose a wonderful project with a host of familiar faces. *GBH* was Alan Bleasdale's first new screenplay for five years. The curiously titled piece was directed by Robert Young and broken down into seven chunks, to be aired by Channel 4 over June and July 1991. The complex tale of politics, ambition, secrets and violence was, as always with Bleasdale, written with a specific cast in mind.

'Most of the guys and gals on *GBH* had worked together on Alan's stuff before,' recalls Alan Igbon. 'We were called the Mersey Mafia. We knew each other, we knew our acting limitations, we knew each other's nuances and we could really pick up off each other. We knew how people reacted and responded and I think that's what made it a smooth run. And that's really what Alan had in mind.'

So Julie was reunited with Tom Georgeson, Alan Igbon, David Ross and Michael Angelis, and was introduced to Robert Lindsay and Lindsay Duncan, with whom she would work again. 'It was like Alan Bleasdale's own repertory company,' says Michael Angelis. '*GBH* was a similar cast, but it was a much bigger piece, so he broadened the spectrum a little bit.' One of those extra faces was the marvellous Michael Palin, playing the counterpart to Robert Lindsay.

Robert is the central character, Michael Murray, a popular and powerful Labour city council leader. 'I was his main confidant, Teddy,' says Alan Igbon. 'Wherever Murray went, Teddy was on his shoulder looking after him: bodyguard, minder, confidant, you name it, dogsbody.'

Bleasdale throws the viewer into confusion with Murray's early confrontation with an ageing headmaster, Mr Weller, played by David Ross. In a stark flashback, it is revealed that Murray was beaten as a child and now abuses his power to put his tormentor in his place. He sends

Weller to teach special-needs children at a school run by affable Jim Nelson, played by Michael Palin. (The Labour Party northwest regional organiser, Peter Kilfoyle, later an MP, was an acquaintance of Bleasdale's and was thought to be the basis for Jim Nelson's character.) Nelson's close friend Martin (Michael Angelis) is a poet and, by continually composing evocative verse, provides an outlet for Bleasdale's lyrical, creative streak.

Nelson is also a left-winger, but he clashes with Murray when he does not support a 24-hour protest strike, organised by Murray who is being manipulated by a group of far-left militants. The Trotskyites hold Murray to ransom with the mention of a dark secret. His life is further complicated by the arrival of a beautiful young woman, Barbara, played by Lindsay Duncan.

Julie plays Murray's idealised and idolised mother, who watches over events from her isolated, tragicomic position. Murray's world closes in on him and, when the story becomes heavy and bleak, Bleasdale masterfully adds hysterical slapstick comedy by giving him two physical ticks. The twitchy left eye is not a patch on the spasm in his left shoulder, which sends his arm shooting into the air, mimicking an exaggerated Nazi salute. Suddenly, *GBH* becomes high farce and Bleasdale deftly handles the dramatic slide from the absurd to the tragic.

In the last few episodes, the viewer's patience is rewarded when all the events become intertwined. Not only is the Labour council infiltrated by the far left, but they in turn are being influenced by MI5. Nelson, the voice of Bleasdale, articulates a case for the redundancy of both political extremes: 'The further left you go, the more right-wing you become.' The series' conclusion sees the city under riot, and all the characters' lives are altered, very few for the better.

Bleasdale does not opt for cliché characterisations and, although accused of basing Murray on Derek Hatton, Liverpool's deputy city council leader in the mid-1980s, his conflicting aspirations, beliefs and loyalties are actually far more complex. If any character seems predictable, the next moment he or she will be doing something utterly unexpected.

For instance, who would imagine that doddering old Weller harboured an unrequited love for Mrs Murray in her heyday?

'There was that memorable scene in the early part where he mouths, "I love you" to her when she's come to see him about her son,' says David Ross. 'I think Alan wanted me to have a love interest with her, rather than it just being a normal headmaster–pupil's mother relationship. When you know someone you're working with, you have an instant rapport – you don't need to act that relationship, which Alan Bleasdale well knows and which is why he writes for certain people.

'Alan's very clever at doing that because he knows the people who will spark off each other without having to write it in really. My character was in love with Julie, and I didn't really need to do anything, because you are slightly in love with her.'

The rest of the time, however, Julie was in full regalia playing Robert Lindsay's elderly mother. Having read the script, Julie was a little shaken by the familiarity of the doughty dame. She took Bleasdale aside and warned him, 'You're going to have to tell me how to play this, otherwise what you'll get is my mother.' This came as little surprise to Bleasdale. 'I don't look exactly like [my mother] when all the make-up and the padding is on, and yet I can hear her,' says Julie.

The actress sat in the make-up chair for hours and came out almost unrecognisable. Sometimes 'one of the crew would say, "Like the latex padding around the chin, Julie." And I wouldn't have the heart to tell him they hadn't put the latex on yet. It was all me!' she says.

Typically modest, Julie does herself a disservice. Rather than let her figure go, she was still displaying the effects of her strenuous workout in *Stepping Out*. Robert Lindsay had never met her before but was thrown into a long, emotional scene on their first day of filming. 'And there was Julie in the make-up and the wig and the glasses and the elderly voice,' he recalled, 'and underneath it all was this stunning pair of dancer's legs!'

Julie found she had much in common with Robert: they are the same age, they both come from working-class backgrounds and had three-year-old daughters, born just three weeks apart. Their on-screen relationship was less harmonious.

'Michael absolutely hates his mother,' says Robert.

'Ah, but she doesn't know it,' replies Julie. 'And even if she did, she could never admit it.' Julie then revealed one of the greatest mysteries of parenthood: 'You always love your children far, far more than they ever love you. It's good to know that, then you don't expect too much.'

GBH was filmed in Manchester during the bitter early months of 1991. 'My God, it was cold that winter. We were always in those big bubble coats,' says Alan Igbon.

Despite the freezing temperature, hearts were warm on set, not least due to Robert Young's relaxed direction and Alan Bleasdale's cheery participation. 'The director was very laid-back,' remembers David Ross. 'There was no tension on set or any difficulties. We all seemed to get on very well – anything Alan brings together I always think is very jolly.'

'As always, Alan was on the set every day, but just watched from the sidelines,' says Igbon. 'If he wanted to convey anything to the actors he'd do it through the director, so there was no conflict. We all know how Alan writes and works, anyway, so it ran smoothly.' Tom Georgeson has a theory as to why the set was so focused yet lively: 'I put this down to a feeling that what we were doing was very worthwhile, and a sense of calm and humorous concentration engendered by the director.'

Although the actual shoot was very smooth, Julie had other concerns. 'She told me her Maisie had leukaemia,' says Robert. 'She explained how she might be a bit vague at times or have to dash off suddenly.' Robert didn't need much imagination to understand her plight; all he had to do was to think how he would feel if it was his little girl.

Alan Igbon also had a child of the same age and shared a bond with Julie. 'Every time she had a day or two off she'd always go back,' he remarks. 'But it was always positive: at the time Maisie was responding well to the treatment. So we all kept our fingers crossed and our prayers were with the kid. We thought it might have adversely affected Julie, but it didn't. Obviously it was on her mind but she didn't let it show or get her down. She was a real trouper.'

They were all aware that Grant's control at home and unwavering strength were behind Julie's ability to perform well while at work. 'Although she had a mother's fear and anxiety, I think she felt Grant was on the case and had quite a lot of support there,' recalls David. 'That was a very difficult time for her but we didn't interfere. We were all very sensitive to the fact that a mother was going through that and we were caring about it, but it didn't affect her work.'

Unfortunately, the upheaval impacted on her home life. 'When I'm working, Grant does everything for Maisie and I get the old nose in the air,' says Julie. The little girl seemed to understand that her mother worked as an actress but, whenever Julie had to go away, more often than not she would play up. 'Having Maisie has taken the edge off my ambition,' she said. 'But I know she's all right without me because she's got Grant. The opposite-sex relationship during childhood is vital. Your mum and dad are the prototype for what happens later.'

When all the hard work finished, the 'Mersey Mafia' celebrated in style. 'I think we had a wrap party for *GBH* at *Coronation Street*'s Rover's Return, and a lot of us got drunk – not Julie, of course!' says Tom Georgeson.

As *Boys from the Blackstuff* presented an authoritative take on the Thatcherite depression of the 1980s, so *GBH* spoke for the political turmoil of the 1990s. Yet the latter stands out as the superior work, partly due to the producers' belief in Bleasdale and consequent budget, but also thanks to the scale of the project with such complex characters and plots. The underlying strength of the series was its ability to encompass an overall view of events without losing any emotional connection to the protagonists. *GBH* remains one of Bleasdale's finest works and stands as the greatest original television drama series to date.

Although she thoroughly enjoyed filming *GBH*, Julie hated being away from home. She was relieved to be back and thrilled to hear how successful Maisie's treatment was proving.

'She takes her medication really well and hasn't been sick,' Julie said in May 1991. 'So far, she hasn't even lost her hair – which was so wispy I thought she'd lose it right away. After a while, you begin to think how lucky you are.' This was a very positive attitude indeed, considering there was a 30 per cent chance that Maisie could relapse. 'You do have to mourn her,' continued Julie. 'You have to go there, because if you pretend the worst is never going to happen then it isn't real.'

Overall, Julie and Grant strove to act as a normal family and treat Maisie to a regular upbringing, rather than wrapping her up in cotton wool, which would have been tempting. 'Part of you wants to give her everything . . . But that's not going to do her any good because suddenly, at the age of seven, we will have this child who's cured of leukaemia but chronically spoiled.'

The one thing she was mindful of was not repeating her parents' mistake of withholding affection. 'Whenever I feel like hugging Maisie, I do it, whether she wants it or not,' says Julie. As well as the big 'cuggles', as Maisie calls them, Julie makes sure she praises her daughter for things done well, rather than just telling her off when she's naughty. 'Self-worth is everything. Without it, life is a misery. If you haven't got that feeling of worth about yourself, then you can't find any worth in other people.'

However positive they stayed, the fact remained that, even if Maisie's treatment continued to go well for rest of the course, she would not be declared cured until three years later. There was still a long road ahead.

21. HITTING THE PRIMARY COLOURS

Julie still had to keep working, because her stint on *GBH* was not paid *that* handsomely. She undertook steady work closer to home when she signed up for the lead role in the great Sir Peter Hall's next stage production, *The Rose Tattoo*.

The Tennessee Williams play, set in a Sicilian community in the 1950s, deals almost exclusively with sex and sexuality. Serafina (Julie's character), is riddled with pretensions and elevates the intercourse she has with her husband above a carnal instinct to a 'miracle' that happens every night, to appease her Catholic guilt. They are a working-class couple, but her airs and graces earn her the moniker, 'Baronessa'.

When her husband dies, Serafina is tormented as nature entices her wild, dark side. She fights to guard the sanctity of his memory against gossip of his infidelity, but only by accepting the truth can she move on. She releases the stranglehold on her teenage daughter's burgeoning desires and gives in to her own yearnings with a Sicilian trucker, Alvaro.

Alongside the emotional upheaval of the play, Williams balances comedy and visual farce. In one scene, Serafina, dressed to kill for Alvaro, changes her mind and struggles to remove an uncomfortable girdle. When he arrives, she has managed to wriggle the offending article down to her knees, where she finds she can neither pull it off nor put it on again. It was a potentially amusing moment, but its prospects were limitless in Julie's hands with her impeccable timing.

However, she doubted her ability to conquer such a wholly demanding role and accepted it only under pressure from Hall, who had faith in her talent and wouldn't take no for an answer. Julie conceded that recent events would help with preparation for the role and the emotional range it required. She said at the time, 'It's not that I bring Maisie to mind during the performance – that would be too painful – it's just that I am more open emotionally than I have ever been.'

Physically, Julie required assistance to achieve Serafina's voluptuous curves: she wore D-cup bras full of bean bags and generous foam padding from the prosthetics department of *Spitting Image*. 'She takes risks most of her contemporaries wouldn't,' says Sir Peter Hall. 'She has no vanity, she'll become somebody else completely.'

With Kenneth Stott, Tina Martin and Sally Bankes also on board, rehearsals started in April. As always, Julie gave 110 per cent to the explosive role.

This time, though, it was apparently too much. 'When we started rehearsing I really hit the primary colours,' says Julie. 'I was completely done in, couldn't walk, couldn't speak, couldn't hear, kept getting dizzy.' The trauma of the past nine months caught up with her and she collapsed with a mystery virus.

Although she missed most of the rehearsals, like her character Julie is dogged and fuelled by passion: the show must go on. Drawing on untapped resources, she summoned all her strength and pulled off a magnificent six-week performance on the provincial tour. Like Serafina, Julie danced near the edge of insanity and exhaustion, but ultimately found the will to persevere.

During the pre-London run, including a stint at the Theatre Royal in Bath, Julie was attacked for camping up the role for laughs. 'It is meant to be funny,' she defended. 'The humour is very black. The whole play teeters on a knife edge between tragedy and comedy. Williams always hated the film [of 1955 with Anna Magnani and Burt Lancaster] because Hollywood took out all the gags.'

On 11 June 1991, *The Rose Tattoo* transferred to London and opened at the Playhouse Theatre for a six-month run. There Julie received rave reviews. 'It is a *tour de force* performance,' claimed the *Evening Standard*. Serafina doesn't so much react as erupt . . . she stalks the stage – shouting, screaming and spitting invective as she hurls her huge body around, like a weary bull turning to face another attack.'

Julie was shattered. 'By the end of the first week I'd never felt so tired in my whole life,' she said one month in. 'At the beginning of the run I remember telling myself I would never go through this again.' She was convinced that taking on the demanding role was the biggest mistake she had ever made and that she wasn't able to portray Serafina.

'I suppose I'm interested in strength being tried, of people being pushed to the limit,' she added. 'It was frightening to take it on but that's what I liked about it. Characters are like love children. You feel an empathy with them.'

The actor Peter Whitfield, who was so impressed by her performance in *Jumpers*, was once again mesmerised: 'She was brilliant in that Hispanic role – she's such a versatile actress, she really makes you believe in the part.'

Compounding issues, Julie again found the role reminiscent of her mother. 'Like Serafina, she was a strong, dynamic woman with a huge spirit,' she says. This was particularly hard, because she had so recently used her mother's essence for *GBH*.

And then there were the issues of motherhood. 'I felt guilty when I was at work. Then, when I was at home, I felt guilty for not giving more to the play. So I was unhappy in both places.'

Finally, after months of putting on a brave face, Julie wearily admitted defeat. Her performance had been praised to the hilt, yet her health and state of mind were suffering too much. She returned to the sanctuary of home in the bosom of her loving family.

Just as the actress hit rock bottom in *The Rose Tattoo*, Maisie's chemotherapy led her to lose her long blonde hair and Julie and Grant were dealing with the fact that they probably wouldn't be able to have any more children.

'There's nothing like a sibling,' she said at the time. 'That's why I feel sad, because I don't know whether Maisie will have a brother or sister.' Julie was in two minds about the possibility: on the one hand she wanted to see Maisie through her illness before considering enlarging the family, as she recognised that it was sometimes difficult for an only child to have a rival for the parents' affections; on the other hand, because Maisie had been the centre of so much intense speculation in her young life, the deflection of another child might have been beneficial. 'In one sense, it's the last thing on our minds, then again, I can't let it go for much longer,' she concluded.

With this weighing heavily on her mind, it seemed that the combination of her virus, work exhaustion, Maisie's hair loss, and stress had interrupted Julie's natural cycle.

'I thought I was pregnant a couple of months ago,' she said in December 1991. 'I was thrilled, we both were. But planning another baby is another matter. And we don't feel like planning it.' With the phantom pregnancy just that, at 41, Julie had to accept that having another child herself was less likely.

Briefly, the couple considered adoption as an alternative, but decided against it, partly again because of the negative effect it might have on Maisie and partly because of Julie's celebrity. 'Grant and I did think about adopting a child at one point,' she would reveal almost a decade later. 'But we were put off the idea by the knowledge that the child would be in the public eye so much ... I wouldn't want to put a child through that – it wouldn't be fair to them.'

Back in 1991 Grant, too, was finding day-to-day life hard. He had to run the house, deal with the daily problems of Maisie's illness and support his stressed partner. Julie admitted that, although it was tiring, at least she had the distraction of work. Grant managed to find an outlet for his feelings at Maisie's playgroup. 'The women love it, because they never have a man there,' said Julie at the time. 'And Grant prefers women because ... whenever he's tried to discuss Maisie's situation with other men, they don't want to talk about it, so he tends to seek out women. He has a good sense of his own sexuality and his own maleness, but he likes cooking and homemaking and isn't ambitious in a career sense. We're a good combination.'

Somehow they struggled through that tough year and Julie learned a valuable lesson. 'Trials and tribulations do bring you closer together. I miss her terribly when I'm working – and I know she misses me. Now I only leave home for two good reasons – either the job's worthwhile, or it pays a lot of money!' she says frankly.

After some much-needed home time, rest and recuperation, Julie accepted one last project for 1991. She was honoured by her peers for her courage and professionalism through such a difficult year with a London Weekend Television Christmas special titled, *Julie Walters and Friends.*

Victoria Wood had contributed the majority of the sketches for the hour-long show, but other material was provided by Alan Bennett, Alan Bleasdale and Willy Russell. Bennett wrote a piece for Julie's character Lesley from *Her Big Chance*; Bleasdale created a mini-sequel for Mrs Murray from *GBH*; and Russell penned a rhyming sketch mocking the arts. Victoria, who was well versed in the medium, conjured up six wickedly witty scenarios and added a song to the repertoire.

'I love her stuff,' says Julie. 'It was a great comfort having Victoria there – it's like slipping on a comfy pair of slippers.' It was like old times for Vic and Jules as they bantered with each other in four different guises. First of all they played two young northern girls in the 1960s, then they aged up to become southern pensioners at a funeral reception. Other skits revolved around the seating arrangements for a family gathering, and a manicure for the forthright Julie, who proffered bizarre opinions on current political situations.

The strangest set-up for the costume department was Julie's impression of a cockney geezer Don, with Vic as his wife Con. Julie says, 'They used a hairdryer on my face to stretch the skin and make it look wrinkled.' The look then remained for a few hours. 'I don't worry about getting old, but I don't want to get there prematurely!' Don was an incontinent, name-dropping, culinary-xenophobic chauvinist, while Con, with her grey perm, showed off her dancing.

Julie also had a few solo sketches, including the batty Barbara Cartland parody and the relaxation guru who becomes increasingly stressed trying to film an advertisement. She says she enjoyed the roles equally, and doesn't have a favourite: 'They're like my babies, you see, I sort of love them all.' Victoria's song for Julie was as sharp as ever, charting a romance from the nervous excitement of a first date to the disillusioned marriage, although, given the recent strain on Grant and Julie's relationship, Vic ended it on a suitably happy note of 'let's stick with this'.

Unknown to Julie, the four authors had all taped private tributes to her, which were inserted into the final programme. While the three men doled out affectionate admiration, Victoria maintained the humour and played up her northern image.

'I was sent a video of the finished show,' said Julie, 'but I'm too frightened to view it. I'm slightly embarrassed. This show is all me, and I keep thinking it won't be good enough.'

Far from Julie's fears, the show, produced by Nicholas Barrett and directed by Alasdair Macmillan, was aired on Sunday, 29 December 1991 to high ratings. Furthermore, it won the Writers' Guild award for Best Light Entertainment Script and received a BAFTA nomination for Best Light Entertainment Programme.

'It's been a very difficult year but my friends have helped me to pull through,' Julie summed up. 'They've given me such support.' Other than the four writers involved in the special, Julie thanked her two best friends, Grant and Ros.

Maisie was over halfway through her two-year treatment and, as Julie said in December 1991, 'So far, so good. She's the best she's ever been, despite all the chemotherapy. Her hair fell out but it's grown back now – it's short and suits her.'

At the beginning of 1992, Julie's finances dictated that she take on more work and was approached for the film, *Just Like a Woman*. In it, Monica (Julie) is a middle-aged London divorcee searching for lodgers to share her home. Gerald is a brilliant and handsome American banker who is thrown out of his marital home when his wife finds another woman's underwear and assumes he is having an affair. He turns up on Monica's doorstep, rents one of her rooms, and the pair begin to fall in love.

Monica is curious to see a mystery woman creeping into Gerald's room, but gets rather more than she bargains for when she investigates this 'other woman'. Gerald explains that it is Geraldine, his transvestite alter ego. Monica is dumbfounded but, when she finally grasps what he has said, she bursts into fits of giggles and offends him. Finally persuading him to show her Geraldine, Monica becomes more open-minded and slowly comes to terms with his fetish.

She encourages his love of dresses, suspender belts, panties and the rest, and the two embark on a passionate affair, having the time of their lives. This happy period is brought to an abrupt end when Geraldine is caught speeding one night coming back from karaoke in full drag. When the policeman discovers Geraldine's secret, he vindictively charges her for soliciting. Gerald's boss uses this scandal as a reason to fire him and pursue a dodgy deal that his ex-employee had been blocking. Gerald's friend and former colleague, CJ, hatches a plan and, with Monica's help, they use his transvestism to expose their racist boss's crooked scheme.

Julie was very choosy about projects, not only with the script and subject matter, but also with the flexibility of the work. This unusual, risqué film piqued her interest but, more importantly, the director Christopher Monger was so keen to have Julie on board that he accommodated her request to film locally and have time off for hospital appointments.

With Julie as Monica, Christopher then had to find an actor willing to play a transvestite. The answer was, ironically, the American heart-throb, Adrian Pasdar, who was first seen as Chipper in Tom Cruise's overtly macho *Top Gun*. 'Adrian is brilliant for the part,' revealed a set insider, 'but I guess the size of his hands and feet might give the game away. As you can imagine, we had a lot of laughs. Julie cracked up in hysterics all the time.' Standing at six feet tall with chiselled features, Adrian did look rather strange as a woman.

'It's difficult for him,' said Julie at the time. 'He's a big, hunky bloke who's wondering what he's let himself in for.' For her part, the actress was having a brilliant time and felt that she would react in the same way as her character given the same circumstances. 'She's shocked, but she thinks it's hilarious, and she comes to terms with it by having a very sexy relationship with the guy.'

Filmed in Barnes, south London, *Just Like a Woman* cost £2 million to make and included some very intimate scenes between the oddball couple.

'I've never come across anything like this and don't understand all of it, but I'm far more open about it than I ever thought I would be,' says Julie, who undertook some research to understand the differences between a transvestite and a transsexual. Instead of the steamy sex-fest she had imagined, Julie was surprised to find the transvestite meeting consisted of men sitting in gorgeous dresses, chatting and drinking tea, many accompanied by their wives.

'These men don't want operations to become women. And more than ninety per cent of all cross-dressers are heterosexual. They dislike male sexuality, but female sexuality is everything. The all-time biggest fantasy for many is to make love to a woman, while dressed as a woman.'

Unfortunately, when the film was released in October 1992, it received mixed reviews. Some critics were just pleased to see Julie on the big screen again, and indeed her performance carried the film. She is terrific as the gobsmacked landlady who discovers that her boyfriend dresses up as a woman, she pulls off a brilliant impression of her most boring lodger and is utterly cringe-making as the floundering business partner in a critical meeting.

Less kind comments pointed out that the film was clumsy and insulting towards transvestites, particularly as Adrian Pasdar was too butch for the role. Unfortunately, his awkward frame tends to make light of the issue, and the direction of key moments, such as his transformation, was, to some minds, handled crudely and tackily. The film is slow in parts and it is too convenient that the Japanese investors with whom Gerald deals are more tolerant of men who dress as women because of their theatre history.

'Someone, somewhere, is due to write another good film soon for that most deserving of actresses, Julie Walters,' wrote *TV Times*. 'But this isn't it.'

Richard Loncraine, a director watching Julie's career closely, with an eye to casting her himself, was equally unimpressed. 'I think it was a case of paying the rent and looking after her child, but I think she made very bad choices in some of the films she made – they just weren't good enough,' he says bluntly. 'She should have been more careful about what she did, because the industry is quite vicious if you get seen in something: it becomes a stigma and it won't wash off you.

'Her child being ill was critical to her career and she made the choice to be a mum. Whilst I admire her for that and for putting her child and family first, I wish we'd seen her in better roles.'

22. CAN JULIE PLAY IT STRAIGHT?

By the time *Just Like a Woman* was ready for its launch, Julie had other concerns. After eighteen months of responding well to treatment, tragedy struck a second time and Maisie suffered a relapse.

'That was much worse than the initial diagnosis,' says Julie. 'She had to go through all the treatment again. And, once it's come back, you feel there's much less chance.'

The strain on Julie and Grant proved as hard as the first time but again, in the face of adversity, she felt it brought them closer. Devastated to be back to square one, Julie clung on to a positive attitude and never shut the reporters out, instead speaking openly about the struggles they were facing.

'I'm taking one day at a time,' she said. 'Time with Maisie is so precious, because you don't know what will happen ... It's funny, I used to worry about what kind of world Maisie would grow up in. Now, I just want her to grow up.'

Desperately trying to look to the future, Julie re-evaluated the Catholic faith that was so rudely thrust upon her. 'When Maisie was ill, I started to feel more spiritual,' she says. 'When you think you are going to lose somebody, that's when you need to put things in some kind of order, which is what I did.' Julie explained that, although she didn't conform to her mother's strict religion, she did believe in something that she found difficult to articulate, but amounted to a moral code of being good.

'I'm a Pisces and I always read my stars in the paper or magazines. I'm quite open-minded about that sort of thing. I don't believe everything I read, but there's much more out there than scientists would have us believe,' she adds, suggesting that fate plays some part in life.

The summer of 1992 seemed to drag on for ever, filled with endless hospital appointments and all-too-familiar feelings. By the autumn Maisie was slowly improving once again and Julie accepted some light work with Victoria Wood, this time for her Christmas special, entitled *All Day Breakfast*.

The theme of the show was a mickey-take of the daytime television institution that was *This Morning* with the husband-and-wife team Judy Finnigan and Richard Madeley. Victoria and Duncan Preston played their roles to perfection, and the rest of the team – Celia Imrie, Susie Blake, Lill

Roughley and Julie – were rounded up in sketches and fake adverts. The latter included digs at current trends and marketing techniques: a sanitary towel absorbing blue ink, environmentally conscious detergent packaging and the absurdly sexual coffee commercials previously used in the playlet 'Staying In'.

Interspersed with the chat-show format were skits. Familiar stereotypes were revisited, such as Julie's opinionated and outspoken knitwear shop owner and Victoria's thick, northern assistant. Victoria's angst with the elderly and her own poor relationship with her mother were shown by Julie playing the ageing battleaxe trying her utmost to make her daughter feel guilty for not looking after her: 'When I go, I don't suppose anybody will find me for several days,' she bellyached.

The real treat was saved for fans of 'Acorn Antiques'. In the dramatic climax of Victoria's soap opera, Mrs Overall, last seen choking to death on her own macaroon, miraculously recovered. The rest of the cast, however, had been killed in a mysterious food poisoning incident on the M42, so Mrs Overall heads off to a new programme – 'The Mall', outrageously based on the BBC's *Eldorado*. Mrs O causes chaos on set once again as props break, cameras are in view and lines are fluffed.

All Day Breakfast finished with a traditional Victoria Wood song, and the show was a huge success. It was aired on the Christmas Day evening slot, which was previously saved for the likes of *Morecambe & Wise*. Produced and directed by Geoff Posner, *All Day Breakfast* won the Writers' Guild Award and the Royal Television Society's award for Best Light Entertainment Programme.

Financially, Julie was forced to keep working but, still shaken by Maisie's relapse, she secured plenty of time off. The first project she did, at the end of 1992, was the challenging role of Diana in *Wide-Eyed and Legless*.

The screenplay is based on the true memoirs of businessman Deric Longden, who enjoyed a strong marriage with his wife Diana, sharing many laughs and indulging their two grown children and Deric's slightly dotty mother.

Unfortunately, Diana suffered from a debilitating disease that baffled doctors and remained undiagnosed. The illness caused intermittent paralysis to her limbs and periodic blackouts. Now known as ME, or chronic fatigue syndrome, it leaves sufferers exhausted and debilitated with muscular pain, after a flu-like viral attack.

The story follows the couple's search for answers amid planning their son's wedding. Finally, Diana realises that this disease will prove fatal and she decides to find a replacement wife for Deric. She chooses a blind novelist, Aileen Armitage, to whom Deric feels bonded. This tender tale of love, hope and survival is told with warmth and humour.

Richard Loncraine, director and screenwriter, had won a BAFTA as Best Director for Dennis Potter's drama *Blade on the Feather* and was approached by the screenwriter Jack Rosenthal to direct this delicate piece. 'I immediately liked it and it just took off from there really,' recalls Richard.

'Julie wasn't attached to the project when I took it on, but I had always wanted to work with her.' Fed up with seeing Julie play stereotypes in the vast majority of her performances, Richard made the surprising decision not to offer her the 'dotty mother' part. 'There was a certain amount of contention as to whether Julie was the right choice for Diana. "Can Julie play it straight, or will she want to camp it up and make it funny?" was the problem discussed.'

Richard understood the concerns, particularly given her last role in *Just Like a Woman*, but he had immense faith in her talent and cast her in the lead. 'I felt, having watched her over the years, that she was a fantastic actress above all, and I was totally convinced that she would control her comedic side,' he says.

'She's a woman who likes to make people laugh, she is very funny, and there were times in the shooting when we did fall about with her sense of humour. But I only had to look at her and say, "Julie," and she looked at me and knew exactly what I meant; that that was wonderful, but it wasn't going to fit into this movie. Sadly I think she's underused in this country.'

In *Wide-Eyed and Legless* Julie was supported by Thora Hird as her mother-in-law and Jim Broadbent as her husband, both of whom she knew well and had worked with previously.

One of the Longdens' sons, Nick, was played by an up-and-coming actor, Andrew Lancel. 'Julie was my first mum. You can't get a better start than with Julie as my mum, Jim Broadbent as my dad and Thora Hird as my gran!' he boasts.

'As soon as I heard the words "ME" my ears shot up, because my brother had lived with it for a long time. The first phone call was to ask if I would like to audition for the role of Julie Walters's son – I don't know an actor in Britain who wouldn't jump at it. I was always a big fan of hers anyway, so to work with her was the cherry on the cake.'

Andrew was quite nervous about meeting his three established colleagues, but they all instantly put him at ease. 'I remember when I first met Julie, she said, "Ah, you'll be my son." I replied, "Yes, was I a difficult birth?" and we just started chatting away,' he says. 'She was really great.

Jim seemed to be a great listener: he would listen to the director and everybody, and then go off and prepare.

'And Thora Hird was fun. I particularly remember her at the read-through. When you get a script, they send you pink pages as the changes are made, then blue pages, then green pages et cetera. Before you get to the read-through, you shuffle them together. But, during the read-through, Thora was on some of the old pages and so she lost her footing a couple of times.

'At the end of it she said, "I'm sorry, ladies and gentlemen. I'd just like to say I spent two hours yesterday collating those pages. I realise now I should have spent three!"'

Another young actor who had followed Julie's career was Peter Whitfield, who was given the part of Fred, and he too was extremely nervous to be working with an idol. 'When we did the read-through the tables were in a quadrangle and I was sitting opposite Richard Loncraine,' he recalls. 'He said, "I want all the main characters facing me," so everyone moved around and I ended up sitting next to Julie, which made it even more daunting!

'When she sat next to me, she said, "Hello, I'm Julie and I'm playing Diana," as if I didn't know! She made me feel at ease because she's so normal and down-to-earth.'

Filming for *Wide-Eyed and Legless* got under way in January 1993, with just a month reserved for the whole shoot. 'It was pretty hectic,' recalls Richard Loncraine. 'We ran out of money and there was a constant battle with the BBC to make it look better. Eighty-five per cent of the film was made in London, we had a few mad days in Blackpool, and a couple in Manchester. We couldn't really afford to accommodate the crew up north, so we had to pretend we were in Manchester in London – we shot interiors in a house in north London and Brick Lane was the location for the dress factory.

'Filmmaking is hard work and quite intense, so I always try to create an atmosphere where the actors and crew work well. Keeping a sense of humour on the floor is crucial to break the tension and ensure people do their best work. Julie, Jim and Thora were all a great help in doing that – they're company players. When we were on location, we just had caravans, so we were usually huddled in small corners somewhere keeping warm. It was a bleak winter when we filmed it, but [Julie] always made it fun. I always felt like I had an ally and if the crew was cold and miserable she would always cheer them up. She's a great trouper and it's rare to find that level of bonhomie and warmth combined with real talent.'

Although Julie was totally dedicated on set, her mind often wandered to Maisie's health. 'Obviously she was at a very complex time in her life,' Richard continues. 'They'd got through the darkest time, but she was still very quiet, and tended to keep herself to herself. She didn't want to come out eating and drinking with the crew. Instead, she'd go home early, get some sleep and be ready for the next day, which is the mark of a true pro. She knows how much her body can take.'

Peter Whitfield, too, remembers Julie's humour on set, and that she was occasionally preoccupied. 'During one of the breaks, the food came out and there was a prawn sandwich. Well, Julie went into a Victoria Wood routine about how the prawns tread water!' he says. 'Then she phoned Grant to check on Maisie. It's amazing to think what she was going through and to carry on working and laughing in between.

'When we finished the shoot at the end of the day, she had to rush off, so she just got changed in the same caravan as us, rather than wasting time finding some privacy. Although she's so famous, she got down to her underwear and wasn't bothered by it – she just wanted to get away.'

Andrew Lancel agrees that Julie could be relied on for impeccable comic timing. 'I just couldn't get the elderly waitress she played on *Victoria Wood As Seen On TV* out of my head during the scene where she walked down the aisle. It took a lot of work, and, when we finally got it right, she comes into my arms – after about a minute, she said, "Right, ready to order?"

'It broke all the emotion and the tension of the scene – she was able to switch on and switch off at just the right time. I watched her from afar, preparing herself for the hospital scenes. She would be joking around and then within a minute she was very focused. It seemed that she was able to just flick a switch. Obviously, the heavier the scene the more she would prepare.'

During filming the cast also met Deric and Nick Longden. 'It was a great buzz that the Longdens came down,' says Andrew, 'but it must have been very weird for Deric to see Jim Broadbent play him and Julie Walters play his wife.

'They weren't intrusive. It was just really nice to have them around. Deric spoke to Jim and Julie a lot. I remember Julie saying lines that she had picked up from Deric that weren't in the book. I met Nick halfway through the shoot, and he said, "That's it, you've got it just right," which was a huge compliment.'

In its adaptation for television, the tale had been sweetened. 'It was a true story, with flowers put round the edging,' says Andrew Lancel. Richard Loncraine is less tactful: 'We met the Longdens and spent some time with them. I wouldn't say that we drew much from them as characters, more the events. I think in truth the real story was less successful as the characters were less lovable than in our film.'

Still, many of the scenes were very moving as the family struggled to cope with this unknown disease and Richard proved a thoughtful and perceptive director. 'He said it was always worthwhile trying to make everything look good, not just bits and pieces,' recalls Andrew. 'He wanted everything to be a "moment". When we picked Julie up off the bed and carried her, we improvised it and played around with it a lot. It was such a simple scene, but it turned out so well they used it in the trailers.'

Richard explains his technique: 'With film, you can't rehearse too much or you'll wear a scene out. You tend to rehearse to make sure everyone's happy that the scene is going to work, rather than getting it word perfect.

'The scene where Diana drowned in the bath, that was tough to do. In a scene like that you work out roughly where the actors are going to be so that you know the mechanics of it, but then you have to leave it up to the actors' skills. We were in a very, very small bathroom in quite a small house – not a set – and there was only room for the camera operator and myself in the room. We did it twice, but I think we used the first take.

'I remember Julie was frightened of going under water, and really quite nervous about holding her breath. I think she might have been a little claustrophobic at the time, but the energy and chemistry and reality she gave to that scene was amazing. Jim and Julie together really made you feel as though you were in the bathroom. You almost wanted to help, because it went on for quite a long time. They got on well and were as warm together off camera as on, and I think it shows on screen. I was in floods of tears at the end of it.'

Julie wasn't so pleased about revisiting that particular 'moment' on screen, however. 'The very thought of flashing my flesh makes me cringe,' she says, and is always embarrassed whenever it is required in filming. 'I remember being hauled out of the bath [in *Wide-Eyed and Legless*], seeing my boobs on screen and shouting, "For God's sake, I'm wearing water wings!"'

Although *Wide-Eyed and Legless* was made for UK television, the American sale to Miramax (where it was retitled *The Wedding Gift*) prevented it from being shown more than once. Moreover, there were complications and further work was necessary for the new market.

'There was a minor hoo-ha about the cinema release in America,' recalls Andrew. 'It was an Equity cock-up and we weren't being paid the going rate, so Richard had to phone up everyone and sort it all out. I then had to redub a couple of lines: one was "flogging" the car, because "flogging" has a very different meaning in America!'

The British critics were impressed with *Wide-Eyed and Legless*, although it was not a financial success. 'What Julie brought to it,' explains Richard, 'was the ability to have comedy that is right on the edge of being big, and tragedy in the same movie. I was amazed at that. I'd seen it in Rude Mechanicals' versions of Shakespeare's plays, but you rarely see comedy and tragedy running parallel. I felt in *Wide-Eyed* that the comedy sat well alongside the drama, because it was played very truthfully.

'When you've got great actors, there's relatively little you need to do as a director – you nudge them a little, you make sure they're OK. With Julie I always felt I was in good, safe hands and, if she felt that something wasn't working, she was probably right. There's always that feeling of security. That's why it's such a joy to watch her – you always know that she won't let you down, as a director or a member of the audience.'

By the time the film was released in 1993, Maisie's treatment had finished, but it would be three more years before she could be given the all-clear. In the meantime, there were more award ceremonies. *Wide-Eyed and Legless* was nominated for the Best Drama BAFTA, and Julie received another nomination for Best Actress. 'It was a shame that she didn't get the BAFTA for it – I think she should have. She played it in a way that other actresses wouldn't. She doesn't hold back,' says Andrew.

After the ordeal of *Wide-Eyed and Legless*, Julie took on an undemanding role in Waris Hussein's *The Summer House*. The made-for-television movie had been adapted by Martin Sherman from Alice Thomas Ellis's novel, *The Clothes in the Wardrobe*.

In this comedy, Lena Headey (from *Soldier Soldier* and *Spender*) plays Margaret, a young woman who has fallen in love with a young man on a recent trip to Egypt, but on her return to Croydon, where she lives with her mother (played by Julie), she is coerced into marrying Syl (David Threlfall), who lives next door. She agrees, although she despises the forty-year-old mother's boy.

Preparations for the wedding get under way, but everyone's life is turned upside down with the arrival of flamboyant Lili (Jeanne Moreau). Lili is Margaret's mother's eccentric ex-roommate, who is determined to stop the arranged marriage and hatches a surprising plan.

With such veteran actors, including Joan Plowright as Mrs Monro, in the cast, it's hard to believe there could be fault with *The Summer House*. However, Lena as the bride-to-be is somewhat distant and arcane; her character's true depth doen't show, resulting in the viewer's frustration at her lack of backbone. Conversely, David is feckless and cloying as her future groom, although Lena seems to offer him little to work with in their scenes together.

The same is true of her performance with Julie, although the older, experienced actress naturally livens even the dullest script, expertly playing the nice-but-dim mother. Jeanne Moreau and Joan Plowright are marvellous as ever, as is John Wood as Lili's ex-husband. Still, the first half of *The Summer House* is desperately slow, with the only intrigue arising from a telegraph from Lili. Thankfully, the film redeems itself as it finally picks up pace for the delicious conclusion, but it is another of Julie's poorer choices.

Returning to powerful drama, Julie next teamed up with Georges Corraface for *Bambino Mio*. Written by Colin Welland, this true story is a well-documented odyssey exploring the semilegal paths and administrative difficulties encountered by a French-British couple, Jean Paul and Alice, when they attempt to adopt a baby from the 'barrios' of Carracas, South America.

Julie plays Alice, a wealthy, middle-aged woman who is left barren after suffering a miscarriage at her husband's funeral. A few years on she is lucky enough to find happiness in love again, with Jean Paul, portrayed by Georges. They have a passionate affair and (despite her horror at being seen naked in *Wide-Eyed and Legless*) the 43-year-old actress appears topless in bed with her lover.

Without wishing to tie Jean Paul down, Alice really wants to share her joy and emotions with a child. She is declined permission to adopt in Britain and France because of her age and single status, but is put in touch with a company who arrange an adoption in South America for a small fee of £10,000.

Alice is thrilled to fulfil her dream, but is a little affronted by the businesslike manner of the proceedings. Eventually the paperwork is processed and she flies with Jean Paul to Carracas to meet her new baby, Chico. After a while the couple encounter complications and are told to fly back to France to await further information. Excited, they decorate the nursery, but the next communication hails bad news. Alice answers the telephone to discover that Chico has died. Julie's performance is gripping throughout as the frantic mother-to-be, but in this scene she excels herself and her reaction is highly emotive.

Jean Paul can't understand the instant bond Alice felt with her child, but persuades her to try again. Another baby is found, but Alice runs into further difficulties as she wants the adoption to be legalised in Britain and then for the family to live in France. The South American authorities then demand that she be married. Finally, the story has a happy ending, though the film avoids excessive sentimentality. Well-placed humour helps lighten the desperation and *Bambino Mio*, directed by Edward Bennett and produced by Kenith Trodd for the BBC in 1993, is a success.

Julie again turns blonde for her craft, and although she speaks naturally with a faint Smethwick twang, she affects realistic French and Spanish accents. The actress was drawn to the film on account of the subject matter: Maisie's illness and Julie's conversations with Grant about adoption made the project all the more poignant.

23. PSYCHO CHILLER OF THE YEAR

In 1994, Julie redeemed herself from some of her weaker decisions and was back in force on the big screen in the disturbing *Sister My Sister*. The film was adapted by Wendy Kesselman from her Pulitzer prize-winning play, *My Sister In This House*, and is based on the true story of Christine and Lea Papin. The creepy existence of the two French domestic staff has inspired three plays, half a dozen films, one opera and countless books, papers and articles. The most famous is Jean Genet's 1948 play *The Maids* and more recent releases include Jean-Pierre Denis's feature *Les Blessures Assassines* and the documentary *En Quête Des Soeurs Papin*.

This psychological drama is made all the more eerie for its factual history. The grisly story began in Le Mans in 1926 when Christine Papin entered the Lancelin household as a cook. Having been raised by nuns, attending Mass every Sunday and proving a hard worker, she seemed ideal for the position. Within a few months, she had no difficulty in persuading the bourgeois family to take on her sister Lea as the chambermaid. They shared a room on the top floor of the three-storey house and their contact with the family was minimal.

The lady of the house was an austere woman, who treated her daughter Isabelle, as well as the maids, with annoyed indifference. Christine and Lea turned to each other for love and comfort, but their closeness soon became obsessive. Christine was increasingly jealous of anyone, particularly Isabelle, who had contact with her sibling. More than just preferring each other's company, the sisters suffered from a condition known as shared paranoid disorder: the French call it *folie à deux* (literally, madness in pairs). Their relationship is believed to have become homosexual and incestuous, and over time, they neglected their duties.

Finally, seven years after entering the house, they committed a savage double murder on 2 February 1933. Christine started the actual attack on the mother, and was then joined by Lea when she turned her attentions to the daughter. In both cases they gouged their victims' eyes out with their fingers, then bludgeoned their heads with a hammer, knife, and a pewter pot that stood in the hallway. The assault lasted about half an hour and left the victims unrecognisable.

Afterwards, the sisters curiously washed the blood off themselves, but made no other attempt to cover up their crime. Instead they stripped naked and climbed into bed together, where they waited for the police.

The murder hit the headlines and the two women became infamous with tabloid labels such as the 'Monsters of Le Mans'. They were tried seven months later and Christine was found guilty and sentenced to death by guillotine. As was the standard for women of the time, this was commuted to life imprisonment, but she went on a hunger strike and died in 1937. Lea was charged only with the murder of the daughter and sentenced to ten years in jail, under the extenuating circumstance that she was manipulated by her older sister. She was released on good behaviour after eight years and settled in the town of Nantes. It is believed that she lived a long life there working as a chambermaid under the pseudonym of Marie.

The director Nancy Meckler was extremely respected in theatre, and had previously directed the stage version of *My Sister In This House*. In 1994, she retackled the subject for her debut movie, *Sister My Sister*. Nancy sought out a strong cast.

'I met Nancy when she was putting on the play, *My Sister In This House*,' recalls cast member Sophie Thursfield. 'I went for one of the sister's parts but didn't get it. Then I got called in to play the daughter when the film version came up, and I thought, Oh yes, I know this story.'

Julie Walters was chosen to play the lady of the household, Madame Danzard; Sophie, her daughter Isabelle; and Joely Richardson and Jodhi May were the two sisters. 'Jodhi, who plays Lea, is incredibly tall and powerful,' says Nancy. 'Joely is even taller than Jodhi. They're like two giants together.'

Everyone involved was fascinated by the perverse story. 'It was a real hoot,' says Sophie. 'When you're doing something that awful, it's a cliché but it is kind of quite funny. Everyone was emboldened by it; there was a great spirit behind it.

'It was an all-female cast and it was one of the first all-female films, with a female first assistant and director. I think it worked very harmoniously because it was small enough and everybody got behind it and enjoyed it. It was one of those jobs where there were no egos. Nancy's from a very specific school of directing for theatre – Shared Experience – and this was her first film,' Sophie continues, 'so she was open and out for learning new things.

'It was interesting, because she works on a very three-dimensional level, much deeper than you would probably normally expect on a film. She trawls the depths of the human psyche and likes to make sure that people know what their character really is about, so there were lots of discussions about the motivation of this story.

'We had two weeks of rehearsals at Pinewood, but she knew that those two weeks were probably all she was getting, so she had to cover as much as she could. Our rehearsals were based on exercises: all playing each other's parts and playing status games, because the status in the house was quite important to understand the minutiae of the games that were played between all four women. It must have been a terrible place to live in, in reality.'

The cast were helped with a portfolio of the case. 'I remember Nancy saying that they talked to a psychologist at Broadmoor who said the murder was quite indicative of homosexual shame,' says Sophie, 'that it was almost ritualistic: they killed them but they kept going back for more. It was awful, but what was really chilling was we had a folder of the forensic photographs from the time. You couldn't see that much because they were 1930s photos, but there was the funeral procession, which was a huge shaming thing.'

After the rehearsals, Nancy Meckler was allocated just six weeks' filming on a shoestring budget. The cast and crew worked twelve-hour days, but no one complained because they were all so enthusiastic about the project.

'We went off to France first of all to do a few scenes outside the house,' says Sophie, 'but these strange events only occurred in Le Mans in the 1930s and it was quite a sensitive subject – there were still people there who could remember, so they wouldn't grant us permission to film there. We filmed in Lannion instead.' The ensemble returned to Pinewood for the remainder of the shoot.

Nancy really liked the idea of the four women as the central characters and used artistic licence to remove the only male role. 'There was a father in the real story,' says Sophie. 'He was the one who actually came home and found the mother and daughter murdered in the hallway and went upstairs to find the two girls sitting, shivering, in the bed.' For *Sister My Sister*, Madame Danzard became a widow and the story focused more on the maids. That said, the relationship between mother and child was interesting and duly explored in the film.

'The woman and her daughter lead this terribly sterile, awful life,' says Sophie. 'The daughter is just a constant disappointment to the mother, and the mother is very exacting.

'We used to giggle, because they were so awful. I was this lump of a girl, and I was given the most savage haircut: I looked like one of the princes in the tower. In fact the producer didn't even recognise me! We used to laugh at the things she had to say to me, like, "Oh, you don't look well in those clothes, do you, Isabelle?" I was such an awful daughter and the mother had this fantasy that her daughter was some day going to get married! I remember the first scene we did, I looked at Julie and she just seemed to completely inhabit this woman from the start.'

'Oh God, you really know what you're doing,' Sophie said. 'You've absolutely encapsulated this woman and all her awful pettiness.'

'I've just been looking at you, thinking the same thing!' replied Julie. Regardless of her many accolades, Julie Walters was still daunted by a demanding role and open to all advice and suggestions.

'Julie and I had quite a difficult card scene,' continues Sophie. 'When you see it in the film, you think, "Oh that's just a card scene," but it took us ages. It was written as a proper card game, which is quite unusual in a film for something to be in real time. You assume they're faking it, but that's another sign of Nancy – it had to be real. So, it was a true game of cards that we were actually playing, and Julie and I just practised and practised and practised.

'We knew that with the tight budget they weren't going to be able to film it for ever, so we weren't going to be able to make any mistakes. And we actually did it! I think our stomachs were churning and our hands were clammy, but we managed to get through it, which was fantastic.'

Fortunately, given the subject matter, all the women were able to lighten the mood, something at which Julie is a dab hand. 'She was such a joy to work with,' enthuses Sophie. 'Every day when she came on set she'd call out, "Good morning, everybody!" And it gave you such a lift. The great thing about Julie is that you think she's going to be nice, but actually, she's even nicer – there's no disappointment there at all. It's such a dull thing to say. I want to say she's a roaring drunk, and she's very tricky to work with, but she just isn't!

'She's got such a great sense of comedy and of comic timing and the ridiculous. There was one scene when we both had to be laughing hard and off camera she would just go into complete hysterics, which really helped. You just felt she was an ally.'

However, as the story progressed and the scenes became more and more disquieting, so it became harder for the actresses. 'Julie got quite upset because she had to be really vicious to the maids,' continues Sophie. 'I remember her saying, "I just feel horrid being that ghastly to someone" – but she managed it!

'By that point, the story was building and coming to an end; Joely and Jodhi looked like zombies and you knew what was going to happen. With just four of you and a director, it felt quite claustrophobic.' Indeed *Sister My Sister*, although muted for the screen, is still pretty gory. 'On the staircase, when it was all coming to a crescendo, it all felt quite real and chilling – there was nothing toned down for the cameras.

'I got chucked down the stairs first, but we both had body doubles. So, when it came to it, the stuntwomen came on. Then we laughed because my body double was sixty if she was a day and needed the help of a walking stick by the time she got on to the set! It was quite weird watching the end of the film and knowing that you're not in it.'

On such a draining movie, Julie would retreat to her dressing room in between shots to lie down and regather her energy. As Maisie was improving and had by now started primary school, even the farmhouse proved chaotic after a long day filming. 'Grant would do loads of things with the school, and sometimes there would be other mothers around the kitchen table when Julie got home,' says Sophie. 'The house had a staircase at the back and she said, "Sometimes I just sneak up so I can be alone." Not to be antisocial, but just to have some time out.'

Sister My Sister was billed as 'The Psycho Chiller of the Year' and, given that other releases in 1994 included the feel-good *Four Weddings and a Funeral* and *Forrest Gump*, and the gritty *Pulp Fiction* and *Natural Born Killers*, it did well to hold its own in that genre. However, the film received mixed reviews. 'Despite an excellent performance by Walters, the slow-moving, dark and claustrophobic piece rarely packs the impact it carried on stage,' said the *TV Times*. 'A piece of cinema of almost stifling intensity and formidably acted throughout,' praised the *Guardian*, while *Variety* dismissed it as, 'a small-scale film with some powerful moments'.

Love it or loathe it, Nancy's stylish and mannered direction undoubtedly added to the unsettled feeling of the whole story and, although painful at times, it certainly delivered the required chills. That said, all four actresses play their parts perfectly, leaving the viewer with no doubt as to how the horror can end. This is in no small part due to Nancy Meckler's meticulous rehearsal method and direction.

'It was quite a testament to the producer Norma Heyman that she got it in the film festival,' says Sophie. 'It was played in Los Angeles and London. It's just a shame it didn't have wider appeal as a film, because I think Julie was fantastic – it's certainly one of her more interesting mother roles. It was just effortless: the body, the voice, the gait – extraordinary.'

Unsurprisingly, given the disturbing subject matter, Julie took some time off after *Sister My Sister* was completed and, when she did return to work, it was in a lighter, Victoria Wood vehicle.

Victoria formulated *Pat and Margaret* during her second pregnancy over 1991 and 1992, loosely basing it on the characters seen in 'Over To

Pam' one of the playlets in *Victoria Wood*. She was delighted when Marcus Plantin, director of programmes for London Weekend Television, proposed turning her screenplay into a £6 million, two-hour film with a cinematic release. Breaking into movies was something about which she had long dreamed, and she felt sure that with Julie in the lead, the American market could be conquered.

Sadly, LWT subsequently dropped the project, leaving Victoria publicly crushed. Rather than abandon it, she bought back the rights and took it to the BBC. Margaret Matheson, the executive producer for *Screen One*, purchased it and offered a £1 million production. Victoria, determined the film should see the light of day, resigned herself to a more modest budget and took a pay cut.

Filming for *Pat and Margaret* got under way in May 1994 and continued for most of the summer. The premise was somewhat predictably inspired by television and featured a mismatched couple, played by Julie and Victoria. 'I must have seen something like *Surprise, Surprise*,' says Victoria. 'I was interested in the idea of people being divorced from their pasts. Even if you invent a persona for yourself, in the end you have to face what's inside.'

To this end, Julie plays Pat, a successful British actress in a hit American soap opera called *Glamor*, and Victoria portrays her sister Margaret, a dowdy, northern motorway-cafeteria employee. Julie is perfect as the snooty star, uttering the egotistical line to her PA, 'When you deal with me, Claire, think "icon".' Victoria openly let herself be compared to Julie, who looked fabulous, and consequently appeared as frumpy and unattractive.

The pair are reunited after 27 years on a *Surprise, Surprise*-style TV chat show, *Magic Moments*. After an awkward embrace live on air, Pat makes it clear to Margaret that she has created a new life for herself and does not care to be linked to this unattractive image of her past. Margaret is not enamoured of the situation either, as she realises that she and her sister share nothing except a few strands of DNA.

However, Margaret is coaxed into staying by Pat's assistant Claire (beautifully played by Celia Imrie) and she phones her boyfriend Jim (Duncan Preston) to explain her absence. Thora Hird, magnificent as Jim's mother hell-bent on splitting up the couple, fails to pass on the message however. Duncan and Thora have a brilliant rapport, affording some of the film's most memorable lines.

Meanwhile, Pat's unauthorised biographer Stella Kincaid, played by Deborah Grant, is thrilled with the scandal and determines to find their mother Vera. There follows a farcical chase up and down the country, which halts overnight, allowing a few home truths to be spilled by the sisters: Pat was thrown out of the house by her mother when she fell pregnant aged fifteen, while Margaret was told that her sister had run away.

Stella eventually uncovers the real Vera, an ex-prostitute turned dodgy property dealer, played by Shirley Stelfox, with whom Julie worked on *Personal Services*. Everything seems destined to destroy Pat's career, until the actress, journalist and wayward mother team up to produce a bestseller. Margaret and Jim patch up their differences, he finally stands up to his mother and the couple start afresh with a cafeteria bought for them by Pat. While Stella looks for a happy ending for her biography, Victoria's writing avoids such a sentimental cliché, and many issues are left unresolved.

As with much of Victoria's work, *Pat and Margaret* shows strong elements of autobiographical detail. The difficult family relationship is a recurring theme, as are the two sides of the sisters – Pat has achieved fame and let it go to her head, while Margaret is content to remain in her uninspiring life. Victoria was baring the opposing sides of her personality: 'It was that battle between the one who can never get on, the sort of impotent person, and the one who's so determined to get on that there's no room for anything else,' she said.

Equally, Victoria had always been painfully aware that, of the two friends, Julie was the one who had achieved international success on big and small screen. Although she insisted that she was in a different genre and that level of renown was not appropriate for a comic, a feeling of inadequacy seems to appear many times in the characters she wrote for the two of them.

Pat and Margaret was broadcast as part of the BBC's *Screen One* series on 11 September 1994. It is an enjoyable film, with good pace, interest and a few unpredictable twists, and consequently proved popular with both the public and the critics. Viewing figures were four times that of the previous week's slot, while the *Sunday Times* raved, 'Victoria Wood's screenplay, written for her and Julie Walters, is the perfect forum for the old partnership to prove its undiminished excellence.' The *Observer* simply proclaimed, 'Victoria Wood on top form.'

Those in the trade also thought Victoria had excelled herself as she was nominated for a BAFTA for Best Actress, and the film received a Best Drama BAFTA nomination and a win from the Broadcasting Press Guild. The only criticism to be heard was the way in which Victoria recycled the same themes and jokes, but that took nothing away from the duo's sparkling performances.

Victoria, finally proven to be an accomplished dramatist, sounded reminiscent of Alan Bleasdale. 'I wrote the role of Pat with Julie in mind because I knew she'd be great to play it,' she said. 'The advantage of working with friends is that they're used to my work.'

Funnily enough, Julie's next project teamed her up with Bleasdale, although not for something he had written. Unusually, he acted as producer for a Channel 4 series called *Alan Bleasdale Presents*. During the four-part programme, Bleasdale showcased new writers, one being Raymond Murtagh with his play *Requiem Apache*.

'It was a one-off play that [Bleasdale] liked,' says David Ross, who was also involved. 'Alan was lovely as a producer. He is as he always is: he's never any different. When he's on set as a writer, he's there to support people, not to cause problems. I suppose when you're there as a producer, you're there to smooth the problems! It was actually a lovely job.'

The story follows Hamish, a former getaway-car driver, who has retired to the country to become a househusband and raise his baby son, while his wife works. Things go awry when Hamish is visited by his old gang and they make him an offer he doesn't dare refuse. The only issue he has to work around is who will look after the baby while he is out. Unable to find a solution, Hamish takes the toddler with him. While Julie's old colleague from *Prick Up Your Ears*, Alfred Molina, plays the lead character, Julie has a cameo as Mrs Capstan.

With Maisie seemingly out of the woods, Julie was less nervous about taking on more work. Rather than a total preoccupation with her child's health, she now only had to wrestle with the regular working-mother guilt of not seeing her daughter growing up. She continued to choose her projects carefully, requesting London shoots when possible and insisting that she see her family frequently.

Drawn, as she was, to true stories, at the end of 1994 Julie signed up for a new film, *Intimate Relations*. The setting is a coastal town in England, some forty years earlier. Merchant seaman Harold Guppy, played by Rupert Graves, disembarks his ship in search of his long-lost brother, Maurice, portrayed by Les Dennis. Perturbed by Harold's past, Maurice's wife will not let him stay in their home, so he seeks local lodgings. He stumbles across the welcoming home of the middle-aged Mrs Marjorie Beasley, a role expertly executed by Julie as the epitome of 1950s motherhood. The family consists of the blossoming-yet-macabre teenager Joyce (Laura Sadler*) and the hen-pecked Mr Beasley (Matthew Walker), who is forced to sleep in his own room without any marital relations.

* Laura Sadler tragically died aged 22 in June 2003 after falling from a balcony.

All is well until, one night, a sexually frustrated Mrs Beasley creeps into Harold's room and forces herself upon him. 'She may have started feeling maternal about him and become mixed up,' explained Julie. 'She has quite a high libido even though she's repressed.' The noise from their rampant intercourse awakens Joyce, who enters the room and refuses to leave until she is allowed into their bed. The depraved tale twists further when Mrs Beasley and Harold quietly resume their antics once they think Joyce is asleep. Instead, the tormented teenager lies awake and plots a way to entice Harold into her own bed.

While maintaining a perverse façade of normality, the trio plunge into a rapidly escalating downward spiral that culminates in a horrific act of violence fitting for this darkest of black comedies.

Julie, who would hit 45 before the film was aired, was once again self-conscious about her body and was prepared to put her foot down should a nude scene present itself. 'I was very nervous,' she confided in promotional interviews. 'Rupert is so good-looking – I didn't want any close-ups with him. Luckily, nobody asked me to take my clothes off because I wouldn't do it these days.'

Intimate Relations was director Philip Goodhew's debut. He successfully laces the sordid tale with lashings of satire and comedy, producing a glimpse into the repressed lust, jealousy and deadly obsession behind the net curtains of this well-to-do family. He also aptly captures the nuances of post-World War Two Britain, with ample 1950s references simultaneously honoured and mocked.

'I worry about overdoing the 1950s,' said Julie at the time, 'Marjorie is funny and the 1950s are such a camp era [but] she has to be played ultra-believable and real.' Julie's hair and make-up are suitably severe and took some time to prepare each morning, although the actress was more than happy. 'Being in make-up is just a nice, easy start to the day – really, a good old gossip!' Many colleagues confirm that this is the best time to catch Julie, when she is at her most relaxed, genuine and spontaneous.

Most of the filming was carried out in London but, unlike the Julie of old, the actress went straight home once the day wrapped. 'I *never* hang out socially. I'm a real old bore,' she continued. Philip Goodhew would often call Julie up to invite her out for a drink with Rupert Graves and him, but he would be too late. 'I would say, "I've already eaten and I'm in bed" – at nine o'clock. I don't sleep so well, so I feel I have to preserve much of my energy,' justifies Julie.

During the location shooting in Abergavenny, Julie missed her family and so tried to arrange for Grant and Maisie to visit during half-term. Ironically, this was not possible due to her daughter's busy schedule.

While promoting *Pat and Margaret*, the BBC featured Julie in one of their promos. In it, she wanders through the rambling corridors of the Beeb in search of the complaints department. Instead she stumbles across an assortment of stars in cameos in this clever short.

Julie remained with the channel and, in 1995, once again turned her attentions to Comic Relief and joined a cavalcade of celebrities singing a few lines of 'Old MacDonald' for a montage of the song. This was a tentative step back to her social consciousness, now that she had time again to think of such things, and she has become a regular face for the cause.

24. WORKING MUM

Since its launch in 1982, Channel 4 had increasingly picked up viewer ratings and television advertising income. By 1995, it became a serious rival to ITV, and continued to be so by producing a varied schedule, attracting a young, upmarket audience. To this end, Alan Bleasdale was commissioned to write a six-part prestigious drama series.

Jake's Progress began life as part of the aborted 700-page novel that spawned *GBH* and, on the back of such tremendous success four years earlier, became eagerly anticipated. It was written specifically for Julie and Robert Lindsay and included several of the usual Bleasdale repertory in supporting roles: Lindsay Duncan, David Ross and Alan Igbon.

Julie and Robert play Julie and Jamie Diadoni, a married couple with a six-year-old son called Jake, living in a rural village. They are a dysfunctional family: Jamie is an attractive and charming dreamer, lusted after by the local ladies; Julie is a hard-working nurse who holds the unit together; and Jake is an exceptionally hyperactive and disturbed child – although the source of his inner turmoil is never very clear. Finances and emotions reach breaking point when Julie discovers she is pregnant again; the last thing she needs is another dependant. The only positive point to the new addition is, as Julie says, to get a child 'who's better than Jake'.

Her boy in question, powerfully played by Barclay Wright, proves his wicked side by unleashing cruel prank after dangerous gimmick on his baby brother, and alongside Bleasdale's darkest humour sits tragedy: Jake dresses up as a little Indian brave and tries to set his cowboy-suited sibling on fire; he methodically loosens every screw in the high chair to watch it collapse. The drama continues to unfold around the incompatible generations.

Thomas Sutcliffe from the *Independent* described this rigorous analysis into the pressures of the modern family as, 'What children do to their parents and vice-versa – the difficult, emotionally bruising experience of trying to build a family, a construction for which the parts arrive piecemeal and for which the instructions are always missing.'

The language of Bleasdale's script is often raw, but always touches a nerve with accuracy. This is complimented by the unusual and memorable score, including John Lennon's 'Nobody Told Me' and collaborations between Elvis Costello and Richard Harvey.

Jake's Progress was filmed in Wexford in the Republic of Ireland during the summer months of 1995, and was a particularly pleasant experience for all involved.

'I was with a new wife who came over to Ireland with me and was appointed as dialect coach for Barclay,' says David Ross. 'Our accommodation was like a little village. There was a riding school, which had rather gorgeous chalets in a quadrangle. We all stayed there: the producer Keith Thompson and his wife Dawn; Alan Bleasdale and his wife Julie; Julie Walters; my wife and I. We all lived close to each other, so it was all very sociable. We used to have a lot of meals together. It was lovely because we were all away from home in Ireland.

'Julie would fly home most weekends, so as not to disrupt Maisie's schooling, but sometimes Grant and Maisie would come over for a change and spend the weekend with us, particularly if there was a holiday.

'Grant's a lovely bloke – a very good-looking, quiet chap. When you're with a group of actors and you're not an actor yourself, even though your wife is the leading lady, you tend not to come in and bluster and dominate the whole conversation. I think he's very sensitive to Julie's world and doesn't say, "I feel left out, I want to put my two penn'orth in." There was a very family feel to it all.

'It was my wife's birthday while we were there, and Julie came over with a bottle of champagne and knocked on the door. My wife had been completely in awe of Julie all through drama school, and it just floored her that someone so famous and wonderful would take the trouble to do such a thing. But that's what she's like, she's a very thoughtful person.'

Alan Igbon has fond, if hazy, memories of this time. 'All I can remember of that is I worked during the days and drank a lot of Guinness at night,' he laughs, 'so I don't recall much except that it was great in Ireland! It was a great crack, a real laugh.'

If there is a criticism to be made about the series, it is that it is slow-paced and self-indulgent, focusing on the trivial and, quite frankly, boring. Competing with Jimmy McGovern's hugely successful *Cracker*, *Jake's Progress* was broadcast over the autumn of 1995, the first episode airing on 12 October. Six weeks later, Alan Bleasdale's reputation notwithstanding, the *Guardian's* TV page asked, 'Is anyone still watching?'

That Bleasdale was revered in the world of British drama perhaps meant no one would stand up to him and give an honest opinion. Uniquely, each episode lasted as long as the author wanted, ranging from 75 to 100 minutes, but this only proved the producer's lack of authority. Critic AA Gill pointed out in the *Sunday Times*: '*Jake's Progress* has a problem, one I associate with success – nobody has dared edit it. Bleasdale is a small-screen God: what he writes is treated as writ.' The series desperately needed someone not in awe of Bleasdale to say, 'Let's cut the first twenty minutes, it's waffle.'

Furthermore, the public were expecting a juicy political saga, but Bleasdale was curiously keen to distance himself from being a revolutionary. 'I have no axe to grind, no answers to give and I don't want to change society. I want to reflect it,' said the author at the time.

Bleasdale was notably enthusiastic about writing for Robert and Julie: 'I try to get inside actors, so they can bring out something I know is within them. Often they're not aware of it themselves,' he said, adding that actors are an essential tool for him as they breathe life into his work.

Tellingly, however, Robert was not so complimentary in return. The original script dwelt on his character's failed rock career – he played a gig to mark the closing of the mine where he had worked. But this scene, along with most of the political references, was removed. 'What I'm getting now from the edit is that Jamie is a bit of a waster,' said Robert disappointedly. 'I voiced my opinions to both the producer and Alan, who've been very sympathetic, but in the end the series is about a boy growing up, and that's right.' Coming to this conclusion, however, Robert admitted that he had doubts he would ever be happy with the finished version and he perhaps should have moved on to another project.

The author clearly worked on the series for some time, writing and disregarding several early storylines. Unfortunately, the result is that Bleasdale assumes the viewer is familiar with the family and can understand private jokes and personal relationships.

The relative failure of *Jake's Progress* reflected more on the author than on those involved and Julie spent the rest of the year happily with her family. At the end of 1995, five years after the diagnosis of leukaemia, and three years after her treatment had finished, Maisie was finally given the all-clear.

'We were told that after five years Maisie would have as much chance of getting cancer back as anyone else,' says Julie. 'We were also told that she should have no lasting ill effects from the treatment and will be able to lead a normal life.'

As a precaution, Maisie continued to have an annual check-up, but otherwise she was declared fit and healthy. 'Sometimes, if she's a bit run down, your heart thumps a little louder,' continues her mother. 'But then, after what she's been through, that'll always be the case. Grant says never a day goes by when he doesn't think about it. It sometimes seems we've had to live with it for most of the time we've been together.'

She finally felt she was able to enjoy being a mother again, with just the usual parenting worries. As Maisie was seven, Julie faced many issues, such as schooling and extracurricular activities. 'I will never lumber my child with such a place,' Julie vowed, referring to the terrible convent upbringing she suffered. 'If she wanted to act, I'd support her,' she said. 'Nobody pushed me. I'm glad. I don't think I'd have done it if they had.'

But Julie's greatest challenge remained the balance between work and motherhood. She became so incensed by the misconceptions of others, who thought she had the best of both worlds, that she wrote an article highlighting the issue for OK! magazine's soapbox: 'I get so angry when I hear women saying they wish they had a man to stay at home and take care of the family and domestic chores, leaving them free to go out to work.' She explained that, while role-reversal reflects increased equality between the sexes, it was far from easy.

'Being away from my daughter is hard for me – it has made me depressed at times, and it has torn into my heart,' she said. 'Because children inevitably gravitate towards the person who looks after their needs all day at home – and in role-reversal, that means the father – the mother can be left feeling a bit shut out at times.' Julie was very open about her feelings, even admitting that she had pangs of jealousy when she returned home from a long day at work to find Maisie clinging to Grant.

'I try to console myself by thinking, "No matter, I'm still Mum." But I'm not really – Grant is ... If she's at death's door, which she has been, she's going to want the person who doesn't go away.'

Julie laid herself bare in the lengthy article and offered much insight into the difficulties she and Grant faced with their situation. She concluded by advising, 'Role-reversal is a lot more difficult than it appears. You have to be willing to stay with it, be open and talk about it with your partner. Don't go into it lightly; it could break your marriage as well as your heart.'

Despite her assertions, Julie still needed to work to pay the bills. While she was always striving for artistic credit, some offers were too good to refuse and she accepted more advertising work, taking over from the Bisto Kids as the spokeswoman for the gravy product and making light of bad breath with a series of Clorets ads.

At the beginning of 1996, Julie joined Danny DeVito in an unusual production of Roald Dahl's *Little Red Riding Hood*. The revisionist version was narrated by Ian Holm and featured a host of actors wearing animatronic animal heads. While DeVito provided the voice for the Big Bad Wolf, Julie played the little girl and her grandmother.

Since Maisie's birth, Julie had been swamped by her maternal instincts. For one who once had never wanted to settle down, she now felt an overwhelming surge towards all children. In 1996, she decided to become more involved in Comic Relief. Taking positive action, she went to Addis Ababa in Ethiopia to make an appeal film for the following year's Red Nose Day.

The actress recognised that visiting Ethiopia changed her life and perspective. 'It isn't particularly beautiful, as it's been stricken by civil war, famine and drought. But the people are really beautiful, especially the children. They've got so little, but appreciate life so much,' she said at the time. When she left she promised never to forget the children she had met and to return one day.

The film, broadcast in March 1997, shows Julie's visit to the Goal Drop-in Centre, which provides cheap food and free education to the street kids. The children work hard all day to earn any money they can, but Julie points out that they still laugh and play and have lessons. The footage of the children playing table football and in class at the centre shows them trying to live a normal life, despite the poverty and hardship they face. Such courage in children so young was poignantly reminiscent of Maisie's battle with leukaemia.

Later in 1996, Julie couldn't resist being involved in the BBC's *Wicked Women* drama series and signed up for *Brazen Hussies,* directed by Elijah Moshinsky. In Manchester, Julie again teamed up with Robert Lindsay and worked for the first time with Alun Armstrong and Crissy Rock.

Julie played Maureen Hardcastle, pub landlady and wife of Jimmy, portrayed by Alun. The pub is as run-down as their marriage and after a chance meeting with an old schoolfriend Sandra Delaney (played by Crissy), Maureen decides that what she needs to combat her husband's stripper nights is a ladies' night, with male artists. Sandra's husband Bad Billy Bowman (Robert Lindsay) helps out, although his own infidelities come back to haunt him. Unsurprisingly – given the title of the series – the women are triumphant, but not before a *lot* of male flesh is exposed.

'When I got asked to do *Brazen Hussies*, I nearly died of shock,' recalls Crissy. 'I didn't know that Julie Walters, Alun Armstrong or Robert Lindsay were in it – they were like Hollywood stars to me. I had admired Julie Walters for years. I was completely star-struck – how do you keep your composure when you're working with someone who's like a god to you?

'We were in this costume place and I was getting changed. Next thing, the buzzer on the door went and it was Julie. She was wearing this mac and I was half-dressed and we just looked at each other.'

'We're going to get on marvellously, us two, aren't we?' laughed Julie.

'What you see is what you get: she's not at all false,' continues Crissy. 'Whenever someone would wave at her, she'd say, "Oh, hello love, how are you?" like she'd known them all her life. She's probably racking her brain to think where she knows them from, but it feels like she knows everyone personally.'

Julie was aware of Crissy's awe and, as the two got on so well, decided to continue a tradition. With her first Hollywood movie in mind, she bought Crissy a present.

'I'm going to say to you now what Michael Caine said to me,' explained Julie. 'Enjoy fame while it lasts and save your memories with this camera.' Crissy was bowled over.

Julie was thrilled to be working with Robert again. 'I've played Robert Lindsay's mother, wife and lover now in three TV series,' she said at the time. 'He always plays little jokes on me when we're acting together, like dropping his trousers in a scene when he's not supposed to!'

Not to be outdone, the cheeky actress gave as good as she got. 'We used to laugh at Robert Lindsay in the scene where he had to strip off in the toilets,' says Crissy. 'Julie used to say, "You get more handsome every day, you!"'

'The four of us used to sit in the Winnebago, and Julie and Robert were like brother and sister, reminiscing about *Jake's Progress*. When we'd finish on Friday, the two of them were off like a bat out of hell, going to the airport and jumping on a plane to be home for the weekend. Then they'd come all the way back again for Monday morning.'

Filming was long and tiring because of the tight schedule, but the atmosphere on set was a laugh a minute, due in part to the friendship between Robert and Julie, and also the saucy subject matter. 'She always gets fits of the giggles, but she taught me that you can have a laugh *and* be serious on set,' comments Crissy. 'You can entertain everyone but, when you're [in front of] the camera, that's when you come alive. She never used to fuss about how long a scene would take. Although she was a big star, she never once had a stand-in while waiting for things to be changed, and she never complained about anything.'

As other colleagues have noticed, Julie was aware of her physical limitations, and combining long hours with travelling the length of the country each week was wearing. 'We shared the same Winnebago and, when Julie wasn't filming or rehearsing, she'd go and have a lie down,' says Crissy. 'She'd be awake, but she'd just lie there, almost like meditation. If she wanted to relax, she wouldn't just slope off: she'd say, "I've got to go and get my beauty sleep now, love."

'She taught me how to control my energy. When you're working playing neurotic women, take after take, she'd say to just lie flat so you didn't feel too tired.'

One particularly touching scene between Julie and Alun moved everyone on set.

'Did you ever love me?' asks Julie.

'I married you, didn't I?' comes the reply.

'I loved you,' she persists.

'Aren't I the lucky one,' he sighs.

It is a sign of Julie's talent that no matter what the scene, in any play or film, she absorbs her audience. As so many directors and colleagues have observed, because she portrays her characters so truthfully from the heart, she becomes so utterly believable.

'When we did the song it was so funny,' remembers Crissy of 'I Will Survive', which appears in *Brazen Hussies*. 'We had to go into a proper recording studio in the BBC where they used to do *Top of the Pops*. We recorded the song and the video for it. It was fabulous, but we never got on *Top of the Pops*!'

Julie and Crissy became great friends during the shoot, mainly because they had lived in the same areas and shared a sense of humour. 'I told her I did stand-up in this club in Birmingham,' says Crissy. 'It was dead rough and this one woman had sovereigns on.'

'Ooh, you've met me Aunty Ruby then, have you?' replied Julie, quick as a flash.

Julie always remained so down-to-earth. 'When it was dinnertime she'd grab my hand and say, "Quick! Run!"' laughs Crissy. 'We'd run to the chuck wagon, and she'd say, "Oh, just throw it all on, love!" Then she'd say, "Now, Crissy, you promise me you're not to let me have any more pudding after this." And of course, she'd have some more!'

'She wasn't worried about her weight, but she used to eat rice cakes for snacks. One time I had a cup of coffee and thought one was a coaster – I put my coffee on one of her rice cakes! She also used to eat bananas because she said they're good for your metabolism.'

Julie clearly took Crissy under her wing. 'Julie's like a mother figure in that she cares about people – she genuinely cares about each person on a one-to-one basis,' Crissy continues. 'There's just this warm aura around her – it's unbelievable. You think it must be hard for her to always be so bubbly, but then you realise it doesn't drop, so she must be a genuinely nice person. When Julie Walters comes in the room, her presence brings a tranquil calm around her.'

When resting in the Winnebago, Julie and Crissy chatted about their home life. 'She used to talk about the animals on the farm and how they would call the pigs names, like Bobo or Tiddles,' says Crissy. As with all filming away from London, when Grant and Maisie could spare the time, they visited the set and Crissy was thrilled finally to meet the family she had heard so much about.

'Maisie looks like a cross between Julie and Grant – it really depends on who you see her with,' she says. 'She's a lovely girl. She's chatty, but not overly so. She's not spoilt and she's really well behaved. She has gorgeous, big eyes that look up at you from under her fringe. She really adores her parents, and Julie and Grant are just great with her. They work well together.

'Maisie's an unusual name. I'd never heard it before. When I was at home in Liverpool one time, I saw this little picture in a frame which explained what your name means. Next time I saw her, I said, "You've got a lovely name – this is for you." She sent me a lovely thank-you letter, which I still have.'

25. AN ENGLISHWOMAN IN NEW YORK

Nineteen ninety-seven offered something a little different to Julie. She was approached by ITV, who asked whether she would like to work with them in America.

'I asked to see the script, but was told that there wasn't one,' she said, 'and in fact this was a job in which acting wasn't involved.'

The brief was more challenging than any role: to experience America fully, she had to roll up her sleeves and put in some hard graft. She was to become a working alien in New York and Miami for one month. The deal included two documentaries following her daily activities and a resulting book; it was too exciting to turn down.

As much as anything, Julie was keen to boost transatlantic relations. 'We all ought to be able to live together and enjoy the differences in race and culture,' she says. 'Loathing comes through fear and ignorance.'

Julie Walters arrived in New York in February to temperatures that hovered around zero, but felt colder than Britain because of the biting wind. The first variety of posts for the actress were to be fulfilled at the Four Seasons Hotel on East 57th Street. Rather than marvel at the architectural splendour of the five-star building, Julie found herself quickly immersed in the 'Dream Team'.

Wearing an outfit of a black overcoat and trousers with matching gloves, cape and top hat, Julie resembled one of the Beatles during the snow scenes of *Help!* when she reported for an eight-hour shift as a doorwoman. Her assignment was on 58th Street because the rear entrance saw more action than the more prestigious but placid front door. 'I had to be a one-woman luggage-carrying, people-directing, advice-giving, traffic-controlling, star-schmoozing, message-taking dynamo,' wrote Julie at the time, 'and this was not even a busy day.'

Her day was briefly brightened when she held a car door open for the A-list heart-throb George Clooney, who was at that time starring in *ER* and *Batman Forever*. She had been some distance away but 'a sudden burst of superhuman powers meant that before he could blink his gorgeous eyes, I was by his side and leading him to the limo,' she wrote in her memoirs of the event.

Another duty that she had to fathom was driving one of the stretch limousines. For someone who had only recently learned to drive in a normal car on the left-hand side of the road, Julie coped admirably –

once she had been shown how to adjust the seat so that she could reach the pedals. That done, 'I glided gently forward, I felt like the captain of the *QE2* steaming out of Southampton Harbour.'

The following day she joined the housekeeping team, and in pairs they had an average of 38 minutes to restore each room to its former glory. Julie felt the least she could do was make a bed properly – after all, she had been proud of her mitred corners as a nurse – but soon found that it had to be the Four Seasons way or not at all. Moving on, she tried her hand at room service, but was more interested in sampling the food than delivering it.

She came away from the Four Seasons impressed by the attitude of all the staff. She admired their pride, no matter how menial or lowly paid their job. Julie felt the Brits could learn a thing or two about 'their national attitude to customer satisfaction, which makes the British, permanently class-ridden, often bitter, sometimes downright rude approach look like something from the Dark Ages, which it probably is'.

From there, Julie braved the bracing weather as she spent some time training to be a ranger in Central Park. Donning the padded green uniform and oversized beige hat, Julie was reminded of her misspent youth watching *Yogi Bear*. When asked to give herself a nickname, Julie did not hesitate and answered Boo Boo (the name of Yogi's sidekick), well aware that the signature suggested she would make a mistake. Armed with the 45-page book of park law and a baton, Julie was taught how to scare potential assailants and rescue someone stranded on the iced-over swimming pool.

In just one day – given her television status – Julie pledged allegiance to the park commissioner and graduated as a fully fledged ranger, complete with her own badge. Fortunately, she was involved in only one incident, and even that turned out to be a false alarm.

Her next assignment harked back to her student days at the United Cattle Products restaurant, as she tackled a quintessential New York deli. Entering the Carnegie Deli on the corner of 7th and Madison Avenue, Julie signed up for a nine-hour day at the place once immortalised in Woody Allen's film *Broadway Danny Rose*. She virtually had to learn a new language to understand the menu; she needed to shout orders at the top of her voice to be heard; and she had to please the customer at all costs, because her pay was minimal and the real money lay in tips, which could be up to 40 per cent. Julie, for all her acting training, found it hard to lose her apologetic manner and acquire the requisite brash New York attitude.

Her final job in the Big Apple initially seemed more in her line of work: she became a news reporter for NBC television for the day. However, she admitted she was used to a world of rehearsals and multiple takes rather than the cutthroat, time-is-money approach of this crew. She was at least presented with an interesting story – Sylvia Alston had transformed a run-down apartment block into an immaculately decorated place to attract locals with talent – and Julie handled the interviews well.

With three interview tapes in the can, Julie raced back to the edit suite at the Rockefeller Center. Disaster struck, as one of the tapes had been accidentally swapped and was on its way to New Jersey. At the very last minute the relevant information was electronically transmitted to Julie and she met her deadline by the skin of her teeth. She closed her one-minute-and-twenty-eight-second piece with the immortal line, 'In Sugarhill, this is Julie Walters for News Channel Four' – and became part of broadcasting history.

The plucky actress was in for quite a culture and temperature shock as she left the wintry bluntness of New York in February for the stranger, sunnier climes of Miami. Julie was aware of the latter's reputation as a crime and drugs paradise, but duly reported to the Dade Police School of Justice and Safety Administration for her first assignment.

She was horrified to find that her induction included an American movie-style run, chanting in step and on beat. From there she moved to the weapon self-defence section of the class and ended with a rehearsal for a felony stop, chasing a pretend armed criminal by car, stopping him and bringing him to justice. As with the New York deli, Julie found there was no place for her inbred British politeness in this job.

Fortunately, the new recruit was asked only to pound the beaches and she started in Haulover Park, north Miami. Aside from fighting the sun's rays as the temperature hit the high seventies Fahrenheit, Julie's worst crime was her wandering eye on the male nudist beach.

Her next task was more physical as she signed up with Pesky Critters, a company who specialise in capturing wild and exotic animals, alive and unharmed. Though she turned 47 on her first day on the job, she soon found herself capturing a sixteen-foot python that weighed eight and a half stone.

The most terrifying call-out was undoubtedly the alligator taking a swim in someone's pool. Although small, he was still six to eight feet long. Julie's boss, Todd, hooked his catchpole noose around the gator's neck and hoisted him on to the poolside. He sat on the animal's back and struggled as the creature whipped its head and tail violently from side to side. Finally gaining control, he instructed Julie to drop her pole and tape up the beast's mouth.

'It's a strange feeling taking out a roll of tape and binding up a deadly alligator as if it was a vase you were sending to your Auntie Vi in Australia for Christmas,' she recalled in her diary. But the actress was so dedicated to doing well that she even leaned forward to bite off the tape without a second thought for the powerful jaws.

Little could match the excitement of *that* job, but Julie's final employment succeeded in taking her breath away. She was a real-estate salesperson – a glorified estate agent – but she was dealing with multimillionaires purchasing multimillion-dollar properties. On entering one mansion she exclaimed, 'It's like the TARDIS!'

Having spent one month abroad, Julie was desperate to get home. She had thoroughly enjoyed her travels and relished the diverse tasks, but just wanted to be back with her family. 'I'll never go away for that long again,' she said on her return. 'I was homesick and missed my daughter Maisie.'

Her assignments were detailed in two entertaining documentaries, *Julie Walters Is An Alien In New York* and *Julie Walters Is An Alien In Miami*, and a tie-in book, *Julie Walters Is an Alien*, published by Hodder & Stoughton. She proved herself to be an amply competent presenter and compelling author, able to make both her viewers and readers laugh out loud. Rather than portray a beautifully written character reading a cleverly crafted script, the programmes depict Julie for who she really is: funny, warm, intelligent and courageous. And she's family-orientated – the preface to the book sweetly includes an illustration of New York by Maisie.

Once back in England, Julie undertook a bizarre film short. *Bath Time* is a black comedy that follows an obsessional man, whose unrequited love for his goldfish finally pushes him over the edge – he tries to commit suicide, but finds it surprisingly difficult. Julie and Alan Cumming appeared in the seventeen-minute piece, directed by Russell Michaels at Elstree Studios.

After a month of being back with her family, Julie was offered a job that again, although it meant filming in Manchester, she could not refuse. *Girls' Night* was the British director Nick Hurran's second feature and tackled the difficult subject of cancer head-on. 'It's a film that speaks about the unspeakable. About the horrible emotions you go through – the hope, and then the reality of the disease,' he said.

The movie is about a pair of best friends and in-laws, Dawn (Brenda Blethyn) and Jackie (played by Julie). They work together on an assembly line in a factory in the north of England, and enjoy nothing more than making fun of the boss and playing bingo. Dawn is married to Jackie's brother Steve and struggles to look after the house and two children.

Jackie's marriage is an argumentative sham and she is having an affair with the bingo club owner Paul.

The girls go on their regular night out to the bingo and, while they're waiting in the queue, a bird defecates on Dawn – a superstitious sign of good luck. As fate would have it, Dawn wins the national jackpot of £100,000, while Jackie is in the back office having sex with Paul. Both women reach their respective climaxes simultaneously.

Dutiful Dawn honours their prior arrangement and splits the winnings fifty–fifty with her friend. Jackie immediately ditches her husband and job, and moves in with Paul, only to find he's not interested in commitment. Meanwhile, Dawn, who has been suffering a lack of control in her hand, suffers a seizure.

During Dawn's stay in hospital, the viewer learns of her history of breast cancer. She thought she had beaten it, but the cancer has travelled, and she now has a brain tumour. She undergoes treatment without telling anyone, but Jackie wises up to the vomiting and hair loss and confronts the doctor. Dawn has given up on the treatment to live her final days with dignity. Jackie is distraught by the revelation, but organises one last girl's night out – to Las Vegas.

No sooner do they arrive in the gambling capital than Dawn wins a fruit-machine jackpot and picks up a cowboy named Cody. Dressing up as rhinestone cowgirls, the girls let their hair down and gamble with love and fortune. Finally, Dawn realises she needs to be with her family and the pair return home. Dawn inevitably dies and Jackie delivers the final eulogy, before embracing life herself. Her decision on the future should be a surprise, but the scene at the start of the film rather spoils the ending.

Julie Walters and Brenda Blethyn were Nick Hurran's top two choices for the powerful leads and he was thrilled when they both accepted without hesitation.

'It's just such an utter dream cast,' he continues. 'My belief is, you always ask. So we sent it out to [Kris Kristofferson], and he came back very quickly and said yes.' Nick filled the supporting roles with the respected actors George Costigan and James Gaddas.

The casting was prime, because Julie and Brenda work famously together. Julie in particular excels herself as Jackie, the one left behind. She and her husband create tremendous tension in their opening kitchen scene, and she is delightfully lippy at work. She also handles with care the sensitive issue of smoking in regard to her friend's cancer.

The subject matter of *Girls' Night* could not be undertaken lightly and it was no coincidence that most of the people working on the film had first-hand experience of these circumstances. The script was written by Kay Mellor (who had written the TV series *Band of Gold*), and was based on her own experiences. 'I wrote *Girls' Night* in memory of my dear friend Denise, who died at a young age,' says Kay. 'It helped me understand how she could accept death so gracefully when everything in me was raging at the injustice of it all.'

Nick Hurran adds that it is even more personal than that: '[Kay] used to visit her friend every day in hospital and they would play "Fantasy Holidays", imagining the holidays they would have when she got better.' The film represents the ultimate holiday she planned with her friend and consequently Kay finds it almost impossible to watch *Girl's Night* without shedding a tear.

'It's a subject that was treated with great respect by all of us,' Nick continues, adding that everyone had some personal experience of cancer. 'There were particular scenes where I knew we had to use three cameras, because the emotions involved meant we were only going to get one hit at it.' One can only imagine how difficult it must have been for all concerned to rake up such deep-rooted sentiments.

With plenty of scope to dwell on the maudlin, Nick was determined to focus on the positive. 'I was very keen for the film to be a celebration,' he said. 'I know it is a harrowing subject, but I didn't want it to descend into sadness. It's about losing someone you love and making the most of them while you still have them.' He explains that it was vital to treat the comedy and drama in the same manner, with the goal of finding and portraying the truth of the situation.

Balancing the two extremes of drama was something in which Julie was particularly well versed. Brenda had an extensive stage career and, although she had only recently broken into cinema, had already notched up an Oscar nomination for Mike Leigh's *Secrets & Lies*. The two exceptional actresses truly touch the audience's heart in *Girl's Night*, proving that small gestures count a lot more than big words.

The project was originally destined for the small screen, but Granada secured backing from the American producer Showtime Network and it became a huge success on the big screen. The film is understandably emotional, but there is one corny line too many about the disease: Dawn says she's lucky because her number always comes up and the girls comment how time seems to stand still in Las Vegas. This occasional crassness is compensated for by such beautiful camera work and thought-provoking performances.

The film was released initially through the film festivals at the end of 1997 and the beginning of 1998, and the greatest response undoubtedly came from the Sundance festival. 'The audience laughed louder than I'd ever heard any audience and wept uncontrollably,' says Nick proudly. 'Then, as the credits rolled, there was a silence like I'd never heard.'

Grant Roffey turned forty in the summer of 1997. He and Julie had been together for twelve years and had weathered many storms. The subject of marriage had come up several times, but neither of them, particularly Julie, felt the need to make their union legal. They had made the ultimate commitment to each other by having a child together and, clearly, the trauma of Maisie's illness only served to make them stronger.

One day, their accountant pointed out a few technicalities that they needed to discuss. 'He said it was incredibly foolish for us not to be married because, if anything happened to either of us, we wouldn't be entitled to all sorts of things,' explained Julie in the *Sunday Mirror*. If Julie died without being married to Grant, the two most important – and shocking – examples were that he wouldn't necessarily get custody of Maisie and he would have to pay inheritance tax on the house and his livelihood, the farm.

'But I was still reluctant to go ahead because I thought we were all right as we were.'

Eventually practicality prevailed.

'We decided that it was better for us to be married in every way – financially and legally.'

Despite her fame, Julie is not someone who embraces celebrity, and the prospect of a lavish wedding with hundreds of guests and a *Hello!*-type spread left her distinctly nauseous. Simplicity was the order of the day, and she had a wonderful idea of combining Grant's milestone birthday, their pending nuptials and another trip to the Big Apple.

'New York is really beautiful – the energy is amazing,' she said, enthused by her recent visit. Keeping their plans strictly hush-hush, the couple arranged for friends to look after their daughter. The only people who knew of their intentions were Maisie, the people looking after her and Julie's closest friend.

'We told Maisie, but she wasn't that interested,' said Julie. 'She was just pleased that she could go and stay with her best friend, Annabel, for three days.'

Grant and Julie organised a whirlwind three-day trip, which only just gave them time to register their intent to marry. 'It was hilarious,' Julie recounted to the *Daily Mail*. 'We had to go to City Hall the day before to fill in the relevant forms. We had to queue up with all these Mexicans who were getting married so they could stay in America.'

Julie Walters and Grant Roffey were married at New York's City Hall on 2 July 1997. On the surface, the civil ceremony seemed to be unromantic, unprepared and rushed.

When they got to the wedding chapel, an administration clerk asked who would be their witness. The disorganised pair had not considered such a detail and ended up borrowing another couple's witness. Seeming more like a comedy than a wedding, the witness got her five seconds of fame when the lady officiating asked if anybody knew of any just cause or impediment why Julie and Grant could not get married.

'Absolutely not!' shouted the woman from Seattle, very melo-dramatically.

Suddenly, Julie, a practical rather than emotional person, was overwhelmed by the event. 'Often the most unromantic situations can become romantic and, because we'd made no effort to make it romantic, it was. Suddenly it wasn't about the money or making sure each of us was secure. It was about officially declaring our feelings for each other.'

After the initial sentiment settled, Julie was aware of a more subtle change: 'It hasn't altered the way we feel about each other, but it has made a difference. I feel that we are finally in a proper framework.' Although Julie retained her maiden name as her professional title, she was quietly tickled to answer to Mrs Roffey on a personal matter.

And that was it. Mr and Mrs Roffey returned to England and kept the news quiet. They told immediate family and friends once they were back in the country, but refused to make it public knowledge. 'I felt as though it would bring us bad luck if we made a big thing about it,' Julie explained. 'We didn't tell anybody beforehand for the same reason.' Amazingly, the press didn't find out until over a year later.

26. ORDINARY WOMEN IN EXTRAORDINARY SITUATIONS

Having turned down other roles in 1997 (including one in *Little Voice*, for which Brenda Blethyn gained another Oscar nomination), Julie was willing to work again for Alan Bleasdale. She received a script from him for a new drama series called *Melissa*, with her part outlined as 'a very plain, drab woman with glasses'.

Rather than be offended, she accepted without hesitation. 'I suppose anyone looking for an actor to play a middle-aged monster dials my number first,' she says. 'I like playing ordinary women. Ordinary women in extraordinary situations, rather than the other way round.' Needless to say, Bleasdale had written the piece for the usual crew, but the subject itself was new territory for the writer.

'There was a detective series years ago written by Francis Durbridge, which was a very good mystery – a whodunnit,' explains Michael Angelis. 'Alan was quite friendly with Francis and so did a spin on it, kind of a prequel: Melissa's background from her point of view.'

'It was quite a departure for Bleasdale,' says Gary Cady, the new kid on the block suggested by Robert Lindsay. 'Everyone expected dark, gritty, northern, working-class realism and instead he picked this very frothy, dated thriller.

'It was a good original idea. Francis Durbridge is a master writer of thriller and Alan is character-driven, not plot-driven. So the idea of taking the frame of a brilliant thriller and adding Bleasdale, who writes marvellous characters, should have been brilliant.'

Bleasdale's first problem was simply that it was just too complicated. 'There's a series of murders which start in South Africa, and continue on the boat over to England and then in England,' says Michael, who plays one of the detectives. 'A group of close friends are slowly being killed off one by one. Jennifer Ehle plays Melissa and one of her best friends is Julie Walters, who actually turns out to be her mother. Interspersed with this are all these murders, and no one can really work out why they are happening.

'It's all very complicated, but it turns out that Julie put Jennifer up for adoption years earlier and has been trying to find her ever since. When she finds her, she finds out how badly she'd been treated as a child and goes over to South Africa to bump off these two people.

'Then, the guy Melissa's married to is blackmailing various people and starts bumping them off. Each week you'd think, What's going to happen next? Even to this day I'm still trying to work it out!'

The next problem was one of class. Bleasdale was used to writing from his working-class roots and seemed unable to summon empathy for the upper classes. 'The whole thing is about a lot of spoiled rich people, but spoiled rich people suffer too,' says Gary Cady. 'When it went out, however, people didn't have sympathy for them: they felt spoiled rich people deserve to suffer.'

Still, although it's easy to see with hindsight why *Melissa* did not work, at the time, the cast were presented with a script from the brilliant Alan Bleasdale, who rarely puts a foot wrong.

Filming took around six weeks in London at the beginning of 1998. 'We were using an office block in Chiswick as a stand-in for police cells,' recalls Gary. 'We didn't really have a studio, it was all on location. We had one day away in Llandudno. We went up there just to walk along the beach, and then we had a nice dinner in the hotel.

'There were a lot of scenes in the back of the car while I was driving. We did the road scenes down in Surrey Quays, because you can block the roads off. So there was Adrian Dunbar, Julie Walters and Diana Weston in the back of the car – the three of them together were hysterical, they were all like naughty schoolchildren. They are all very funny people, just wise-cracking all the time.

'For me it was a bit exhausting. I was the one with all the lines and I had to drive. I was trying to concentrate while they were all mucking about and laughing. At one point I just had to scream at them, "Will you just stop being so funny!", because it wears you out after a while.

'We were in [a] crazy red Jaguar, that I kept smashing up, with a great big camera strapped to the bonnet, and these three in the back being hysterical – it had kind of an odd, surreal feel to it.'

Although the cast ably amused themselves, the subject matter was not the cheeriest. 'It got pretty grim for Julie,' says Michael Angelis. 'It was a very heavy piece and, because Jennifer Ehle gets killed about halfway through, Julie had a lot of morgue acting to do, looking at bodies and all that sort of thing – it was quite tough.'

Gary remembers the conclusion vividly. 'There's a scene right at the end where Julie's character takes her own life,' he says. 'She crushes a glass in her armpit and bleeds to death, and very, very slowly you just see the life draining out of her. I remember watching her do that scene – it was incredibly moving.

'That was a fairly intense scene all round as my character has just found out the love of my life had lost her life, and then we found out who did it. The camera moved around to each one of us, getting our reactions in turn. The director, Bill Anderson, was very sensitive, he just put the camera on the person that was ready to be filmed. He tried to get a filmic sense to the production as much as possible.'

Predictably, the author appeared at many of the rehearsals, but kept his distance. 'Alan called me at home about a week into the shoot just to say he'd been watching the rushes and he was very pleased with what he saw,' says Gary.

No amount of first-class acting could overcome the underlying problems of the series but, worse still, *Melissa* was let down by ill-advised airtime. 'It just didn't have the impact it should have done,' says Gary Cady. 'The response was disappointing and I think the schedule was partly to blame. Because they were expecting this big new Bleasdale, they cleared the schedule for five days from Sunday night. It was meant as a huge compliment – they'd never done that before – but in retrospect the scheduling was wrong.

'Because it was a thriller, you really needed to see every part as it unfolds, and nobody stays in for five nights in a row. It would have been better if they had picked one night and shown it weekly. Then they would have got people hooked, watching the characters and the plot unfold, and it would have been a success.'

It was a great shame that *Melissa* was not more popular, but most people saw it as just another blip in Bleasdale's career and it did not put anyone off working with him again. The regulars were in fact pleased to see that Julie was much more her normal self. 'She did get a bit mumsy at one point,' confesses Michael Angelis, 'but she seems to have lost that and is back to how she used to be – Julie's always been the best fun in the world, a great laugh, but obviously there was a period when Maisie was ill and she had a lot on her mind and she quietened down a bit.'

Indeed, Julie was facing the normal trials and tribulations of raising a prepubescent daughter. 'She's just like any other ten-year-old,' said Julie at the time, 'except that her illness brought out tremendous courage and compassion within her. She can't bear to see anyone suffering.'

A mother cannot protect her child for ever, as Julie was beginning to find out. Maisie wanted to become a weekly boarder at her school, which played on Julie's conscience. The mother, who had come so close to losing her child, naturally wanted to spend as much time with her daughter as possible. Yet Julie also understood that, as Maisie was an only child, she desired a little independence and the company of her peers.

'I said to Grant that, if she does go and board during the week, it will be like the first step towards her leaving home and I'll feel as if a part of her has gone,' said Julie. 'I don't want that to happen, but I do want to choose the best thing for her.'

Next in Julie's work line-up was another of Alan Bennett's monologues. *The Outside Dog* was part of his second series of *Talking Heads*. The producer, Mark Shivas, was unaware that Bennett had been working on a new batch. 'It was an amazing surprise to get them,' he said. 'They are darker than the previous six, but still wonderful television.'

Julie's character in *The Outside Dog* was certainly much more sinister than the unsuspecting porn star of *Her Big Chance*. British tabloids had been sensationalising, and causing panic over, serial killers for many years, but the most recent case was Rosemary West, who was jailed for life in November 1995, and her husband Fred, who hanged himself in his cell. The couple had buried their multiple victims under the patio at their house in Cromwell Street.

Although Bennett claims immunity to topical themes, *The Outside Dog* seems to draw from the contemporary media scaremongering. In the piece, Julie's husband is suspected of a string of murders of local women. Although determined to believe in him, she finds incriminating evidence; the ending is left ambiguous as to whether or not she will denounce her husband. Julie handles the tense piece magnificently and the viewer is left feeling rather suffocated.

In contrast, her next project was a much lighter affair, both in terms of content and workload. Victoria Wood, who had been awarded an OBE in December 1997, was approached by the BBC to write a sitcom.

'I knew it was about a group of women in a factory canteen, so I asked myself, "Who are they? And how many?"' said Victoria. She had originally planned on seven main characters but found that too many to work with in a half-hour programme. She settled on five with several hangers-on.

She began to write prolifically – in fact the first three episodes served only to set the scene in her mind and were subsequently scrapped. As the characters developed it was clear that she was writing for certain people, namely the group with whom she regularly worked and a few loyal extras. Victoria herself takes the main role as Bren; her colleagues include Dolly (Thelma Barlow) and Jean (Anne Reid), bickering menopausal women; Twinkle (Maxine Peake), distinctly uninterested in work and more concerned with her sex life; and Anita (Shobna Gulati), who is so dense, she's on a different planet. Duncan Preston appears as the maintenance man, Stan; Celia Imrie is the manic human-resources manager and Andrew Dunn is the supervisor, Tony, who develops a relationship with Bren.

Of course, Victoria often adds an autobiographical touch with an impossible mother, and so she created Petula. 'When I first came up with the idea, I was determined not to use Julie,' she says. 'People must think I can't work with anyone else.' However, as the character gathered momentum and the words spilled on to the page, the casting was inevitable: 'I genuinely couldn't think of anyone else who could do the part better.'

Julie was delighted to appear with Victoria again, and relished the part of her mother, Petula Gordino. 'No one could call her remotely glamorous,' she says. 'She was just another in a long line of grotesque old crones.' Petula sees the world in a different light from everyone else; she embellishes and falsifies most things, just occasionally telling the truth in order to confuse. 'She is someone who lives on the edge of society.'

What is amazing is that, although Victoria was the star and writer of the show, she insisted on giving the funniest lines to others, more often than not to Julie. 'I always think, Christ, if I'd written that, I wouldn't let anyone else have it. But she doesn't seem to mind,' Julie marvels.

Petula never fails to upset the balance of Bren's world whenever she appears: 'I've had postnatal disinterest for thirty years,' says the mother, who put her daughter in an orphanage as a child and then forgot the address.

The series was called *dinnerladies* and took up the majority of Julie's summer of 1998 with filming at the BBC. The cast rehearsed from Monday to Thursday and recorded on a Friday evening. Using a new technique, Victoria and her long-standing director Geoff Posner immediately analysed the show and rerecorded any weak sections on the Saturday night.

Each episode dealt with the effect of different visitors on the core members of the dinnerladies cast. Petula was a guest on the show with reasonable regularity, simply because she caused so much disruption. Her main appearances are in the episode titled 'Scandals', in which she brings shame on the factory by shacking up with a sixteen year old toy boy, and in the fifth episode, 'Party', Petula brings a strange friend Babs to the Christmas do. As with the majority of Victoria's work, the subjects of television, women's problems and any number of double entendres were liberally strewn throughout the script.

The six episodes of *dinnerladies* were broadcast during November and December 1998. The BBC touted it as the revival of the Great

British Situation Comedy, but Victoria sensibly shunned any such connection. 'I don't feel anything is riding on it except I want people to like it,' she said then. 'I want it to be half an hour of television that people like, that's all.'

The series received mixed reviews. Wood loyalists instantly predicted it would be a hit, with 'writing that is not a million miles from brilliant', while the backlash commented on its playground humour and tedious, old-fashioned feeling. Paul Hoggart wrote a fair summation for *The Times*: 'There were a few dud lines, but since Wood's script packed more inventive original and funny gags into one episode than most British sitcoms manage in a whole series, it seems churlish to complain.' The public watched Victoria's new creation with support, although viewing figures dropped from an initial 12.24 million to just under 9.5 million by the end of the series.

By 1998, Julie had reached the menopause and was grateful to have other women in the same situation for a chat. 'During the making of *dinnerladies* we were like a bunch of old biddies sitting around and discussing our symptoms,' she laughs. 'Fortunately, these days it isn't a taboo subject and people are open about it and honest, and able to laugh at the whole thing, too.'

It wasn't just among friends that Julie openly discussed the changes she was experiencing and she divulged her secrets to reporters, hoping to help other women in the same boat. 'I don't like the idea of having HRT [hormone-replacement therapy] so I've been using progest cream, which is a progesterone replacement,' she said, matter-of-factly. 'I don't like the idea of having oestrogen replacement. There's a lot of nonsense talked about HRT helping women to fight off osteoporosis, but they are now discovering that it's not actually a lack of oestrogen that leads to osteoporosis, but progesterone.'

Julie also passed on her discovery that green tea alleviates hot flushes, to which she was prone. 'It's good for you,' she explained. 'I had terrible hot flushes and tea, ordinary tea, made it much worse. I love tea and someone suggested green tea because it doesn't affect you in the same way, even though it still gives you a lift.'

Julie's workload had been quite heavy throughout 1998, but *Titanic Town* was a project so close to her heart she couldn't refuse. It was a gritty drama adapted from the novel of the same name by Mary Costello, the daughter of an early Ulster peace campaigner. The film is based on the true story of a family's survival through the troubles in Ireland during the early 1970s, although some of the lines between fact and fiction are a little blurred.

Julie plays Bernie McPhelimy, a formidable housewife who moves her family into the Catholic neighbourhood of Andersonstown in west Belfast, once famed as the location of the *Titanic's* construction, but now reduced to a battlefield of bullets. She will do anything to protect her four children, particularly as her husband has an ulcer and is in and out of hospital. The family try to continue life as normal but, with shootings literally taking place on their doorstep, it is sadly predictable that someone close will be the next victim.

One of Bernie's oldest friends is killed in crossfire while out shopping. Distraught at losing her former bridesmaid, Bernie admits she's grateful it wasn't her son, who had been standing right next to the woman. Sick of the violence, particularly during the day when children are around, Bernie attends a Women's Institute peace group. She finds their approach ineffectual and determines to set up her own cause to stop the fighting.

Though she has all the best intentions in the world, Bernie is naïve and her words are easily twisted by the media to make her look anti-IRA rather than pro-peace. Given that the IRA claimed they were fighting the British Army to protect Republican civilians, her attempts are not well received in the area. Bernie becomes caught up in the complex peace talks, and is manipulated by both sides, all the while alienating and angering her neighbours.

Meanwhile, her eldest daughter embarks on a sexual adventure, only to get her heart broken. The young couple prove excellent debuts for Nuala O'Neill and Ciaran McMenamin. Bernie is virtually oblivious of her family's needs – campaigning for peace is all she is concerned with. When she tries to organise a petition, as suggested by the British officials, she meets resistance, but through perseverance persuades thousands to sign. Eventually, she believes her own publicity and thinks she really can find the elusive solution to an age-old struggle.

After her daughter snaps and tells her the truth, Bernie is further humiliated when she realises the tirade was witnessed by the ever-present British Army. She understands that she will receive threats on her life, but when the estate turns nasty and there is an attack on the family home – culminating in the hospitalisation of her son by an axe-wielding neighbour – Bernie gives in. She resigns from the peace movement and the family are forced to move.

The fact that nothing has changed leaves an unsatisfactory ending for the viewer and, without any questions really answered, one wonders what the film was hoping to prove. Although the subject matter was undoubtedly worthy and thought-provoking, *Titanic Town* is flat and heavy-going. Thankfully, Bernie is not portrayed as a saint – while she's obviously brave, she's also impulsive, Valium-popping and revelling in the limelight.

The director Roger Michell (*Notting Hill*) injects into the grim activities a shot of black comedy, while his successful use of hand-held cameras helps keep the bloodshed blunt and hard-hitting, yet not gory. The inordinate amount of blue language is actually more offensive than the violence.

Ciaran Hinds, a politically aware student in Belfast during the 1970s, relished the role as Julie's suffering husband. What really appealed to Julie herself was the resemblance of Bernie to Mary Walters. 'This one *really* reminds me of my mum,' says Julie. 'She was strong – she'd have protected us to the end.'

Drawing on her mother's stoicism, Julie achieves a marvellous performance and helps carry the film. She is utterly believable in her anguish: she only wants to protect her children, yet she is the one causing them pain. Her dichotomy is highlighted early on when she discusses the problem with friends, simultaneously watching her daughter return home late after being out with a boy. 'All I want is a peaceful life for my children, I am gonna kill you, wee girl,' she utters, icily, in the same breath.

Julie adds a splash of physical humour when Bernie misplaces the IRA's list of demands at her first summit with British officials and rummages in her handbag, although the *Guardian* film review criticised this style of comedy as 'Julie Walters in curlers doing one of her turns'. These were the only negative comments, and overall the reviews, especially in America, were positive: 'One of this season's most welcome comebacks', commented Lou Lumenick for the *New York Post*, while Stephen Holden wrote, 'a powerful performance', for the *New York Times*.

Once again making waves, in December 1998 Julie appeared in Angus Deayton's *The End of the Year Show* alongside Clive Anderson, Robbie Coltrane and Graham Norton. Getting into the Christmas spirit, Julie also featured in her first pantomime since the bawdy *Dick Whittington* in Liverpool, some 24 years previously.

ITV produced a feature-length special of *Jack and the Beanstalk*, written by Simon Nye (the man behind *Men Behaving Badly*) with an all-star cast: Paul Merton is the narrator, Neil Morrissey is Jack, Adrian Edmondson is Dame Dolly, Griff Rhys-Jones is Baron Wasteland and Julian Clary is the Giant's assistant. Julie was tickled to be asked to play the role of Fairy Godmother.

'I loved it,' she said. 'It was such a laugh. I got to wear this amazing costume covered in white feathers. I think I was meant to look like a swan, but I ended up looking more like an old duck.' In this boisterous and fun version of the traditional tale are a few elements usually unknown in the fairy tale, such as Denise van Outen as the character Jill and Morwenna Banks as Goldilocks. The hilarious result, filmed live at the theatre, was aired at teatime on Christmas Day.

As Julie entered 1999, she commented, 'There are very few things worth leaving home for, so I do turn down a lot more than I take on,' adding that she wanted to spend as much time with Maisie as she could while her daughter still wants to be with her.

However, after a peaceful start to the year, Julie was bombarded with irresistible projects. Victoria Wood was working again for Comic Relief; Julie was also involved. Victoria agreed to be the guest editor of the special issue of *Radio Times* in March 1999 and not only changed the entire content, but also conducted a mock interview with Julie Walters. The actress's fictional life was one of a gin-swilling diva, who was hated by film crews and, despite being rendered infertile after a netballing accident, had chalked up seven husbands, including Bobby Crush and Larry Adler.

Victoria then wrote a parody of *Hetty Wainthropp Investigates* – about a pensioner cum private investigator – for a variety of her regular actors and a few wild cards. Taking the lead role as Wetty Hainthropp, Victoria proved a perfect mimic of Patricia Routledge. The improbable plot lent itself to the incestuous antics of her spoof soap operas, as Alan Titchmarsh's evil twin brother kidnaps Delia Smith and Rolf Harris, steals Matthew Kelly's greasepaint and practises maths to rival Carol Vorderman, all in a bid for stardom. His downfall, as Wetty points out, was the classic mistake of stealing fish fingers from the bag of the very woman he tries to kill.

The sketch sat neatly alongside other Comic Relief classics from the year, including an all-star spoof of *Doctor Who*, a special episode of *The Vicar of Dibley* where Dawn French meets Johnny Depp, the cast of *Men Behaving Badly* in a 'lost pilot from the 1960s', live sketches from *The Fast Show* cast and a quick-fire combination quiz show, *Have I Got Buzzcocks All Over*.

27. MRS OBE

In the spring of 1999, Julie rather unusually became involved in a period piece: *Lover's Prayer*. The nineteenth-century Russian romance is relatively straightforward – a young innocent, Vladimir, is hired as a page for the wealthy family next door. The middle-aged lady of the house is a princess with a severe drinking problem and failing health and Vladimir becomes infatuated with her teenage daughter Zinaida. He hopes to win her heart, but learns a painful lesson in the art of love, not least when he discovers that one of his rivals for her affections is his own father.

Julie was cast as the alcoholic mother and starred with James Fox, Geraldine James and Nathaniel Parker, while the young lovers were played by newcomers Nick Stahl and Kirsten Dunst. Produced under the title *All Forgotten*, this was the debut for the screenwriter and director Reverge Anselmo, and filming was far more complicated and bizarre than the storyline itself.

'It was a very, very odd experience,' says Nathaniel Parker. 'None of us really knew what we were getting into. Reverge had about $30 billion in the bank and didn't really know what to do with it all. He had never written or directed a movie before, but decided that was what he wanted to do.'

The script wasn't even finished when they started rehearsing, and as the actors tested the roles, Reverge continually made amendments. 'He combined *The Woodlanders* from Chekhov and Dostoevsky's *First Love*; it was mostly *First Love*, but he brought in some other ideas,' continues Nathaniel. 'There was one point where I asked, "If you don't like the script, why are you doing this?" But I think he did like the script – it was just the more he got into it, the more changes he wanted.

'I remember we were doing a rehearsal in London. It was jolly and we were all getting along. At the end I asked, "Who's producing it?" and Reverge said, "I am." I said, "No, I mean which company?" and he said, "Mine." '

The combination of Reverge being fairly new to the job and the fact that he wanted to retain complete control left the cast and crew bewildered and frustrated. 'There was a fair amount of friction – it wasn't always the most settled of shows,' says Nathaniel.

'Reverge had one of the best cameramen on board, a terrific crew and a terrific cast, and an all-right script that we all hammered out and tried to make sense of. But he was a bit threadbare in the directing. Actors do tend to need directing, even someone like Julie, who is brilliant at what she does – if you've got a director worth his salt, he will bring that brilliance out.

'To give Reverge his due, he did care passionately about the film and he did send me a very sweet letter when he was cutting it to say, "I think I understand what you were getting at before." I think people skills just wasn't one of his strong points.'

Lover's Prayer finally started filming in the spring of 1999, on location in the Czech Republic. 'They built these incredibly elaborate sets about an hour and a half out of Prague,' recalls Nathaniel Parker. 'They'd built two dachas – Russian country homes – and they were really lovely: you could have stayed there. And we were in the countryside with horses and farmers, everything was wonderful.'

Fortunately, although some of the actors were new to the game, they were supported by the exceptional British veterans. 'We were lucky to have people like Julie,' he says, 'as she doesn't have any barriers as an actress. She doesn't think, This is Shakespeare or Brecht or Beckett, which a lot of actors do. Someone like Julie Walters just does it, she says her lines, with a flicker or under her breath, or whatever she thinks the part or the character requires. She doesn't hold back and if she thinks she can help you she will – she's very generous like that.'

As with all her work, Julie knew the fine line between the serious business of acting and the humorous time in between. However, playing the lush of the house allowed her to combine the two. 'There was one scene where we had to have a dinner, a rather tense dinner,' Nathaniel elaborates. 'It was shot first thing in the morning at eight o'clock and we had a full three-course meal, including buckets of real caviar. Everybody, including the crew, tucked into it.

'Julie managed to take the tension out of the scene and made sure we acted the tension, but didn't feel it. If you have a drink problem you don't necessarily know what you're doing – so she brought everything she could to the role, from burping and farting to picking her nose. It took us so much by surprise: she was sitting there in her full regalia, black beads and lace and tight corsets, just burping and farting!

'Nobody had any control over her, she was a law unto herself! And thank God, because she brought a completely different element to what had been a very tense shoot and turned it on its head.'

Unfortunately, due to a dispute between the production and distribution companies, the movie missed its commercial release, appearing in a handful of film festivals and then going straight to video.

Filming lasted about three months but, for the last few weeks, Julie was juggling two sets as she had started work on her next project: Alan Bleasdale's adaptation of *Oliver Twist*.

'I only got mixed up once,' laughs Julie, recalling a time in the wardrobe department for *Oliver*. 'I asked where on the costume my character was going to keep her snuff. Then I realised it was the other character, the one in *Lover's Prayer*, who took snuff!'

'When ITV rang and asked if I'd dramatise *Oliver Twist* I said yes immediately,' Alan Bleasdale said in promotional interviews. 'I'd been waiting twenty-five years for this phone call. When I put the phone down, I did cartwheels around the house!'

Bleasdale has been a lifelong fan of Charles Dickens and has often been complimented as a modern version of the great Victorian writer. 'This is partly because he [Alan] often writes about class, or has class as an important factor in his work,' explains Julie. 'But it is also because he is very good at writing fabulous mad characters, just as Dickens was.'

The producer Keith Thompson also understands the comparison. 'Alan writes about big issues. He deals with issues of social consciousness and he creates extraordinary, larger-than-life characters. These are all descriptions that could equally well be attributed to Dickens's work.'

Bleasdale had first read *Oliver Twist* as a teenager, but now reread it with a different vision. He was quite daunted by the enormity of the project. 'I was scared, because with Dickens you're entering the playground that basically consists of Shakespeare, Dickens and Tolstoy,' he said, nervous of competing with such masters. 'Dickens is undoubtedly one of the greatest writers who ever lived and facing up to him was hard to do.'

Given the challenge, many in the industry were surprised that Bleasdale wanted to tackle such a project, but as a Dickens fan he couldn't wait to get started. '*Oliver Twist* is fundamentally about childhood and that's a subject I've written about before and keep returning to,' he adds. 'Even some of my adult characters never seem to grow up.'

Charles Dickens wrote the novel in monthly instalments and literally made the story up as he went along, without any forward planning. This meant that by the time he reached the end, he had backed himself into a corner, from which he could escape only by writing a few pages of back plot. For the sake of the television drama, however, Bleasdale had to deal with this history first. He explains why Oliver is born out of wedlock to Agnes Fleming in a workhouse, and how he becomes an orphan. The result is two hours of thrilling drama before young Oliver Twist even takes his first breath.

Bleasdale was determined to override traditional Dickens clichés, such as the casting and portrayal of Oliver. 'I've tried to give the character a toughness, a hardness and a sense of determination,' he says. For the young lead, they searched high and low, and came up trumps with Sam Smith. Bleasdale wrote with his usual actors very much in mind for the other characters.

'Fagin has to be witty and seductive and have the most incredible charm,' says the screenwriter. 'I'm always desperately keen to write powerful parts for Robert Lindsay and this part is just perfect for him.' He wrote roles for Lindsay Duncan, Alun Armstrong, Michael Kitchen and Tim Dutton, while he brought in newcomers Marc Warren, Andy Serkis and Emily Woof.

'Julie was on board in my imagination before I'd ever written a word,' says Bleasdale. 'As soon as she pops into my head, the lines I know she'll say just have a way of falling on to the page.' There was no way he could leave her out of such a mammoth undertaking.

As with many of his regulars, Julie relishes every new role that comes her way courtesy of Bleasdale. 'Now we have what I call a "faxual" relationship,' she joked in the *Sunday Mirror*. 'We fax each other a lot. When scripts come through for me, I can't wait to see what the lines are because I just know they're going to be good.'

Julie devoured the part of Mrs Mann, savouring the dichotomy between the old bag who runs the workhouse and shocks people, and the funny, flirty lady fooling around with Mr Bumble. 'You feel sorry for her, too, because she's married to a man who's always at sea,' she commented, 'and she's looking for love and romance, but she's never going to find it.'

Keen Dickensian followers will spot that, although Mrs Mann appears in the novel, she is not the workhouse matron Mr Bumble so desires. The character is instead based on Mrs Corney, but Bleasdale took the liberty of switching the names for a modern audience. 'I couldn't cope with Bumble and Corney,' he says. 'It sounds like a very bad couple of third-rate comedians in the 1940s.'

And who better than David Ross to play the lecherous Mr Bumble? 'I put them together in *GBH* and they work really well together,' says Bleasdale. 'They just make me laugh and these two characters are brilliant comic inventions by Dickens.'

The screenwriter was particularly mischievous with this pairing. 'David Ross is a very funny man and a great actor,' said Julie, although she couldn't help but notice his fascination with women's bosoms over the years. 'Alan's written that characteristic into the part of Bumble, and I roared with laughter when I read it.'

David himself was jubilant. 'Alan deliberately gave me the opportunity to get into bed with Julie!' he enthuses. 'He said, "I've been waiting for this for years," because he knows there was this time at college when I could never take my eyes off her chest – well, it was quite an eyeful! So he engineered that she and I would have a pseudo-sexual relationship so that I could say I'd got into bed with Julie Walters after thirty years of pretending to try!'

But Mrs Mann is married and accepts Mr Bumble's playful behaviour only because her husband is at sea and she is lonely. 'She goes along with this, and flirts when it suits her,' told Julie. 'When Sea Captain Mann dies, she looks at Mr Bumble and thinks, Well, why not? But all the time he's not really what she wants.' Ultimately Mrs Mann feels that Mr Bumble is somewhat below her in the class stakes, but gives in to her lust. Having succumbed and descended to his level, she is horrified to learn on her wedding day that he doesn't love her and only wants her for her housekeeping. 'She still goes ahead with the wedding, but from then on she makes his life an absolute misery, and he never quite knows why,' concluded Julie.

David savoured their complex connection. 'It went from being coy and seductive to those final scenes in the snow where they weren't speaking at all and they had both gone into severe decline,' he says. 'You had the whole gamut of a relationship between Mr and Mrs Bumble. I know a number of people, whose judgement I value, have said that the chemistry between us was rather marvellous.

'Julie admires and respects me, which makes her relaxed and makes her have fun with me, because she's not frightened or intimidated. It means that we can spar on an equal footing. When she threw me over the bench in that sequence when we came out of the room having had a row, we had such fun – she laughs like a drain!'

Filming for the workhouse scenes took place in Alston, Cumbria, while the majority of the shoot, including Fagin's London underworld, was carried out in Prague. 'The old buildings down by the Thames just don't exist any more – they were all destroyed – so we had to go elsewhere,' explains the producer Keith Thompson. 'The Czech Republic offered us a lot of different textures: cobbled streets, alleys and semi-derelict buildings.' And so the back streets and alleyways were recreated in the derelict town of Zatec, just north of Prague.

Most of the interiors were shot in the expansive Barrandov Studios in Prague. 'The reason we chose the Czech Republic in the first place was purely financial, as we saved money on studio space and construction,' explains Keith. While the studios at Barrandov are cheaper than those in

England, the country boasts a sophisticated infrastructure for the industry. Barrandov was built in 1931, they still make a large number of movies there and it is positively steeped in the history of filmmaking. Consequently the local community is geared towards supporting expertise.

Finances were certainly key due to the sheer size of the affair. 'It was a massive cast; the whole production was quite expensive,' says Marc Warren, who portrayed Monks. 'Once we got to Prague and we were all away together in hotels, it boosted the atmosphere and we had a fantastic time. It's a beautiful city, anyway, so it was like a working holiday – a real joy.'

David Ross concurs: 'We had a wonderful time. Between takes, when you have twenty minutes while they're relighting, you sit down and have a chat and catch up on mutual friends et cetera. I often saw Julie in the make-up chair; that's when she's always her most jolly, chatting to the make-up artists, having a bit of fun and really being a live wire.'

Along with the sets, the costumes and make-up were elaborate, with no expense spared. 'As Mrs Mann drinks a fair bit, we put broken veins on her to give her that gin-laden look, but we kept [Julie's] warm, round face,' explains the make-up and hair designer Lesley Lamont Fisher.

'After the marriage, when things immediately go downhill, she has a quite severe hairstyle . . . It's a small touch, but a good one, and Julie carries it off to great effect.'

Not someone who succumbs to narcissism, Julie admits that sometimes she shudders at the physical sight of her characters. She has been known to turn to Grant and whisper, 'God, I'm deeply unattractive in this, aren't I?' Few actresses would have been happy to be seen in quite such an unflattering light, but Julie shone as Mrs Mann, bad teeth, warts and all.

Once again, Julie proved herself in one of Bleasdale's indomitable roles. 'I think one of the reasons why she is one of the greatest actresses is not only can she talk a lot, but she listens very well and is very giving. She's such a vulnerable person, you want to look after her all the time,' says Hugh Lloyd, who relished working with her for the third time (after *Me! I'm Afraid of Virginia Woolf* and *Say Something Happened*).

Equally, Julie continued to be patient and nurturing to new actors. 'When we did the scene where I have to have a fit in front of her, she was fantastic, faultless, and very supportive,' recalls Marc Warren. 'She said lots of nice things and gave me confidence.

'The first scene we did was coming into the barn and we were getting drenched because it was pouring with rain outside. Obviously this was done with visual effects, but they absolutely flooded us – we were soaked to the skin and it was freezing. We kept doing this scene and I was having trouble remembering the lines, because Alan writes really particular dialogue, which is fantastic, but sometimes the unusual phrasing is quite hard to remember.

'They were shooting my way and Julie was doing the off-camera looks to me. She was being incredibly funny and said something that made me laugh. But that's the take they kept in the piece.'

Of course, it wasn't just on set that she amused the masses. 'When she was telling an anecdote, you wouldn't speak: it was just pure entertainment sitting listening to her,' continues Marc. 'She was hysterically, side-splittingly funny.'

One day, Julie, who normally held court, was caught unawares. 'I was sitting in the make-up caravan and they gave me tea in a china cup with "Mrs OBE" on it. I thought somebody was playing a joke,' says the actress.

But this was serious. After thirty years in the business, Julie Walters was due to be honoured with an Officer of the Order of the British Empire medal for services to drama. The ceremony would be held in December, just after *Oliver Twist* began its run on ITV – but Julie had other plans before then.

No sooner had Julie returned from several months filming in Prague, than she started work on Victoria Wood's second series of *dinnerladies*. Due to the disappointingly mixed reception the first series had received, Victoria broke one of her cardinal rules to prove a point. 'I don't normally do anything twice,' she says, 'but I felt for this to give it its best benefit I had to do more. The first six were like an experiment.'

To ensure that her concept worked fully, she wrote ten rather than the standard six episodes. Rehearsals began in the late summer of 1999, with filming in the autumn and winter. The second series had much greater depth, with characters experiencing true emotional turmoil rather than trivial mishaps.

In her writing, Victoria slips in a dig when Petula says, 'I had a baby once before, but I never really got involved.' Bren also uncharacteristic-ally defends herself when the social worker pressures her to provide a home for her ageing mother.

Petula unwittingly helps her daughter's financial concerns: in the pilot episode of the first series, Petula asks Bren to dispose of a mobile phone for her. In the second series, it turns out that the phone belongs to a criminal who has since been murdered and Bren and Tony become heir to his loot.

However, this time Bren's major events are deciding on a future with Tony, and the death of her mother, which rather abruptly ended Julie's involvement. One of Julie's favourite inane Petula comments remains, 'Bren, if you pop into the caravan, on the chemical toilet underneath one of my cardigans there's a shepherd's pie. The meat won't go another day but you can probably scrape the potato off.' Julie was sad not to recreate Petula, but chirpily says, 'I'll always find time to do something Victoria writes, however small.'

The show as a whole received a better reception the second time around and most critics agreed that it had drastically improved. 'The tired and bedraggled *dinnerladies* we used to know has re-emerged, transformed into a brilliant and sparkling piece of comic writing,' proclaimed Simon Edge for the *Daily Express*. 'The dialogue raced along at three times the pace of the first series.'

Still, Caroline Aherne's comedy series *The Royle Family* cleaned up at most of the award ceremonies, garnering most of the accolades in its genre except the BAFTA, which went posthumously to *Father Ted*'s star Dermot Morgan, who had unexpectedly died shortly after completing the series. Nevertheless, thrilled with the overall response to *dinnerladies*, Sir Christopher Bland, the chairman of the BBC, hinted that the series might become a long-running hit. Victoria, on the other hand, felt she had succeeded in her quest and quickly crushed that idea, stating, 'I've done what I wanted to do now.'

Julie appeared once more on television in 1999 as she narrated the BBC-produced documentary about sitcom, *Laughter in the House: The Story of British Sitcom*. In it, she traces its roots in *Hancock's Half Hour*, through to groundbreaking series such as *Steptoe and Son* and beyond. But that was not to be her last appearance on television that year.

On 2 December 1999 Julie Walters was recognised as one of Britain's most gifted character actresses as she attended Buckingham Palace to receive her OBE. For the first time ever, the ceremony was televised in a bid to modernise the monarchy and publicise aspects of the Queen's working life.

Getting her womanly priorities straight, Julie had consulted Victoria Wood about what to wear. The comedienne had been honoured two years previously, pipping her friend to the post. 'She said not to wear a hat – hats are for the old ones,' Julie told reporters on the day. 'So I'm not wearing a hat and I was quite relieved to see the Queen wasn't wearing one either.

'I've been practising curtseying since four o'clock this morning. Then, before the investiture, with the other ladies, we were all bobbing up and down like pistons. We were all nervous – especially the men – and the people getting bravery awards had sweat pouring off them. And, after you've met the Queen, you have to walk backwards, and that's quite difficult in front of the Queen. I was sure I was going to fall over.'

Julie behaved herself impeccably for the monarch but, when asked what she was currently filming, couldn't resist teasing the Queen by saying, 'A television series with Victoria Wood. I am playing her mother, an old bag lady who lives in a caravan on a petrol-station forecourt.'

Julie was accompanied by her proud husband and daughter. 'Maisie was hoping for the Queen's autograph,' laughed Julie. 'The family are thrilled with the award – I only wish my parents were alive.'

28. THE DANCER

Before the end of 1999, Julie had signed up for her next project, due to start filming at the beginning of 2000. For once, she didn't have to be made up to look like an old hag. Instead, as she turned fifty, she had to learn a complicated dance routine.

The role was that of a ballet teacher in Stephen Daldry's debut film, with the working title of *The Dancer*. The coming-of-age drama sees eleven-year-old Billy, the youngest son of an English coal miner, looking after his senile grandmother after the death of his mother. The boy has a terrible relationship with his brother, and his father is constantly worried about money. Set in Durham during the miners' strike of 1984, the film captures the regular angry clashes between picketers and riot police as Billy's father and brother are among the protestors.

Billy is pushed into the macho pursuit of boxing by his father, but one day at the gym, after hours, the ballet class catches his eye instead. The dance teacher's forward young daughter, Debbie, encourages Billy to join in and, on seeing him struggle in his boxing boots, the tutor, Mrs Wilkinson, dares him to put on some ballet shoes. She is a hard-nosed, straight-talking, chain-smoking woman who recognises Billy's raw talent. Not one to suffer fools gladly, she always finds fault with her students – Billy is no exception – but equally she cheers him along with a friendly wink. The youth is also encouraged by his friend, who is struggling with his sexuality.

Billy faces head-on the prejudice of the working classes of the time to a male entering such a 'feminine' activity. Indeed, when his father finds out his son is dancing, he is furious and bans him from the class, using lack of funds as an excuse. Determined, Mrs Wilkinson tutors Billy for free and prepares him for the national auditions to the Royal Ballet School. Billy eventually becomes fed up of Mrs Wilkinson's constant nit-picking and tells her to stop tormenting him just because she failed as a dancer herself. Outraged by the child's painfully accurate impertinence, Mrs Wilkinson slaps him. Their aggression released, the pair resolve their differences and continue to practise.

Sadly, on the morning of the auditions, Billy is at the police station with his father, retrieving his brother, who has pushed the picket line too far. Angry, Billy takes his frustration out in a fabulous dance scene set out on the streets and in the back alleys. Later, Billy's father catches him dancing at Christmas. Rather than acquiesce and stop, the young lad defies his father and dances in front of him. It is then that the miner realises that his son's talent might free him from the danger and grinding tedium of a miner's life, and supports him. Finally, despite a shaky audition appearance, Billy looks set to succeed in his dreams after all.

The Dancer was developed by BBC Films, with the help of the new Film Council. David Thompson, head of BBC Films, was pleased with the project: 'It is another example of our commitment to backing the very best of British film talent, and we are particularly pleased as this is Stephen Daldry's first feature film.' Stephen, like Sam Mendes (*American Beauty*), Roger Michell (*Notting Hill*) and Nancy Meckler (*Sister My Sister*) before him, was a talented theatre director who had turned his attentions to film.

Julie always enjoyed working with such renowned directors and didn't hesitate to accept the role of Mrs Wilkinson. 'I think there is a bit of a trend with theatre directors coming into cinema. Generally speaking, theatre scripts are more complex than film scripts, so they're going to want more intelligent scripts,' she explained to reporters.

Julie was touched by the depths of this particular offering, recognising it as 'a diamond in the rough' compared to all the mundane scripts she receives. She was particularly taken with the fact that Mrs Wilkinson – in a similar way to Mrs Mann in *Oliver Twist* – was disappointed and jaded on every level.

Furthermore she was intrigued by the curious relationship her character had with Billy. 'She was so unmaternal, and he's a boy without a mother. She treated him not like a child, but more like a lover, a man,' she explained.

And finally, she liked her character's ambitions and determination that Billy would succeed where she had failed: 'This talent in this boy. She can just smell it when he walks in the room. She's obsessed, over and beyond what he wants. It's what *she* wants.'

While Julie jumped at the role, she realised the film would fall without a strong performance from the actor playing Billy. Her initial talks with Stephen were blunt. She told him not to worry about her role, but concentrate on finding Billy. 'He's got to be able to act because the scenes are quite complicated emotionally, and he's got to be able to dance well enough to get into the Royal Ballet School,' she told the director. '*And* he's got to come from the northeast!'

This indeed was a tall order, and Stephen and the producer Jon Finn went in search of the elusive Billy. During the research for the role, the scriptwriter Lee Hall rang the Royal Ballet to ask if any of the company's dancers came from a northern mining town. He was introduced to Philip

Mosley from Barnsley, south Yorkshire, who detailed his experiences and provided inspiration for parts of the script, including the scenes of Billy dancing on cobbled streets. With a firm idea of what they were looking for, the team auditioned around two thousand young hopefuls.

Then they stumbled across Jamie Bell. 'If I hadn't found Jamie, the film couldn't have been made,' says Stephen honestly. 'He had to do so much.' Yet, for someone who needed to be so talented, Jamie was an unlikely choice. He didn't come from a stage school and had never acted before.

'There was just a freshness about him and an honesty that he brought,' marvels Julie. 'It was wonderful working with him and I love the way he dances.' Sparks ignite when Jamie and Julie perform together.

Rather than acting, dancing was Jamie's forte, his story bearing a certain resemblance to the plot. Born in Billingham in 1986, Jamie grew up in a family of dancers, including his grandmother, mother, aunt and sister. Having watched his sister's classes for years, at the age of six he was finally encouraged to start dancing himself. Like his character, Jamie kept it a secret from his mates at school, but once word got out they teased him and called him 'Ballerina Boy'. Fortunately, Jamie was resolute: dancing was for boys as well as girls and, having starred in a movie aged fourteen, he had the last laugh.

'It was Stephen's first film, but you would never know it,' says Julie. 'Because he's a theatre director, it's just fantastic for actors. It's the best.' Alongside Jamie's natural ability and the professionalism of Julie and Gary Lewis, who played Jamie's father, Stephen's directing was the key to the film.

'With Julie, you get buckets of emotion,' says Stephen. 'But I would tell her, "Keep this as tough as you can."' It was a measure of her ability as a serious actress that she did not ham up the role, for the chain-smoking, gutsy mentor could easily have turned camp.

Julie knew she could handle the acting, but the dancing concerned her. In the film, dance is an expression of yearning and a symptom of frustration. Mrs Wilkinson is clearly unfulfilled, which is why she dances. 'I'm too old to be learning stuff, really,' admits Julie. 'I spent weeks and weeks on one tiny bit of dance. It was so fast.'

As usual, she does herself a disservice. Although primarily an actress, Julie has always been able to sing and dance, as she amply proved in *Stepping Out* in 1991.

One of the highlights of the film is undoubtedly when Jamie and Julie rehearse to T Rex's 'I Love To Boogie'. The producer confirms that Julie faced her demons head on and never let it get her down. 'Actually, she said she hates dancing,' says Jon Finn. 'We didn't have much time to shoot the film, so it was really remarkable how she would always be up and willing to just go for it.'

That she struggled with the routines certainly doesn't show in the film, but, when she saw the final version, she had other concerns. In her naturally self-deprecating fashion, Julie is comically harsh on herself. 'I almost cried when I saw myself dancing,' she says. '*Fantasia* came to mind. This sort of balloon-type person with tiny feet. I saw the menopause personified as I came towards myself.'

Dancing aside, the hardest scene with Jamie was when she had to slap him. 'I didn't want to have to do that,' says Julie. 'I said, "For God's sake, we must be able to do this without hitting him." But Stephen said, "No." Then Jamie said, "Argh, you really hurt me that time!"'

Although Jamie wasn't even born when the miners were striking, the memory is crystal clear to Julie. 'I remember feeling angered at Thatcher, and seeing the results of it,' she says. 'Those communities being destroyed. ... If you can make people think about it, in an entertaining way, that's great. It's better than preaching about it.'

The Dancer was chosen as the closing screening of Directors' Fortnight at Cannes in May 2000. Stephen was delighted at the honour, but the moment was marred when he was forced to change the title of his masterpiece. The winner of the prestigious Palme d'Or at the end of the festival was Lars von Trier with *Dancer in the Dark*, starring the Icelandic singer Björk. To avoid confusion, and using the young dancer's full name as inspiration, Stephen's second choice was quite simply, *Billy Elliot*.

Julie turned fifty during the filming of *Billy Elliot*. Of course, it was like water off a duck's back with her *laissez faire* attitude. 'I think the last time I noticed my age was when I was about seventeen and since then I haven't given it a thought,' she said as she approached the half-century landmark. 'I certainly wouldn't want to be thirty again, or even forty.' She very philosophically likened life to a journey and commented that she wouldn't want to go backwards.

In the industry of show business, age and looks are fairly critical. Although sporty as a teenager, once she left school Julie dropped fitness like a hot potato but, in the late 1990s, Grant introduced her to yoga, which had a certain appeal. 'Exercise is something I can't stand normally, but yoga I think I can handle,' she said. 'What I like is it involves the minimum of effort, yet you feel stretched and very calm afterwards.'

Julie has never conformed to traditional glamour roles, but has rather thrived on the challenge of acting grittier – often uglier – parts, so the passing of years has not dented her appeal. 'Middle-aged women are cast as ogres or comic turns, if they feature at all,' she commented. 'In the States, most women my age in the business have had plastic surgery.' Cosmetic enhancement was not an issue that Julie had ever remotely entertained.

'Having said that, it's ironic that I've never been busier with work,' she continued. 'I just love the escape of being someone else. It gives you a voice to say things that you wouldn't normally say, a voice of emotions you can't express. I'm lucky because I've been able to do what I want.'

Her other passion is her family. Having fought all domestic and maternal urges until later in life, Julie had considerably cut the window in which she could have children. With Maisie being so seriously ill at such as young age, the couple had also had other, more important, issues to concentrate on. 'I always wanted a bigger family, but Maisie more than makes up for not having more than one,' she said.

Having hit the menopause, she occasionally struggled with latent urges. 'When you're in the middle of "The Change" it isn't really an option anymore, is it?' she said frankly. 'But it's really OK because I had a child and it was the best thing that ever happened to me.

'I think the end [the menopause] is harder than the beginning [puberty]. Personally I can't wait for the whole bloody thing to be over. I just hate the unpredictability of it. One minute you feel sublime, the next you're sobbing in the toilet. It can be very wearing indeed for the person you live with.' As Maisie rattled towards puberty, Julie felt sorry for Grant, sitting between a moody adolescent and an emotional woman with hot flushes.

'There is a certain sense of mourning that there will never be another child, but I'm not mourning for my lost youth,' she said, returning to the theme of her small family. 'There were babies on the set of *Oliver Twist* and for a few moments I felt quite broody towards them. But it was only for a few moments and there was no longing. I was broody but not in any practical sense ... And then there's the problem of age as well. If we adopted a baby now, I'd be coming up to sixty by the time it was ten.'

Instead, Julie put her maternal drive to use elsewhere. She was very moved by Save the Children's Forgotten Children campaign – their aim was to highlight the plight of some 20 million children around the world who had been forced out of their homes by conflict. Julie was initially wary about joining the cause. 'I had a terrible aversion to swanning around looking like a middle-class actress, patting children on the head,' she said. 'But having a child changes you. It makes it impossible to hear about children suffering without wanting to do something.'

To that end, Julie visited Kosovo during the Balkan crisis in the spring of 2000, to meet the lost children of the war and speak out on their behalf. Her compassion for the children was overwhelming, and the feeling was mutual as they gazed at her like a favourite aunt from a strange land.

Julie visited the paediatric ward at Gjakova hospital during her trip. 'As soon as I walk in, the atmosphere takes me back to when Maisie was diagnosed with leukaemia at two and a half. I remember how frightening and shocking it was,' she wrote in her diary of the time. From her own experiences, she understood that often the greatest courage comes from children. She was particularly stunned by her encounter with a boy named Gazmend, who was the same age as Maisie. 'From the moment I look into Gazmend's face, I can see this little lad has been through something terrible,' she remarked.

'He says he doesn't want questions. He just wants to tell his story in his own words. And then it all comes flooding out.' Gazmend had witnessed a massacre in his town and, as he and his family tried to flee to Albania, saw Serbian soldiers drag his father away. 'He is literally vibrating with emotion,' she continued. 'He's strong and brave, but when he talks of his dad he cannot fight off the tears.'

On her return, Julie launched the Forgotten Children campaign in April 2000. She publicised her trip on television, on radio and in the national press, and encouraged the public to 'put their faces behind the campaign' – almost literally – by sending in photos of themselves as part of a unique petition.

'In Kosovo I was horrified by the stories children told me about how they were forcibly expelled from their homes,' she announced at the launch. 'It's unthinkable that so many children around the world, from Angola to Sri Lanka, have had their lives torn apart and turned upside down because of wars being waged by adults.

'Save the Children's Forgotten Children campaign is vital in putting these children on the map and ensuring that they get the protection they are entitled to. Children can't afford to waste their precious childhoods starring down the barrel of a gun. They have got to be protected.' Her protest was powerful and 25,000 people, including seventy top celebrities, joined the fight.

The following year, Julie's political conscience was once again awakened as she joined an all-star cast of musicians and comedians to celebrate the fortieth birthday of Amnesty International. The concert, entitled *We Know Where You Live: Live!*, took part at London's Wembley Arena and was hosted by Eddie Izzard in the spirit of the classic *Secret Policeman's Balls* of the previous thirty years.

It was no coincidence, then, that Julie's next project of 2000 tapped into her current frame of mind. She chose the role of Kate Keller, a woman with an overwhelming capacity for familial love, in Arthur Miller's *All My*

Sons. The searing melodrama was the playwright's first major success in 1947 and was being revived by the Royal National Theatre in the intimacy of the Cottesloe Theatre, London, in July.

All My Sons is a compelling story of love, guilt and the corrupting power of greed. Joe Keller is alleged to have supplied World War Two fighter planes with defective engines, leading to the deaths of innocent pilots. His business partner takes the blame for the crime, but Joe has to live with the fact that his son, a pilot, is thought to have been killed in action. His wife, Kate, can't accept her son's death and is equally distraught that his fiancée has transferred her affections to his brother. The confrontations that ensue lead to the uncovering of a shameful family secret.

'I'm incredibly touched by the way she tries to hold on to her son,' said Julie. 'I remember that feeling of not being able to go forwards or backwards, that paralysis.' She was equally moved by the character's strength and unconditional love for her husband. Julie recognised that, like so many women, Kate managed to hold everything together.

The play teamed Julie up with eminent actors and newcomers alike, including James Hazeldine, Ben Daniels and Catherine McCormack. It was directed by Howard Davies, whom she greatly respected and admired. 'He's incredibly incisive,' she says. 'He's so *there*. You're in your own little capsule as an actor, but he seems to be able to see it all ... I've never felt so prepared in my whole life.'

Howard helped Julie establish her own method of summoning up her character's anguish, using a strange image from her childhood: she keyed into an image of a solitary sandwich left on a wall, and conjured up the feeling of being sad and totally alone. Julie worried about overplaying the part and becoming too close to Mrs Overall in 'Acorn Antiques'. 'I know she's there, she's part of my shape, I can't help it,' she admits. 'I'm terrified when I come on with the tray and the headscarf. I think, Oh God, I'd better stand up straight!'

With the previews at the end of June, the play opened on 6 July and ran until 18 October. Although Julie hadn't been on stage for nine years in a dramatic piece (since the emotionally draining *The Rose Tattoo* and notwithstanding her comic turn in *Jack and the Beanstalk*), she felt at ease. 'It's great to be back in the theatre,' she said at the time. 'I'm much more at home here. I suppose it's because I'm big and loud, and you have to tone everything down when you do films or television.'

The only night she really felt anxious was when she heard that the author was in town. 'Usually I like knowing when people are in, but with him I didn't want to know beforehand,' she says. 'I was worried I'd get the lines wrong, or put in a "well" or a "but" that wasn't there. But he loved it; he cried at the end. He signed my copy of the play. He was lovely.'

Arthur Miller had reason to be impressed. Julie amazed the critics with her resounding portrayal of a mother in torment. She received praise from all corners, and *The Times* described her performance as 'an unforgettable portrait of a material fixation'. When the show transferred to the more impersonal Lyttleton Theatre, London, Julie left the cast and was replaced by Laurie Metcalf from *Roseanne* for the rest of the run.

Having made the leap back into theatre, Julie became hungry for more. 'Helen Mirren said I should have a go at Restoration comedy,' she mused. 'Something like *The Country Wife*, perhaps. That would be good fun. And I wouldn't have to cry every night.'

Although busy, Julie still found time to squeeze in a fun event called 'CelebriTea'. On 5 September 2000, Julie had afternoon tea at the Terrace Café and gave a talk about her work, answering a few questions from the floor afterwards.

At the end of the month she was then required for promotion of *Billy Elliot*. She, Stephen Daldry and Jamie Bell were all present – and slightly bewildered – at the glittering premiere. The Cannes screening had ensured slow-burning media excitement about the film and now it was being compared to the huge success of the previous low-budget British smash hit, *The Full Monty*. Stephen himself was rapidly acquiring – in both the UK and the US – a profile on a par with that of his close friend Sam Mendes, whose debut film, *American Beauty*, swept the 1999 Oscars.

'I don't have any idea why it's taking off like this. We're all completely amazed,' said producer Jon Finn. The next thing they heard was that President Clinton had asked for a private screening at the White House, while the influential *Hollywood Reporter* proclaimed that it was 'one singular sensation!' It seemed the film could do no wrong.

However, when *Billy Elliot* went on general release in October, one thorny issue emerged. Jean Ure, author of a children's book called *A Proper Little Nooryeff*, found the plot uncannily similar to her fiction, written some twenty years earlier. Her story also follows a young dancing boy struggling to overcome the taunts of his friends, and spurred on by a formidable dance teacher. Although set in London and not to the intense backdrop of the miners' strike, the novel was written in the early 1980s and so is contextualised by similar political and social divisions.

'I've closed my mind to thinking about it, otherwise, I would spend all the time thinking, My God, they have stolen my idea. That would be counter-productive, and I wouldn't be able to get on with my writing,' concluded Jean Ure. Fortunately for all involved with the movie, she stopped short of accusing the production team of plagiarism and the film proceeded without obstruction.

The BBC were so pleased with their run of Victoria Wood Christmas specials that they couldn't resist offering her another one. The comedienne gladly obliged, and produced *Victoria Wood With All the Trimmings*, a fifty-minute sketch show brimming with parodies, pastiches and personalities, all laced with a Christmas theme. Famous and familiar faces included Derek Jacobi, Richard E Grant, Alan Rickman, Delia Smith, Bob Monkhouse, Michael Parkinson, June Brown, Pete Postlethwaite and Robert Lindsay; the regulars Julie Walters, Celia Imrie and Duncan Preston; and a pair from *dinnerladies*, Kate Robbins and Maxine Peake.

Victoria always looked for a novel way to present such shows, like the *This Morning* take-off for her Christmas special, *All Day Breakfast*, eight years previously. This time, she established her noncelebrity status by arriving at the BBC rehearsal studios for the special on a bus, wrapped up in a duffel coat. Displaying her ability to move with the times, she taps into the current confusion over digital television programmes and explains that the making of her show will be filmed for the new channel, 'BBC Backstage'. From there on she has free rein to poke endless fun at the BBC, with each sketch mocking a fictitious channel.

Although it was a successfully funny show, Victoria was disappointed that she was once again beaten by Caroline Aherne, whose half-hour Christmas episode of *The Royle Family*, shown immediately after *All the Trimmings*, received higher ratings.

In March 2001, Victoria and Julie would revive *Wood & Walters* as a special about wartime wives in aid of that year's fundraising activities for Comic Relief.

29. THE BIGGEST, FATTEST CHERRY ON THE LOVELIEST CAKE

For one who flits in and out of the limelight, Julie started 2001 with a high profile, and it only increased as the year progressed.

At the end of the previous year, she had been in talks with the director Chris Columbus to appear in his movie dramatisation of JK Rowling's popular debut novel, *Harry Potter and the Philosopher's Stone*. The book sees a young orphan, Harry, realise his true heritage and enrol in Hogwarts School of Witchcraft and Wizardry, where he and his friends, Ron Weasley and Hermione Granger, embark on a series of magical adventures.

As Rowling was signed to a seven-book deal – one for each year that Harry was at the school – and given the phenomenal success of the first four literary instalments with children and adults alike, the films looked set to be a worthy ratings rival to the long-awaited *Lord of the Rings* film trilogy.

Julie signed up for the part of Mrs Molly Weasley in the upcoming quartet of *Harry Potter* movies. Her appearance in the first film was little more than a cameo, but her role as the mother of Harry's best friend increases as the stories progress.

With a teenage daughter, Julie was well versed in the enchanting world of Harry Potter. When she signed the deal she admitted she had been forced to read the first book simply to converse with Maisie and her friends.

Her daughter, who had read all the books, was very pleased. 'I only had two lines, but it made my daughter very proud!' It was one of those things that if you didn't do, you'd never hear the end of it. It was quite nice to be involved in something fun.'

Amusingly, Julie was not the only award-winning actor to be bullied into joining the cast by a child. The distinguished actor Richard Harris was offered the coveted role of Albus Dumbledore, headmaster of Hogwarts. 'I was asked to play the part and I wasn't going to do it for various reasons,' he said. 'Then my eleven-year-old granddaughter Ellie telephoned me and said quite simply, "Papa, if you don't play Dumbledore, I will never speak to you again!" So I didn't have much choice in the matter.' (Richard Harris was able to reprieve this role only once more, in *Harry Potter and the Chamber of Secrets*, before his death shortly after his seventieth birthday in October 2002.)

Alan Rickman was similarly persuaded to play Professor Snape. 'I have lots of nephews, and relationships with friends' children. They weren't so much excited as insistent that I do the part,' he recalls.

So Julie joined an all-star adult cast including John Cleese, Robbie Coltrane, Zoë Wanamaker and Dame Maggie Smith, while the children were played by spunky newcomers Daniel Radcliffe, Rupert Grint and Emma Watson. Of course, with such a generation gap, the fame of the elders was somewhat lost on the younger actors. 'I'd never really seen much of Julie's work,' confesses Chris Rankin, who plays the third of her six sons, Percy. 'I'd seen a few episodes of *dinnerladies*, and my mum's an English teacher who used to teach *Educating Rita*, so I'd seen that on television at home, but I think, to start with, my mother was more excited than me!

'Just after I started work on *Harry Potter*, her Michael Parkinson interview was aired and after that I was much more interested in her career.' Julie's warmth naturally transcended the ages. 'She came across as a wonderfully down-to-earth person, who loves her job, and loves having fun.

'She seemed like the perfect Mrs Weasley just from reading about her and watching some of her work,' he continues. 'The first time I met Julie was on a freezing cold Sunday morning in January 2001, in the first-class compartment of the GNER train that we were using as a green room while filming at King's Cross Station. James and Oliver Phelps (the Weasley twins), Rupert Grint and I were sat having a hot drink, when one of the production runners brought her in. Before she was through the door, she was saying, "There's my boys, there's my little boys!"

'She was absolutely wonderful to talk to – I think that we'd all been slightly apprehensive, because she's such a famous actress, but we all had a wonderful time that morning, and continued to do so.'

However, Julie ran into problems almost immediately due to the exaggerated matronly figure she adopted for the part. 'The padding was full of birdseed, which was very worrying at King's Cross, with all the pigeons,' she says. 'I thought it would be like *The Birds*. And when they brought the owls on ...'

Chris adds, 'I remember Julie keeping hold of her Mrs Weasley sags, saying, "Keep those pigeons away from me!"'

When she was able to film, however, Julie's one scene uses magic to get the children on to Platform 9¾ for the Hogwarts Express; they have to run straight into a brick wall. 'That was bizarre to say the least!' says Chris, but the cast are sworn to secrecy about how the special-effects department achieve the visual trickery.

Despite her minimal work on the first film, Julie made a lasting impression on the new generation of actors who worked with her. 'I've had the privilege on the *Harry Potter* films to work with some of the world's best actors and actresses,' enthuses Chris. 'Julie is definitely top of the list: she's hilarious, kind and caring, she treats everyone the same from the cleaners to the director, and she's amazingly talented. It's a pleasure to be able to call her a friend.'

In February, Julie continued to make waves. The BAFTA ceremony was brought forward in advance of the Oscars – and possibly to influence them – and *Billy Elliot* held its own. It was named the Outstanding British Film of the Year; Jamie Bell scooped Best Actor (above stiff competition from Russell Crowe in *Gladiator* and Tom Hanks in *Cast Away*); and Julie Walters won the Best Supporting Actress category (beating Dame Judi Dench, Lena Olin, Zhang Zi Yi and Frances McDormand). Letting her hair down, the actress got happily – and deservedly – drunk that night.

Julie was also nominated for Best Supporting Actress at the Screen Actors' Guild (which went to Judi Dench for *Chocolat*), the Golden Globes (which she lost to Kate Hudson for *Almost Famous*) and the Oscars. It seemed that the appeal of *Billy Elliot* was less for the Americans as Jamie Bell and the film were overlooked at the Academy Awards, and Julie was once again pipped to the post, this time by Marcia Gay Harden for *Pollock*.

Still, the actress never thought the low-budget British film would take her *this* far and was thrilled to meet one of her favourite actresses at the Oscars. 'Like everyone, I love Judi Dench ... We were having our hair done ready to go, and she sent me a note saying, "I can't stop weeing!"' Bizarrely, Julie popped a piece of coal into her designer handbag as a 'working-class good luck charm', but later found to her dismay that its dust had ruined the lining of her accessory!

Although the award ceremonies were exciting and Julie was praised for her work, during the after-show mingling, she was often over-shadowed by Grant. 'He loves all that,' she says. 'In fact it's him everybody wants to talk to all the time because he's a farmer.' Maisie, who by that point was virtually a teenager – at twelve and three-quarters – also revelled in the glamour and glitz of the occasion.

Julie was then recognised for her role in *All My Sons* in February 2001. The prestigious Laurence Olivier Awards were held at the Lyceum Theatre on 23 February, at which the play won four awards: Best Actress for Julie Walters, Best Supporting Actor for Ben Daniels, Best Director for Howard Davies and Best Set Designer for William Dudley. Again, Julie beat strong opposition, including Jessica Lange and Helen Mirren, but unfortunately she was unable to attend the ceremony to receive the award in person. Instead, she sent a message to the audience, saying the prize was the 'biggest, fattest cherry on the loveliest cake'.

Julie Walters had not been so popular since the height of her fame after *Educating Rita*. Typically, she barely noticed the fuss and, throughout the early winter months of 2001, kept her head down, working on a new project.

This was the television drama *My Beautiful Son*, which united a curious mix of leading British and American talent, including the *Royle Family* star Ricky Tomlinson, George Wendt from the US sitcom *Cheers*, the *Mad About You* comedian Paul Reiser and the Oscar-winning Olympia Dukakis (*Moonstruck*). Julie was drawn to the script for three main reasons: first, the role was another tough, working-class mother; second, it was inspired by real-life events; and finally, the subject dealt with overcoming leukaemia.

Filmed to kick-start the autumn season on ITV1, *My Beautiful Son* was based on a true story about a wealthy New York psychiatrist (Paul Reiser), who is diagnosed with leukaemia. He needs to find a direct blood relative – namely a sibling – for a crucial bone-marrow transplant, but discovers from his mother (Olympia Dukakis) that he is adopted.

Determined, he tracks down his birth mother (Julie Walters) on a run-down Liverpool estate and flies out for a reunion, which isn't as successful as he hopes. The American–English and rich–poor culture clash initially prevents any empathy with his family, but over time they bond. When they discover his true motive for the journey, the relatives undergo the required tests for tissue compatibility before a series of clever plot twists.

The evolving rapport between Paul and Julie and unforeseen developments more than make up for the occasional plot contrivances to produce a gripping, sensitive drama.

At only eight years older than Paul, her on-screen son, Julie was once again aged for the role. 'They bleached my hair and made the roots show,' she explained to the *Sunday Herald*. 'They highlighted everything that was starting to go, to make it look much worse. I know I'll look like that one day but I don't care.' Julie has often been subjected to the unusual spectacle of facing her future self in the mirror for roles, but reliving the past was another matter.

'In the script there was a graphic description of a bone-marrow transplant,' she says. 'While Maisie didn't have a transplant, they did take a sample of her bone marrow without anaesthetic. I can still remember the big needle, which really upset me at the time.'

Fortunately for Julie, there was a friendly face on set: Alan Igbon, with whom she had worked on three Alan Bleasdale dramas. They caught up over coffee at the read-through. 'It's amazing but Julie doesn't seem to have changed at all,' he says. 'Although she's a big star now, she's the same as the days back in the theatre at Liverpool; she doesn't look any different, she doesn't sound any different and her attitude's not changed.

'When I look through the album of all the set shots over the years, we have all aged after twenty years, but Julie looks the same.' Could that be because she played a wrung-out mother in all four roles?

As Maisie entered her teenage years, she had a much better relationship with her mother than Julie ever did with Mary Walters. However, there were some similarities.

'Look, Mum,' said Maisie, 'I love you, but I don't want to be like you.'

'Do you know what?' replied Julie, smugly. 'That means you are exactly like me, because at your age I wanted, above all else, not to be like my mum!'

As Maisie matured, Julie found it easier to explain her working patterns to her daughter. 'Juggling motherhood with work is hard. I miss Maisie a lot and I don't like being away,' she reiterated. 'Now she's thirteen she's actually fine. She says, "OK, Mum, see you tomorrow." Unless there's a problem, if she's unhappy then I really know it.

'Sometimes she says, "I don't want you to go," and that's the worst thing. Then I'll give her a cuddle and say, "I don't want to go, either, but I've got to and I'm really sorry." But generally I don't go away that much. I'm usually in London, which isn't far from home. I don't want to give up acting – it's what I am. So I've tried to cut it down.'

With a short break after *My Beautiful Son*, Julie just couldn't say no to the opportunity to work with Lewis Gilbert for a third time. She was very excited: after all the director was now in his eighties and the film marked his return to the business after an absence of over a decade.

'Making films gets easier the older you get,' says Gilbert. 'You just sit back in the director's chair and shout orders. I hope to be making movies until they carry me out on a stretcher. I'd like to be in *The Guinness Book of Records* as the world's oldest movie maker.'

Like *Educating Rita* and *Stepping Out* previously, Lewis Gilbert's latest film, *Before You Go*, started out as a stage play. *Before You Go*'s original guise was as Shelagh Stephenson's *Memory of Water*. The dramatic potential of female siblings has fascinated playwrights and filmmakers for generations, and Stephenson was no exception.

Her play originally reunited three sisters at the family home for their mother's seventieth birthday, but she soon decided a funeral would make a better story. The siblings reunite to bury their mother, settle old scores, and bond as only girls can. Unfortunately, the revised plot became remarkably similar to *Hanging Up*, released in 2000 and starring three Hollywood A-listers (Meg Ryan, Lisa Kudrow and Diane Keaton); here the three female siblings reunite to look after their dying father, the inspirational Walter Matthau.

In *Before You Go*, Julie plays the eldest of the Heaney sisters, Teresa, a zealous housewife, devoted to her mother and dominant over her homeopathy salesman husband Frank (Tom Wilkinson). Joanne Whalley is the successful middle daughter Mary, a doctor who has been having an affair with a married colleague, Mike (John Hannah), for years. Catherine, portrayed by Victoria Hamilton, is the baby of the family, and blames her current druggy, aimless lifestyle with her lover Xavier in Spain, on a poor childhood.

When their mother Violet dies, the three return to the family home on the Isle of Man to prepare for the funeral. Wily Teresa swiftly discovers a biscuit tin full of papers, which she hides from her sisters. Mary is furious that the tin has disappeared and, worse still, has to sleep in her dead mother's bed. There she is haunted by the ghost of Violet (Patricia Hodge), clad in her favourite pale green cocktail dress. Violet's mission is to help her daughter resolve her problems with her married lover, who will not leave his wife. But the secret lies in the biscuit tin, and Violet hopes that Mary will finally be able to forgive her for an unresolved childhood incident.

The sisters were once close, but have grown apart as adults and, as in any family, memories of the same events differ. Ghostly Violet tells Mary, 'You invent these versions of me and I don't recognise myself!'

The highlight of the film is cute, though predictable: the three sisters get drunk while sorting through their mother's clothes and have a riot dressing up in her garish gowns, much to the bemusement of Frank and Mike.

But Walters, Whalley and Hamilton are an odd trio, and the difference in their characters' ages is offputting at first, making the plot hard to follow. Equally, Tom Wilkinson and John Hannah receive a rough deal because they are permanently on the sidelines. As such a mixed bag of comedy, weepy, and supernatural melodrama, this stage play does not transfer well to the screen. Lewis Gilbert hoped that by coming out of the house he could pick up the movie's pace, but the excessive number of dramatic scenery shots can lead the viewer to suspect that this was a requirement of the movie, in which the Isle of Man Film Commission invested heavily.

Unable to break away from its roots, *Before You Go* is overly theatrical as the accomplished cast speak emphatically in prolonged speech or extended soliloquies. The *Observer* critic, Gaby Wood, summed it up neatly: 'The sharp Joanne Whalley comes across as ponderous, Tom Wilkinson seems bland, John Hannah has lost all his lightness, Victoria Hamilton overacts excruciatingly every second she's on screen, and Julie Walters is wasted.'

Before You Go was released in cinemas in June 2002, but was quickly withdrawn, slipping quietly on to DVD. Although the film was not a success, it was an understandable, yet unfortunate, choice for Julie, whose underexposed performance was otherwise first-rate.

30. DIAL M FOR MURDER

Over the summer of 2001, Julie and many of the 'Mersey Mafia' were supposed to regroup for another Alan Bleasdale venture. The left-wing author had created a new political drama, along the lines of *GBH* and *Boys from the Blackstuff*, this time attacking Tony Blair's government and brand of New Labour.

Bleasdale wanted to make a real impact with his latest work and negotiated a generous budget with the BBC to make a seven-part series called *Running Scared*. 'I am working on a much bigger canvas with this,' he said. 'It couldn't be more different than *Jake's Progress*: it has a large number of characters and deals with a great many issues.'

He enticed the BBC with the first three episodes, and quickly penned the next three, just leaving the grand finale unfinished. Predictably, his lead characters were written for Robert Lindsay and Julie Walters, who provide the focus of the piece – a love story about a couple who meet up after twenty-three years. 'He left Liverpool and made a fortune during the property boom of the 1980s,' said Bleasdale. 'It looks at how their passions are re-ignited. I must stress he has moved a lot further to the right than the Labour Party. But he does have redeeming qualities.'

Bleasdale wanted to get close to the political action, so he consulted his old friend Peter Kilfoyle, who had recently resigned as Labour defence minister on the grounds that the party was deserting traditional supporters and its 'heartland'. The author expanded Kilfoyle's stance further, accusing the government of scrapping socialist principles in favour of retaining power. Bleasdale, who has always been considered a mainstream Labour supporter, surprised and unnerved the party with his proposed attack.

'I never look at my work as being controversial,' he said. 'I don't set out to create a row: I just write things as I see them. I think it will annoy everyone!' He added that it shouldn't surprise the Labour party as they appeared to have identified the issues outside London, but, he quipped, 'I think I'll have to go and live in southern Ireland for a while!'

The series was indeed set to spark a major row because it was scheduled to coincide with the general election.

But it was the BBC who started running scared. In September, they told Bleasdale that severe cuts would have to be made if he wanted his series to be aired.

The author defiantly told them that he couldn't conform to their rules and there would be no more changes. 'I'm used to battles, but in the past there have always been friends I could count on,' he said. 'Those people are no longer there. I have been in this game for thirty years, and the battles do not get any easier.'

This disclosure that the BBC would only show the programme if severe cuts were made infuriated the Tories, who had suffered humiliation in *Boys from the Blackstuff* twenty years earlier. The dispute brought preproduction work to a halt, with no hint as to whether it would ever resurface. With Bleasdale's battles in mind, it is no surprise that Julie lent her support to the actor's union Equity over a proposed strike in September.

Unexpectedly out of work over the winter of 2001, Julie signed up with BBC2 for an unusual drama entitled *Murder*, in which she would play the lead role of Angela. 'It's a fantastic script, beautifully written,' said the actress. 'It just stuck out from the other stuff that comes through, which is why I agreed to do it.'

As the title suggests, the piece is about a murder but, unlike a simple detective whodunnit where the viewer works with the police to crack the mystery, *Murder* offers an in-depth study on the aftermath of the crime, exploring the impact socially and mentally on several lives, seemingly unconnected at first.

The first episode shows, in graphic detail, the point at which 21-year-old Chris is killed. He is found by a passing jogger, Robert Weldon, and soon the lad's mother, Angela, is told the tragic news. The piece centres on Angela's emotional journey, and how she deals with her grief and the powerlessness of it all, but others are inadvertently encompassed by the event.

The case is added to DCI Billie Dory's growing list, but the investigation is ousted to the periphery of the story and, instead, there is more of Billie's dissatisfaction with work. Meanwhile, a freelance journalist, Dave Dewston, has wormed his way into the house and the lives of the grieving family in his bid for an exclusive. Finally, a local newsagent, Akash Gupta, is dragged into the story as Chris's murder is splashed across the front page of the local paper.

As the four-part drama unravels into a character study of each person, the viewer becomes aware of the far-reaching implications of one crime.

'Unless we've had a personal experience of murder, we think we understand it because we've all seen investigations on TV or read about them in the newspapers,' said the producer, Rebecca de Souza, in BBC interviews. 'They are generally presented in a particular way. The focus tends to be on the victim and the police investigation. We wanted to explore the idea that, alongside the immediate family, many people are affected by murder – some in surprising ways.'

Murder was written by Abi Morgan, with whom Rebecca had worked on *My Fragile Heart*, and as part of her research Morgan interviewed parents whose children had been murdered. 'Their stories were so incredible. There was a strong sense that they had been touched by madness,' says Abi. 'I wanted to capture the intensity of what they were living through as well as the odd normality of it.' The acclaimed director Beeban Kidron (*Oranges Are Not the Only Fruit*) was asked to tackle the weighty project.

Pulling no punches from the opening sequence, the series is not for the faint-hearted. The murder is told in gruesome flashback and is juxtaposed with the mundane reality of the continuation of daily life. Kidron uses crude tactics to make her point – beetroot juice mingles with blood, the mother-and-son relationship is shot with a misty lens – but the unsubtle overemphasis is both inevitable and acceptable to illustrate Angela's overwhelming devastation.

As *Murder* is character-led rather than plot-led, it was important to have strong actors in the lead roles. Robert Glenister, who had worked on *My Fragile Heart*, is the jogger-turned-hero. 'He's actually rather dull,' says Robert. 'What really attracted me to the part was this change that he went through. This shy, retiring bloke all of a sudden becomes Brad Pitt for a day!' But then the enormity of the event hits Robert and he suffers from post-traumatic stress disorder.

Billie, the detective on the case, is a busy woman who remains clinical and removed from her work. Imelda Staunton was offered the part. 'I would never cast me as this. The description of her didn't sound like me at all,' she says, although she was so intrigued by the hard nut that she couldn't turn it down. Imelda especially liked the fact that, although the detective had several cases on the go, the mother's persistence penetrated her tough exterior.

David Morrissey from *Captain Corelli's Mandolin* relished the plot as much as his role as the desperate journalist, Dave. 'It's a very conventional piece but it's unconventionally told, and that's what I like about it,' he says. 'It's about one person's actions against another and the domino effect of that . . . I like that overlapping of stories.'

Om Puri, famous from *East Is East*, but a veteran of more than one hundred films, was equally excited to play the local newsagent who is unwittingly drawn in, not least due to Julie's participation. 'That was one of the main attractions of this job,' he says. 'She's just a wonderful actress. She's focused, sensitive, unassuming, sophisticated, dignified – I simply run out of adjectives when I try to describe her!'

For the third time in a year, Julie plays a mother who has lost a child. Far from being bored or blasé, the actress turns in an unbearably moving performance that drives the series on.

'It's difficult to describe Angela in a sense, because she's going through such extreme things,' says Julie. 'Before the death she would have been warm, a good mother who enjoyed life, independent, strong, someone who values life and the good things about it.' Julie then tries to analyse the various stages of Angela's mental journey: through the shock, grief and turmoil, which is then followed by anger and the confusion at the irrationality of the act, and finally her need to act on the deed and repair her life. On top of the gamut of emotions, Angela also has to deal with the press and the police. Julie honestly conveys the devastating heartache; her loss is so personal, yet it becomes public gossip in the tabloids.

Although she was enamoured with the poignant writing, Julie was unprepared for being dragged through the wringer herself. 'Usually, a project has one upsetting day, but with *Murder* I was dealing with some kind of angst and anger every day,' she says. The filming lasted three months and maintaining such a high level of grief was draining. The rare moments of humour did little to lighten the despair. Although Julie usually embarked on some kind of preparation, she felt that having a child and imagining that loss would suffice – she had come close enough to such pain as it was.

Unable to switch off after a day's shoot, Julie spent much of the filming period feeling miserable. Finally, a friend questioned her motives in playing the role if it left her so exhausted. 'The only explanation I have is that it's to do with my mother, who I kept thinking about. She died in 1989 and I thought I'd mourned all of that, dealt with it, but maybe I haven't and maybe you don't ever.'

It has been a recurring theme of Julie's work that, as time passes, she draws more and more upon the memory of Mary Walters as an inspiration.

That she poured her heart and soul into the work is clear, but it's a measured performance: she has hysterics but never histrionics; she wails but never exaggerates. And, although it is admittedly fairly depressing viewing, Chris Longridge from *Heat* magazine successfully summed it up as 'dramatically satisfying doom and gloom'.

Somehow, the cast managed to lighten the intense atmosphere between takes. Julie gave credit to other cast members: 'Imelda Staunton's just the funniest person in the world. She made me laugh from morning to night. She was fantastic. And Beeban Kidron, the director, was just amazing. She pushed everyone to the nth degree.'

Critics and public alike agreed when it was aired during May and June 2002. The following March, Julie received the Royal Television Society Best Actress award for *Murder*. As she beat Lesley Manville in *Bodily Harm* and Jessica Stevenson in *Tomorrow La Scala*, the host announced, 'The winner's performance of guttural grief was searingly honest. The concentrated power of the performance was harrowing and sometimes difficult to watch.' Julie's portrayal of Angela also secured her success in the same category at the BAFTA TV Awards one month later, surpassing Sheila Hancock, Vanessa Redgrave and again Jessica Stevenson.

31. THE MAGIC RETURNS

'After doing something like *Murder*, which was brilliant but draining, it's ideal,' said Julie on reprising Molly Weasley in *Harry Potter and the Chamber of Secrets*. 'It's not a very big part but it's perfect for me. A small part in a big movie means more time at home with Maisie and Grant. What could be better than that?'

Although still a minor role, it was bigger than her first outing as Mrs Weasley and took the first half of 2002 to film. This suited Julie down to the ground because it meant she didn't have to take on much else in the year, nor did she have to travel, because the base was an old airfield outside Watford, called Leavesden Studio.

In the second outing, the famous young wizard, Harry, is unconventionally rescued from his horrible muggle (nonmagical) aunt and uncle's house by Ron and the Weasley twins in a flying car. The boys 'drive' back to their home, The Burrow, hoping that their parents haven't noticed they – and the car – are missing. Mrs Weasley has been worried sick all night and gives her sons an ear-bashing; with the same breath she turns to Harry and smothers him with motherly love.

She becomes his surrogate mother and insists that he stay in their chaotic house. While Harry is in awe of all their magical accessories (mirrors that talk back, clocks that point to 'Time To Make Tea' and 'You're Late'), Mrs Weasley cooks a generous breakfast and Mr Weasley, played by Mark Williams of *The Fast Show*, returns home from his job in the Misuse of Muggle Artefacts Office and quizzes Harry on muggle life.

The house set was perfect, exactly as any reader of the book would have imagined it. 'I walked into it and it was so cosy and brilliantly designed that I could have cooked the breakfast there myself,' says Julie. And Molly Weasley quickly became the ultimate combination of all Julie's warm characters, mixed with her own maternal feelings, which was fine by the director, Chris Columbus. 'I felt that we were all allowed to interpret our characters as we saw them,' says Chris Rankin, 'and, if Chris didn't agree, he'd say what he thought and we'd work out a meeting point somewhere in the middle. He's very relaxed: I never saw him raise his voice, get cross, swear, or be at all negative in the two years we worked together.'

Under such calm direction, the actors found their work a pleasure. 'On smaller scenes, like The Burrow, there were minimal crew and cast, so everyone took their time and we had a lot of fun,' Rankin continues. 'Julie and Mark were *so* much fun to work with – both of them are wonderful improvisers, so often, when a take went wrong, it'd carry on for a couple more minutes before we'd cut and go back. I remember trying desperately not to laugh out a mouthful of baked beans in many takes!

'There's a line in that scene where Ginny Weasley comes in and says, "Mum, have you seen my jumper?" and Julie's reply, "Yes dear, it's on the cat," was just one of her many superb one-liners that popped up in the takes that were never scripted.

'The whole Weasley clan get on just like a real family. I found that once I got to know Julie, she was like a second mother and we have kept in touch since filming finished: she rang me up to wish me good luck for a drama college audition I went to, she's sent me cards congratulating me on A-level results and even owns two pairs of my nan's fingerless mittens, as does the rest of her family!'

Julie's only other scene in the second instalment was at the book shop where the celebrity wizard author Gilderoy Lockhart (wonderfully portrayed by Kenneth Brannagh) was holding a book-signing. Mrs Weasley clearly holds a torch for him, but as a married woman is embarrassed by her crush.

Fortunately for Julie, Mrs Weasley did not have to endure arachnid Aragog's lair in the Forbidden Forest. 'Spiders absolutely terrify me,' she says. 'I went to see the film *Arachnophobia* to confront my fear, but it didn't work – I was nearly sick with fright.' Julie jokes that it must be genetic as Maisie's just as scared – an eight-legged arachnid can reduce them both to quivering wrecks.

With two more *Harry Potter* films on the way, Julie's role will soon increase as Mrs Weasley becomes Harry's guardian.

At the beginning of 2002, Julie was once again a force to be reckoned with at the award ceremonies when she won the Best Actress BAFTA for her performance in *My Beautiful Son*. When asked by a reporter where she keeps her awards, she was initially reticent. 'I'm not going to tell you, because Olympia Dukakis was asked about her Oscar. She said it was on the window sill in her study and two days later she was robbed,' said Julie, before eventually conceding, 'They're all over the place. Some are on the shelf by the stairs, some are in the conservatory, some are kind of dumped, actually. I can't think where my OBE is, but when would you wear it? Accolades are wonderful but you can't put too much store by them. There are lots of good performances that don't get anything. The real prize is getting more work.'

Enforcing her firm grasp on reality, Julie never forgot her roots and, in 2002, inundated with work and awards, she found time to help potential talent in her birthplace, Smethwick. She wrote a message to businesspeople in the area in the *Smethwick Pride*:

> *I am a patron of Smethwick Achievers, an exciting initiative that supports talented local people from all walks of life as they strive to realise their ambitions and dreams. Smethwick Achievers is a bursary fund established by Smethwick Regeneration Partnership to help nurture local talent.*

She goes on to list the people they have helped since being established in 1999, including a world-class weightlifter, an autistic young artist, a cyclist, a lawyer, a novelist, a dancer and various academics, musicians and singers.

She concludes:

> *That's why I am appealing to local businesses to support Smethwick Achievers in the long term so we can continue to help as many talented local people as possible. Do you think you can give someone a leg up? Whether it's a lot or a little, it will all help to make the stars shine brighter in Smethwick. With best wishes, Julie Walters.*

Unfortunately for Julie, while she was nonchalant about her celebrity status, those around her sometimes couldn't help themselves.

'I was having a cap fitted,' said Julie, with no hint of embarrassment in one of her interviews to promote *Murder*, 'when the nurse stopped what she was doing, looked up at me and said, "I know you!" ... There I was having this thing fitted and she realised she'd seen me on the telly!'

In the second half of 2002 Julie worked on another fun project although, unlike the enchantment of *Harry Potter*, *Calendar Girls* was based on a true story.

Angela Baker was a member of the Women's Institute in Rylstone, Yorkshire, and, when her husband John was diagnosed with lymphoma, the women rallied together and raised money for leukaemia and lymphoma research. Sadly, John died in July 1998, but the group, who had all lost friends and families to cancer, were determined to fund research to find a cure.

So one of Angela's friends, Tricia Stewart, hatched an outrageous plan.

Eleven mature women aged 45 to 66 stripped and posed naked for the 'Alternative WI Calendar'. Terry Logan, husband of Lynda (Miss July) took the tasteful sepia photographs, which captured the women performing their regular WI activities, such as baking, knitting and flower-arranging, preserving their modesty with a few well-placed props. A yellow sunflower appeared in each shot – John Baker had grown them during his illness – and December was a group photo.

They hoped to raise £1,000 for the charity, but when the calendar was launched in April 1999 it became a surprise hit, selling 88,000 copies in the UK, twice that of the racy Pirelli calendar. By January 2000, profits allowed them to donate more than £300,000 to the Leukaemia Research Fund. In May 2000, an eighteen-month version, called 'The Ladies of Rylstone', was published, selling more than 200,000 copies worldwide.

In the hyperbole following the calendar's achievement, the women were inundated with film offers. Tricia Stewart was approached by Suzanne Mackie, producer of Harbour Pictures, who proposed an ideal scenario: a movie made by this British production company with the international backing of Buena Vista, part of the Walt Disney empire.

Because any film would be largely based on the Baker family, the painful death of John and the rousing community reaction, Tricia passed the request on to Angela and her two adult children. 'It's totally Angela and her family's decision whether they make a film. It's her story,' said Tricia.

Angela was understandably cautious. 'I had to consider my children, Matthew and Rachel,' she said. 'It will be a big thing. It's hard because an actor is going to play John and I don't know how they will do it.' Harbour Pictures arranged several meetings at which they reassured Angela that the subject would be handled with the utmost sensitivity.

Things were progressing smoothly until Moyra Livesey (Miss May) received a phone call from a friend. He was a builder who happened to be working on Victoria Wood's property nearby and she too was interested in meeting up with the women. Moyra held a group gathering where Victoria made her proposal. Living just a few miles away, the comedienne felt this was the perfect opportunity finally to make her break into feature films: although she was planning to finance it herself, Victoria allegedly offered more than double the upfront figure from Harbour Pictures.

Angela was left to weigh up all the pros and cons. Clearly, everyone was anticipating that a throng of mature women undressing for a charitable cause would repeat the phenomenal success of the stripping steelworkers of The Full Monty in 1997, which cost £2 million to make and grossed £250 million. However, that was feasible only with worldwide promotion and distribution. On balance, therefore, the offer from Harbour Pictures held greater potential.

The women, Angela's two children and Terry Logan took a democratic vote. Five favoured the offer from the local comedienne of a quintessentially English film, but the majority went for the less altruistic big name. Victoria quietly withdrew her offer. Bitterly disappointed, she gracefully wished the WI members the very best of luck.

Six of the original team, now known as Baker's Half Dozen, signed the royalties to the Leukaemia Research Fund and Harbour Pictures commenced work on *Calendar Girls*.

Angela was ready to move on. 'We've not fallen out,' she said in April 2000. 'We've just had a disagreement and now we'll just forget it. We're still out to make as much money as possible for leukaemia research.'

The movie aims to avoid an overtly documentary-style approach, and instead treats the subject with humour and sensitivity. 'This is a wonderful story because it has heart, courage, group spirit and something that showed you can come out of a tragedy and do something positive,' says the producer Suzanne Mackie. The scriptwriter Juliette Towhidi, who incidentally comes from the same writing stable as Simon Beaufoy, creator of *The Full Monty*, started work on Angela's moving tale.

Almost two years after the initial discussions, the low-budget flick was ready to start filming. Directed by Nigel Cole, who was enjoying success with *Saving Grace*, starring Brenda Blethyn, *Calendar Girls* boasted the best of British actresses. 'I find it incredible really,' says Tricia Stewart, who is played by Helen Mirren (*Prime Suspect* and *Gosford Park*), 'but I'm not totally surprised because we felt it was going to be that calibre of film and have top British stars.' Interestingly, when the women first discussed the possibility of a film, their preferred list of actresses included Helen Mirren and Julie Walters.

Touched by the tragedy she narrowly missed with Maisie, Julie accepted the lead as Angela Baker (Miss February). The impressive cast also includes Linda Bassett, Celia Imrie, Penelope Wilton, Geraldine James, Annette Crosbie, John Alderton, Ciaran Hinds and Philip Glenister.

The Baker's Half Dozen spent some time recording their voices so that the actresses could perfect their accents. Shooting commenced at the end of June 2002 on location in the Yorkshire Dales. Burnstall, Kettlewell, Linton, Coniston, Skipton, Ingleton and Settle were all backdrops for the movie. As the 200-strong cast and crew descended on the scenic setting, they brought some much-needed business after the problems for companies during the foot-and-mouth outbreak of 2001.

Around a thousand extras were required and locals were recruited alongside women from the WI nationwide. Further filming continued at Shepperton Studios in London, Paramount Studios in Los Angeles and on location in America.

Although the film centres on a nude calendar, all actresses retained their modesty in the way the original models did and, along the lines of *The Full Monty*, all camera angles were flattering to produce a feel-good piece suitable for a wide audience. The much-anticipated release of *Calendar Girls* will be in December 2003 and the movie looks set to put the stars, director, WI and Yorkshire firmly in the spotlight.

Spurred on by her recent efforts to help Save the Children and Comic Relief, Julie once again displayed her compassion for children as she joined a number of celebrities, including Victoria Wood, Emma Thompson, Richard E Grant, and the pop bands Pulp and Ocean Colour Scene, in the lobbying group, Baby Milk Action (BMA). The nonprofit organisation boycotted Nestlé in protest at their unethical promotion of powdered baby formulas in the Third World. BMA claims this lures mothers away from breastfeeding, which deprives the baby of vital antibodies, and, moreover, puts the child at risk as the water used may not be boiled correctly, leaving it unsterile and therefore unsafe.

Still with her charity hat on, in December 2002, Julie opened a new breast unit at Birmingham's Women's Hospital. She was shown round the state-of-the-art equipment and spent time talking to staff and guests. The modern facilities mean nearly 26,000 women each year will be treated with hi-tech kit in more comfortable surroundings.

With the release of *Harry Potter and the Chamber of Secrets* in mid-November, the nation was gripped with Pottermania and Julie became a familiar face for a new generation. She was given a bouquet of flowers from the hospital consultant radiographer's eight-year-old daughter, Kate, who was probably more in awe of Molly Weasley than Julie Walters.

But fame is something that Julie doesn't really care for. She has never craved a high profile and takes on a project only on its own merit. She will happily work when something interesting presents itself – namely from one of the two Alans, Victoria Wood or the *Harry Potter* series, or a subject close to her heart (such as leukaemia) – but otherwise she's content to relax at home with Grant and Maisie.

In April 2003, Maisie turned fifteen and Julie was aware that she was approaching adulthood. 'I value my time with Maisie so much,' says the actress in interviews. 'She's growing up fast and we love each other's company. I don't want to be somewhere on the other side of the world when we could be together having fun.

'If she wants me for a friend, I'll be there, but I don't intend to try to be her best friend. You have to get away from your mum. That's the whole point of growing up.'

As well as helping Grant on the farm, Julie truly found her homely side. 'I do turn down work to do nothing,' she says. 'I like to read, be domestic, just live and look after Maisie. I've always got stuff to do and I'm perfectly happy being home.' She particularly enjoys pottering in the garden. 'Well, I call it gardening, but it's just pots on the patio,' she continues. 'What I love best is garden centres. I love wandering round Notcutts.'

Having had some precious time off, Julie was looking forward to reprising Molly Weasley once more, when work on the third *Harry Potter* film commenced at the end of February 2003. Before that, she squeezed in a short appeal for Comic Relief's 2003 Red Nose Day – this time filming took place closer to home as she described the benefits of the UK funding.

The core cast for *Harry Potter and the Prisoner of Azkaban* remained the same, except for the sad loss of Richard Harris. The revered Irish actor Michael Gambon (*Gosford Park* and *Charlotte Gray*) was persuaded to fill Albus Dumbledore's shoes, and he was joined by other newcomers to the *Potter* series including Gary Oldman (*Hannibal*), Timothy Spall (*Nicholas Nickleby*), David Thewlis (*Timeline*), Pam Ferris (*Matilda*) and Paul Whitehouse (*The Fast Show*).

The main difference behind the scenes was the change of director. Chris Columbus told the producers he wanted to return to America with his family, which would prevent him from doing further work on the series. Accepting his decision, they searched for a replacement and chose the Mexican Alfonso Cuarón, whose films have ranged from the 1995 family film, *A Little Princess*, to 2001's erotic hit, *Y Tu Mamá También*.

The result of this slightly unusual collaboration will only be seen when the film is released. 'We couldn't be more excited about *Harry Potter and the Prisoner of Azkaban* being in the hands of such a relentlessly imaginative director as Alfonso Cuarón,' said producer David Heyman.

'To be entrusted with such rich and beloved material, and given the opportunity to collaborate with this extraordinary cast and crew on the next *Harry Potter* adventure, is an honour,' responded Alfonso graciously.

This instalment sees Harry, Ron and Hermione returning to Hogwarts as teenagers for their third year of study. Gary Oldman plays Sirius Black, a renegade wizard who has escaped from the prison in Azkaban and is thought to pose a great threat to Harry.

With the release set for June 2004, Warner Brothers have broken the one-a-year pattern. Unconfirmed rumour has it that this is so that they could concentrate their resources on the *Matrix* sequels and *Terminator 3*, all out in the summer of 2003. With JK Rowling continuing to write more adventures – the fifth book, *Harry Potter and the Order of the Phoenix* was published in June 2003 – it is clear that the movies will continue for many years to come.

However, with an elongated filming schedule, the actors playing the teenage trio will age faster than their characters, which could pose a problem. Julie, however, was happy with the series, as it was guaranteed work that is close to home. She will definitely be seen in the fourth instalment.

EPILOGUE
I'M NOT GROWN UP YET

Outside acting, Julie started work on a novel in 1997 and continued during her sporadic moments of free time. 'I've written 58,000 words, but over five years! The deadline was about three years ago,' she said in 2002. The novel covered familiar territory: two actresses go to New York. However, 'One has lost touch with reality, disappears and is picked up by a man.'

When she finishes the book, it is bound to be a success. Her innate sense of humour comes across well on the page and her two books, *Baby Talk* and *Julie Walters Is an Alien*, were sharply written and laugh-out-loud funny. Although the masterpiece-in-progress is an adult book, Crissy Rock recalls Julie saying that she would 'love to write a children's story one day'. It may be that the actress will turn author for her 'retirement'.

Julie certainly wouldn't consider directing, a common way for actors to mature and expand in their art. 'I'm not the type,' she says firmly. 'You've got to really know what you're doing and be quite controlling. I am quite controlling, but not in that way. It's a very lonely job and I don't like being out of the crowd.'

Moreover she still doesn't feel grown up and still loves acting – so that she can escape into a fantasy world.

Aged 53 in 2003, she has plenty more acting years ahead of her. 'I'm still quite driven in my career,' she says, 'and I can't imagine a time when I wouldn't want to act. But I also realise that it isn't everything: life comes first.' With that in mind, she doesn't envisage herself acting in her eighties. 'Hopefully I'll be gardening, travelling the world by then, writing my novels. I'd like to think there'll be too much real life going on for me to want to do much acting,' she adds.

Thankfully, for fans and followers of her extended career, if either of the Alans or Victoria was to offer her a part, she'd be hard pushed to turn it down. As Bleasdale points out, Julie has always acted 'old and mad better than anyone else', but there is nothing like experience to achieve perfection!

In the 2001 Orange Film Survey, Julie Walters was named Number One Greatest British Film Actress, beating Dame Judi Dench and Emma Thompson among other great actresses. While her ability is not in question, if there is a criticism to be made of Julie, it is that she has allowed herself to become stereotyped. Invariably, she either plays a 'tart with a heart' or, of late and more prolifically, 'somebody's mother' with a healthy dollop of angst.

Blame should be apportioned equally. On one hand Julie's favourite writers create these characters, time after time, with her specifically in mind; on the other hand, Julie not only willingly accepts these roles from old friends, but also seems purposefully to seek them out. *Titanic Town*, *My Beautiful Son* and *Murder* spring to mind as tales of maternal anguish *not* linked to Bleasdale, Bennett or Wood.

This is not to say that Julie hasn't occasionally tried to break the mould. *Educating Rita* and *Billy Elliot* are arguably the most successful results of such experimentation.

In a recent fantasy-film poll, the public voted to see her and Sean Connery in a crime caper where he is a gang boss and she is his safe-cracking wife. Julie's audience clearly wants to see more of her in high-profile work, for example in an action movie. If Dame Judi Dench can appear in the *James Bond* series, why does Julie Walters OBE stick with the comfortable – if lucrative – Mrs Weasley in the *Harry Potter* films?

One should remember that during the initial furore surrounding *Educating Rita*, Julie turned down reams of supposedly unsuitable adventures and romances – genres in which she has yet to make her name. Furthermore, she has been willing to 'age up' ever since her appearance as a grandmother in *Scully* in 1975 (while it was undoubtedly a brave move for a 25-year-old, unfortunately, the identity stuck).

Then again, there's more to Julie than her career and she openly admits that motherhood took the edge off her ambition. Moreover, when Maisie's illness struck, Julie's desire for diversity was understandably dampened and she chose the ease of familiarity.

So what will be Julie Walters's legacy? In May 2001, the actress said she would probably be immortalised in *Educating Rita* or as Mrs Overall from 'Acorn Antiques': 'I can understand why people get annoyed at being remembered for one thing, but a lot of actors aren't remembered for anything. I don't mind.

'Rita was a good old gal. The intentions behind it were good. And I love Mrs Overall. She's in every part I do. I love the fact that people still remember it, and come up and quote bits.' Julie has since reinvented herself as Mrs Weasley and there's no doubt that the younger generation will always associate her with that role.

Fortunately, Julie's ability beyond her stereotyping is recognised by the new wave of actors. 'My personal idol is Julie Walters,' says the award-winning actress, Anna Friel, who started with a small part in *GBH* in

1991. 'She's amazing, she hasn't put a foot wrong in my eyes. She's funny, tangible and compassionate. Incredible.'

While cornering the market in portraying quintessentially British working-class women, Julie's immense talent means that she can handle any role. Unfortunately, directors are sometimes nervous of her force.

'She's a hard person to cast,' explains Richard Loncraine. 'She's so powerful, you can't put her in too small a part because she's so strong. She dominates in the right sense of the word, because she's such an enormous personality, but you've got to find the right cast. I'd use her tomorrow in either comedy or drama if I found the right part. She's right up there with Dame Maggie Smith or Vanessa Redgrave, but somehow people who perform comedy just aren't taken as seriously, which is not fair.'

Therein lies the other misconception of Julie. Her comic timing is murderously accurate, but she is also a compelling dramatist. Those who have been fortunate enough to direct her appreciate both sides of her genius, but the public, and even some peers, are often left with an uneven opinion.

'Julie's work has been in a number of different spheres and unfortunately the business is very snobbish,' says Simon Stokes. 'She's an actress of great depth and range, and those who only look at "Acorn Antiques" miss out on a lot of her repertoire. She is leading in her generation.'

While Julie was taught how to act in a dramatic role, the funny side always has to come naturally. 'Comedy is harder in some ways,' she says. 'You're very aware if something's working straightaway, and so are the audience. I think it's something you can't learn. It's an instinct, which makes it rather elusive.'

John Goldschmidt agrees and believes this inherent aptitude is the key to her success. 'I think people who have a comedic talent make for the best dramatic actors,' he says. 'Comedy is so much more difficult to do, that if you can do that, you have the ability to play real tragedy successfully.'

In the short but sweet words of Lewis Gilbert: 'It's very difficult to make people both laugh and cry, but Julie can.'

CAREER CHRONOLOGY

List is in the order of production, most recent first; date is of release

Harry Potter and the Prisoner of Azkaban	Film	2004
Calendar Girls	Film	2003
Harry Potter and the Chamber of Secrets	Film	2002
Murder	Television	2002
Before You Go	Film	2002
My Beautiful Son	Television	2001
Harry Potter and the Philosopher's Stone	Film	2001
Comic Relief (*Wood & Walters*)	Television	2001
Amnesty International's *We Know Where You Live: Live!*	Television	2001
Victoria Wood With All The Trimmings	Television	2000
All My Sons	Theatre	2000
Billy Elliot	Film	2000
Laughter in the House: The Story of British Sitcom	Television	1999
dinnerladies (Series Two)	Television	1999
Oliver Twist	Television	2000
All Forgotten a.k.a. *Lover's Prayer*	Film	1999
Comic Relief (*Wetty Hainthropp Investigates*)	Television	1999
Jack and the Beanstalk	Theatre	1998
Titanic Town	Film	1998
dinnerladies (Series One)	Television	1998
Talking Heads 2 (episode 'The Outside Dog')	Television	1998
Melissa	Television	1998
Girls' Night	Film	1998
Bath Time	Film short	1997
Julie Walters Is An Alien In Miami	Television	1997
Julie Walters Is An Alien In New York	Television	1997
Brazen Hussies	Television	1996
Comic Relief	Television	1997
Little Red Riding Hood	Film	1996
Jake's Progress	Television	1995
Comic Relief	Television	1995
Intimate Relations	Film	1995
Requiem Apache (as part of *Alan Bleasdale Presents*)	Television	1994
Pat and Margaret	Television	1994
Sister My Sister	Film	1994
Bambino Mio	Television	1993
The Summer House	Television	1993
Wide-Eyed and Legless a.k.a. *The Wedding Gift*	Television	1993
Victoria Wood's All Day Breakfast	Television	1992
Just Like a Woman	Film	1992

Julie Walters and Friends	Television	1991
The Rose Tattoo	Theatre	1991
GBH	Television	1991
Stepping Out	Film	1991
Victoria Wood	Television	1989
Frankie And Johnny in the Clair de Lune	Theatre	1989
Mack the Knife	Film	1989
Killing Dad (Or How To Love Your Mother)	Film	1989
An Audience with Victoria Wood	Television	1988
Comic Relief	Television	1988
Victoria Wood As Seen On TV (Christmas Special)	Television	1987
Buster	Film	1988
Help	Television	1987
Talking Heads (episode 'Her Big Chance')	Television	1987
Personal Services	Film	1987
Prick Up Your Ears	Film	1987
Victoria Wood As Seen On TV (Series Two)	Television	1986
The Birthday Party	Television	1986
When I Was a Girl I Used To Scream And Shout	Theatre	1985
Tribute to Sir Michael Redgrave	Theatre	1985
Macbeth	Theatre	1985
Dreamchild	Film	1985
The Secret Diary of Adrian Mole Aged 13¾	Television	1985
Fool For Love	Theatre	1985
Victoria Wood As Seen on TV (Series One)	Television	1985
Car Trouble	Film	1985
She'll Be Wearing Pink Pyjamas	Film	1984
Love and Marriage	Television	1984
Unfair Exchanges	Television	1984
Say Something Happened	Television	1982
Intensive Care	Television	1982
Open Space	Television	1983
Open Door	Television	1982
Boys from the Blackstuff	Television	1982
Educating Rita	Film	1983
Wood & Walters: Two Creatures Great and Small (Series)	Television	1981
Happy Since I Met You	Television	1981
Days at the Beach	Television	1981
Having a Ball	Theatre	1981
Wood & Walters: Two Creatures Great and Small (Pilot)	Television	1981
Educating Rita	Theatre	1980
Good Fun	Theatre	1980
Nearly a Happy Ending	Television	1980
Flaming Bodies	Theatre	1979
The Changeling	Theatre	1979
As You Like It	Theatre	1979
Ecstasy	Theatre	1979
Talent	Television	1979

Me! I'm Afraid of Virginia Woolf	Television	1978
In at the Death	Theatre	1978
Glad Hand	Theatre	1978
The Liver Birds	Television	1978
Empire Road	Television	1978
Soldiers Talking Cleanly	Television	1978
Breezeblock Park (Mermaid Theatre)	Theatre	1977
Watchwords	Television	1977
Funny Peculiar (Mermaid Theatre)	Theatre	1976
Androcles and the Lion	Theatre	1975
One Flew Over the Cuckoo's Nest	Theatre	1975
Edward Lear	Theatre	1975
Week Ending	Radio	1975
Bingo	Radio	1975
Breezeblock Park (Liverpool Everyman)	Theatre	1975
Scully	Vanload	1975
The Pig and the Junkle	Theatre	1975
Funny Peculiar (Liverpool Everyman)	Theatre	1975
Cantril Tales	Theatre	1974
Dick Whittington	Vanload	1974
The Taming of the Shrew	Theatre	1974
Love on the Dole	Theatre	1973
Playboy of the Western World	Theatre	1972
Summer Folk	Theatre	1971
A Midsummer Night's Dream	Theatre	1962

BIBLIOGRAPHY

Brandwood, N., *Victoria Wood – The Biography* (Virgin Books Ltd, 2002)

Coleman, R., *Phil Collins – The Definitive Biography* (Simon & Schuster Ltd, 1997)

Coveney, M., *The World According to Mike Leigh* (HarperCollins, 1997)

Games, A., *Backing Into the Limelight: The Biography of Alan Bennett* (Headline, 2001)

Halliwell's Film and Video Guide, 1999 Edition (HarperCollins, 1999)

Halliwell's Who's Who in the Movies (HarperCollins, 1999)

Hamlyn History of the Twentieth Century (Reed International Books Ltd, 1995)

Walters, J., *Baby Talk* (Guild Publishing, 1990)

Walters, J., *Julie Walters Is an Alien* (Hodder & Stoughton, 1997)

INDEX